Robert
FLAHERTY

a guide to
references and resources

A
Reference
Publication
in
Film

Ronald Gottesman
Editor

Robert FLAHERTY

a guide to references and resources

WILLIAM T. MURPHY

G.K. HALL & CO.

70 LINCOLN STREET, BOSTON, MASS.

Library of Congress Cataloging in Publication Data
Murphy, William Thomas, 1942-
    Robert Flaherty: a guide to reference and resources.

    (A Reference publication in film)
    Bibliography: p.
    Includes indexes.
    1. Flaherty, Robert Joseph, 1884-1951.   I. Title.
II. Series.
PN1998.A3F552   016.791.43′023′0924   79-3873
ISBN 0-8161-8022-9

This publication is printed on permanent/durable acid-free paper

MANUFACTURED IN THE UNITED STATES OF AMERICA

Contents

Preface

This book began as a review of Robert Flaherty's films with a
survey of related literature for the purpose of compiling a study
guide that would be useful to students and teachers, film scholars
and other researchers interested in learning about this remarkable
man and the enormous legacy he has left to film history. To execute
this research it was necessary to screen all of Flaherty's films and
those of others in which he was involved; to examine Flaherty's writings and those of his acquaintances; to compare the biographical
studies and survey published literature; and to investigate the
"Flaherty Papers" and other unpublished sources for additional information. The results are presented here as biography, criticism, and
bibliography.

The biographical narrative describes the major events in Flaherty's
life as they have influenced the production and content of his films.
To judge the films alone on face value and not understand the circumstances in which they were made is to ignore a great deal about the
continuity of Flaherty's creative processes. The critical discussion
details the reception of Flaherty's films by contemporary reviewers
and their place in the critical literature as it has changed over the
years. It is in criticism rather than in biography that the foreign
language material was able to enrich the discussion. Above all, the
criticism section focuses on Flaherty's relationship to the documentary and especially to John Grierson whose writings have formed the
foundations of documentary film as it is known today.

The two major English-language studies of Robert Flaherty are
Richard Griffith's The World of Robert Flaherty, published in 1953
(entry 203), and Arthur Calder-Marshall's The Innocent Eye: The Life
of Robert J. Flaherty, published in 1963 (entry 249). A close inspec-
tion of Griffith's book, written by one who was Flaherty's friend, reveals that it is much more of an anthology of Robert and Frances
Flaherty's writings together with Pat Mullen's than a critical synthe-
sis or interpretive monograph. Griffith's personal affection for
Flaherty severely limited the book as a work of scholarship, and it
in fact lacks scholarly apparatus. Many of Griffith's judgments,
however, are helpful and provocative introductions for more critical
analysis, and the extracts of writings are useful substitutes for the
student who does not have access to a large research library.

Preface

Calder-Marshall's book, considered the standard biographical study, is essentially a reworking of Paul Rotha and Basil Wright's manuscript on Flaherty (entry 237), dated 1959, copies of which are on deposit at Columbia University and the Museum of Modern Art in New York. The primary difference between the manuscript and the printed version was the omission of most of the critical discussion which the publisher felt was of interest to but a handful of film scholars. The narrative and citations in both versions suggest that many bibliographic and manuscript materials were not consulted. European writings, for example, aside from British sources, were mostly ignored. The Innocent Eye is best, however, for the British period of Flaherty's life, 1931-1939.

The annotated bibliography lists almost three hundred items about Flaherty and his films plus over fifty items credited to Flaherty himself. If any bibliographical entries have been omitted, they are mainly newspaper references of which there are hundreds if not a thousand or more. They are most valuable for judging the contemporary reception of Flaherty's films by newspaper reviewers; the least valuable ones are either wire service stories which were printed ad infinitum or the rewriting of studio promotional material. Annotations are given for published and unpublished materials that have been examined by the author. Unannotated entries represent those materials that were unobtainable by the author, in which case the source of the citation or reference is given. The bibliography contains references to most of the significant literature for the study of Robert Flaherty as of 1977.

The film synopses are based on the author's recent screenings, and the production credits include names that appear on the screen credits as well as those gleaned from other sources.

Research on this book was greatly facilitated by the knowledgeable staffs of the National Archives and Records Service, the Library of Congress, the Butler Library of Columbia University, the Museum of Modern Art, and the American Film Institute. Although the suggestions and guidance of many individuals were both helpful and encouraging, I wish to especially thank David Culbert, Patrick Sheehan, Gordon Hitchens, Lawrence Karr, and Giuliana Muscio for the resources they made available to me, Enid Barnes and my wife Ruth for technical assistance with the manuscript.

Introduction

There is much justification for the argument that Robert Flaherty invented the documentary form with the release of his films <u>Nanook of the North</u> (1922) and <u>Moana</u> (1926). As unique films for their time, together they established a genre which critics, led by John Grierson, could recognize as something new under the sun. Flaherty inextricably linked the new genre with the filmmaker's art; he instinctively discovered the documentary's basic principles just as D. W. Griffith discovered film language; he created a public audience for documentaries; and he continued to test the form's conventions. As the documentary movement expanded and diversified, Flaherty assumed a place on its outer fringe where his films spoke volumes to those filmmakers who were willing to learn from his example.

Flaherty is chiefly remembered for only four feature-length films: <u>Nanook of the North</u> (1922), <u>Moana</u> (1926), <u>Man of Aran</u> (1934) and <u>Louisiana Story</u> (1948). Additionally, he directed <u>The Land</u> (1942) and three shorter films and codirected <u>Elephant Boy</u> (1937). His film career also included several aborted and unfinished projects. This seems like a relatively small output for a film career that spanned thirty years. His work was inhibited by difficulties in obtaining sponsors and by the length of time it took him to make a film; generally from one and one-half to two years. No doubt he would have made more films had sponsorship been more forthcoming and had he compromised his strong sense of independence. Even though small in number, one would be hard pressed to find a more influential body of films.

Robert Flaherty made films out of a compelling need to create. If motion pictures had not been invented, his poetic feelings would have found expression in other forms. For example, he was also a violinist, a novelist, and story teller. Although much has been made of his desire to explore the world, he chose to work in films in order to express his creative personality. His first interests in film, to be sure, evolved from his activities as an explorer in the wilds of Canada. But a mature recognition of his inner feelings as an artist gradually replaced his youthful desire to explore unknown lands. As Flaherty matured he began to trust these feelings more and more. His films became products of his intuition and instincts.

It is not surprising that a man like this would shun film theories, even those that governed documentary film which is typically
smothered in theories and politics. Where other filmmakers have used
the documentary form as a means to a political or social end,
Flaherty avoided the role of propagandist. Occasionally when a cause
was forced upon him he accepted it gracefully, thankful to have the
work, but his heart lay elsewhere.

If Flaherty's life has become synonymous with documentary film,
it may be useful to first explain this indeed flexible term which has
come to mean many things to different people. In film parlance "documentary" originally derived from the French description of travelogues
("documentaire"). Grierson first applied the word to <u>Moana</u> in 1926,
which he said had documentary value. Later, he defined the documentary film as the "creative treatment of actuality." Many writers on
documentary film in the 1930s defined it by its purpose: to foster
the betterment of mankind in his social milieu. For many writers,
therefore, the documentary film had to argue a cause. It was a sub-
jective and interpretive view of reality, born out of Flaherty's art
and nurtured by the politics of social reformists. Only since the
advent of television journalism does the documentary purport to be
objective and evidential, thus obscuring its classical origins.

Biographical Background

The Early Years

Robert Joseph Flaherty was the descendant on his father's side of an Irish Protestant who had left Ireland during the great "potato famine" migration of the late 1840s and settled in Quebec, Canada. Some of Flaherty's associates saw in this Irish heritage his love for conversation, drink, and music, and the origin of his temperament. As a humorous self-assessment of his own temperament Flaherty was fond of quoting an inscription over the old Spanish Gate in Galway, Ireland, the port of embarkation for the Aran Islands, which read: "From the fury of the ferocious O'Flaherty's, Good Lord deliver us."[1] His father, Robert Henry Flaherty, became a well-known figure in the iron ore exploration of Canada and worked in the mining industries in Minnesota and Michigan. His mother, Susan Kloeckner, was of German extraction and a practicing Roman Catholic. Their son Robert was the first of seven children, and he was born on 16 February 1884 in Iron Mountain, Michigan.[2]

As a child young Robert accompanied his father into the upper reaches of Minnesota and Michigan and over into the Canadian frontier. Prospecting for minerals and living in cabins and camps, they traveled by foot, canoe, and snowshoe. Young Robert was often the only child in the camp, and his companions were miners and Indians. During these formative years Flaherty developed his love of the wilderness and his interest in the people who lived there. "Young Bob was bred," his brother once wrote, "to the hard realism of frontier life. Mining camps were the background of his boyhood. When he was thirteen the whole family migrated across the Canadian border.... [Our] father took charge of a mine named the Golden Star on Bad Vermillion Lake, far in the vast hinterland of forests, lakes and streams that lie between Lake Superior and the Lake of the Woods. It was romantic country. We came to know the Indians well, their forest trails, their mysterious lakes and streams, their birch bark canoes." "By this time," his brother observed, "the seeds of exploration had been pretty well planted in young Bob."[3]

Bob went to school at Iron Mountain, but at least two of his school-age years went without formal education. He read books about adventure and outdoor life by such writers as Francis Parkman, James

1

Fenimore Cooper, and R. M. Ballantyne. To add more sustenance to his formal education, his family sent him to Upper Canada College of Toronto. This was a rather aristocratic prep school where the sons of the British colonial and Canadian upper classes wore caps and Eton collars.[4] Many who knew Bob Flaherty doubted that either he or the school could tolerate each other for long, given his outdoor tempera-ment and the restricted academic atmosphere. Nevertheless, he lasted more than two years, and his popularity won him many friends and ad-mirers. Flaherty's next step in academe was the Michigan College of Mines where he enrolled in order to fortify his interest in mining and prospecting with technical skills. After seven months he was asked to seek his fortune elsewhere. He had none of the qualifica-tions considered necessary for an academic mineralogist.[5]

At the College of Mines, however, Flaherty met Frances Hubbard, the daughter of a distinguished mineralogist. Later, as his wife and colleague, Frances was to have a major influence on his develop-ment as an artist. Educated at the fashionable Bryn Mawr School For Girls, Frances seemed an impossible match for this rough and tumble backwoodsman. Perhaps it was the beauty and solitude of the forests and lakes where she and Robert saw eye to eye. Certainly her well-to-do family had some doubts about this itinerant, and tried to dis-courage the marriage. But after a long courtship, conducted in part by correspondence, Robert Flaherty and Frances Hubbard were married in New York City on 12 November 1914.

Meanwhile, Flaherty had gained experience on his own as an ex-plorer, surveyor, and prospector for the Canadian Grand Trunk Rail-way and Canadian mining syndicates. This work took him to British Columbia and the western reaches of Canada. He staked metal claims in partnership but nothing ever came of them. In 1910 Flaherty was twenty-six years old, without a steady job, and his profession was uncertain. His journeys and travels had more or less specific objec-tives such as metal discovery or surveying. For the time being the sponsor's objectives became Flaherty's; the journey itself, however, gave him great satisfaction. These missions into the wilderness were excuses for traveling and exploring which were only periodically re-lieved by the necessity of finding someone to stake him.

In August Flaherty was hired by Sir William Mackenzie, the entre-preneur whose grand vision of industrial development was to influence the economic history of Canada. Mackenzie hired Flaherty to prospect for iron ore deposits along the Hudson Bay where the Canadian Govern-ment intended to build a railroad. From 1910 through 1915, Flaherty made four expeditions for Mackenzie to the Canadian sub-arctic, expe-ditions which were to determine the future course of his life. First, the expeditions brought Flaherty into contact with Eskimo culture. Second, they enhanced his knowledge about the human condition in a natural setting. Third, the evenings he spent in virtual isolation encouraged him to contemplate the day's events by writing in his diaries, from which he developed skill as a writer. Finally, and surely the most important, they brought Flaherty and the motion picture camera together in a union that endured for the remainder of his life.

In the summer of 1910, Flaherty left for Mattagami, traveled down the big Moose River, bound for the Nastapoka Islands, about 1100 miles from the fringes of civilization. His first stop was the old trading post at Moose Factory. He described it as "an enchanting panorama enchantingly unwinding--tepees, overturned canoes, green cultivated fields, meadows, hayricks, grazing cattle, prim cottages and rough-hewn cabins.... A few curious half-breeds and their wives stood at the edge of the bank as we climbed from the landing. The men slouched, hands in pockets, gazing intently, and the women in the abashed manner of the country, peered from the hooded depths of their plaid shawls."[6] Flaherty believed these Indians had lost their dignity through contact with white civilization. The Eskimos, on the other hand, even at the trading post seemed to keep their dignity and independence. Flaherty's observation of the interaction of diverse cultures became a continuous theme in his life. This first expedition was unsuccessful inasmuch as the iron ore deposits on Nastapoka turned out to be too poor for commercial exploitation. One especially important piece of information that Flaherty acquired on the trip was the suggestion of some Eskimos that the Belcher Islands were actually a large land mass although they only appeared as pin points on admiralty maps.

Returning to lower Canada, Flaherty pursued his interest in the Belcher Islands. He convinced Mackenzie there was a large land mass out in the middle of the bay, and that it might well contain a continuation of an iron ore lode beginning in Minnesota. With growing confidence in Flaherty's ability as an explorer, Mackenzie authorized him to try and reach the Belchers on a second expedition. He departed in the summer of 1911 and wintered in Fort George on the southern part of the bay. Much to his disappointment, however, the ice over the bay kept breaking up, and Flaherty had to cast aside his plan to cross the frozen sea by sledge. So as not to make the trip a complete loss, Flaherty planned to traverse the Ungava Peninsula up the eastern side of the bay. This frozen wasteland was barely mapped and its geological resources largely unknown. It was a difficult journey marked by bad weather and an extended winter, difficult terrain, snow blindness, and uncertain food supplies. He and his Eskimo hunters completed the journey, nevertheless. Flaherty did not reach the Belchers but he had seen land no white man had ever seen.[7]

The third expedition, 1913-1914, was notable for two important reasons: one was Flaherty's "rediscovery" of the Belcher Islands; the other was that for the first time he took along a motion picture camera. The main island of the Belcher group, which Flaherty discovered, was actually more than seventy-five miles long and over twenty miles wide. Moreover, Flaherty found rich deposits of iron ore just as he suspected. In gratitude the Canadian Government named the largest island after him.[8]

Although Flaherty had taken a Kodak still picture camera with him on the two previous expeditions, Mackenzie evidently deserved credit for suggesting that Flaherty take a motion picture camera. In a BBC radio interview Flaherty described it this way:

> "Sir William said to me casually, 'Why don't you get one of these new-fangled things, called a motion picture camera?' So I bought one, but with no thought really than of taking notes on our exploration. We were going into interesting country, we'd see interesting people. I had not thought of making a film for the theaters. I knew nothing whatsoever about films."[9]

An account recently uncovered put it slightly differently: "you're going," Mackenzie said, "into interesting country—strange people—animals and all that—why don't you include in your outfit a camera for making films?"[10] On at least one other occasion Flaherty intimated that he himself had made the original suggestion.[11]

In preparation for the 1913 trip Flaherty acquired a Bell & Howell movie camera. In addition, he went to Rochester for a three-week course in photography, the only formal training he ever received in this field. He also took equipment for printing and developing his exposed film stock and had every intention of making a film about the Eskimos.[12] Actually other matters relating to exploration and his attempt to reach the Belchers absorbed his time, so it wasn't until well into the expedition, February 1914, that he began to work with the motion picture camera. In his book Flaherty described scenes of filming Eskimo dances, the building of an igloo, sledging across ice and snow, and seal-hunting during February and March. Many of these scenes anticipated exactly what was filmed six years later for Nanook of the North. On 10 June while preparing for a deer-filming expedition, he mounted his tripod and camera on a sledge. Flaherty described a rollicking chase, filming the deer, the sledge, huskies, and the passing terrain, climaxed by a headlong plunge into a deep snow drift. While all had a good laugh Flaherty was confident he had secured sensational footage of a typical Eskimo hunt scene. Two days later, near the end of the trip, the sledge broke through an ice-covered stream, and the exposed camera footage was destroyed.[13]

With the remaining footage, Flaherty returned to lower Canada for the winter. "The film" he said, "was edited and put in form. It was too crude to be interesting. But I was to go north again in the spring—this time to explore and winter on the Belcher Islands. I determined to attempt a better one."[14] Flaherty became highly enthusiastic about the possibilities of motion pictures in education, in the teaching of geography and history. "Someone might well make it a life's work," he told his wife. "Why not me?"[15]

It was remarkable that despite the demands World War I had made on Canada, Mackenzie should agree to finance another expedition to the Belchers. That he did so was a strong indication of his growing confidence in the resourceful young man. There is no evidence to suggest that Flaherty had strong political feelings concerning the war. He just continued pursuing his own interests.

In the early summer of 1915 he again departed for the North, accompanied by his new bride, his brother, and a friend. They went as far as Moose Factory and Charlton Island, where Flaherty left with his boat and an Eskimo group for the Belchers.

He continued filming more of the landscape and more Eskimo scenes such as a walrus hunt. However, his main activity was still exploration, mapping, and mineral sampling. When this work was finished he devoted more and more of his time to what was swiftly becoming his favorite obsession.

Flaherty brought back to Toronto some 30,000 feet of unedited black-and-white 35 mm film.[16] He assembled a "rough cut" or a workprint which was sent to Harvard University for a screening. While packing the negatives he dropped a cigarette on the floor igniting the film scraps, which immediately burst into flames. He tried in vain to put the fire out and was hospitalized from burns. Most writers on Flaherty neglect to point out that the film stock was composed of a nitrocellulose base (a highly flammable substance akin to gun cotton) which was the staple of the motion picture industry from 1889 to 1951. Flaherty must have had a lapse of common sense to be smoking around nitrate flim. A work print remained but it was not feasible at that time to strike a duplicate negative.[17]

Flaherty was heartbroken over the loss of his film, for he felt he had secured good footage of the Belchers, of walrus hunting and native life together with the scenes showing the dismasting of his exploring ship, Laddie. He hoped this would form the nucleus of a motion picture. Undaunted, he showed the workprint around to private groups "just long enough," he said, "to realize that it was no good." It was too episodic, like a travelogue, he felt. "But I did see that if I were to take a single character and make him typify the Eskimos as I had known them so long and well, the results would be well worth while." The destroyed film was not the first Nanook of the North, and it would appear that its loss was no great tragedy for film history. At least the experience increased Flaherty's determination to go back to the North and make a better film. The growing demands of the war made it difficult to secure backing for another expedition. But Flaherty never lost hope. During the intervening years he wrote articles and gave talks about northern exploration and he continued to show his only film positive.

Flaherty was thirty-two years old when he finished his last expedition for Mackenzie in 1916, and had achieved a measure of success

as an explorer. He was even elected to the Royal Geographic Society.
But a more compelling interest began to replace mineral exploration
in a barren landscape. He became more interested, indeed fascinated,
in the primitive peoples as well as their geography. He had been
given a rare, close look at Eskimo culture and now he wanted to tell
the outside world what was so much a part of his private life. Once
when someone asked him why he spent so much time filming the primeval,
he replied "I grew up with primitive people, Indians and Eskimos. I
was thirty before I knew much about what you call civilization. May-
be I don't know it even now."[18] His diaries from these expeditions
are filled with expressions of his admiration for the skill, ingenu-
ity, strength, and courage of the Eskimo people. For months on end
small groups of Eskimos were his only contact with humanity. He
absorbed their spiritual elan. He began to see the world as they
saw it, he began to see them as they saw themselves. Griffith
pointed out that the word "Eskimo" is from the Indians' perjorative
description "eaters of raw meat." "Flaherty," he continued, "came
to think of them by the name they call themselves: "Innuit," which
means 'we, the people.'" For at that time they did not believe in
other societies, other worlds. Finally, Griffith concluded "Flaherty
found in the Eskimos a humanity so golden that he carried it with him
even afterwards as a touchstone of judgment. To him, the Eskimos were
we the people, as we should be." Flaherty himself said: "I wanted
to show the Innuit. And I wanted to show them, not from the civilized
point of view but as they saw themselves, as 'we the people.' I
realized then that I must go to work in an entirely different way."[19]

During these years in the North, Flaherty also became a collector
of Eskimo art. The drawings he acquired in 1913-14 were published in
1915 as The Drawings of Ennoesweetok of the Sikosilingmiut Tribe of
the Eskimo.[20] His collection of several hundred carvings is highly
regarded.

NANOOK OF THE NORTH

In his book My Eskimo Friends, Flaherty literally skips over the
four years of his life from the fourth Mackenzie-sponsored expedition
to his trip, beginning in June 1920, for the sole purpose of making a
film. During these intervening years Flaherty suffered the fire disaster, showed his single positive print to geographical societies,
explorer clubs, and other interested groups, lived with relatives in
Connecticut and Michigan, wrote two articles on his explorations, and
continued to search for a sponsor for a film about Eskimos.

The persuasive Flaherty convinced Captain Thierry Mallet of
Revillon Frères to sponsor such a film. The French-owned company was
the main rival of the Hudson Bay Company in fur trading, and the film
project was looked upon as a publicity venture. The final credits
would indicate: "Revillon Frères Presents." He convinced Mallet's
company to put up $35,000. Flaherty was to receive $500 per month,

$13,000 for equipment and credit costs, and $3000 for "remuneration of natives."[21] The film did not have a title at this time.

After an arduous journey of two months, laden with equipment, Flaherty arrived on 15 August 1920 at Port Harrison on the upper northeast corner of Hudson Bay. This was the first time in his career that his sole objective was to make a film. He remained in these environs for one year. He immediately began to choose a "cast," making good his intention of focusing on one Eskimo family. He chose an Eskimo named Nanook who evidently had something of a reputation as a hunter and all-around character. With Nanook came his family, and their dogs, kayaks, and sledges. With Nanook's help he chose other Eskimos as helpers.

Flaherty brought with him all the equipment necessary for the filming, printing, developing, and projecting--in effect, a portable laboratory and theater. He took two cameras designed by Carl Akeley for use in Africa, but actually they were good for cold temperatures because they required a minimum of grease and oil for lubrication. Additionally, they were two of the first constructed for gyratory movement to allow pans or tilts without much vibration. Flaherty used this kind of tripod for all his films and was something of a pioneer of its use. To print his negative to a positive he found that the generator light fluctuated too much. As a solution he mounted the printer to the wall, cut a hole the size of a 35 mm frame, placed a piece of muslin over the aperture, and filtered in daylight.[22] He also built a drying room annex. Flaherty trained Eskimos to assist him in the laboratory aspects of the film.

By modern standards Flaherty's equipment was relatively primitive and the frigid conditions imposed a severe hardship. For example, the film stock became very brittle at 37 degrees below zero and would actually break into flakes. They had to warm the film in the igloo or hut and wrap it inside their clothing until it was exposed. Flaherty also said it was necessary to take the motion picture cameras apart in order to carefully remove the condensation that had formed when bringing them in from the cold. An often-told tale concerns his Graflex still picture camera which he could not reassemble. He entrusted it to an Eskimo assistant named "Harry Lauder," and the Eskimo managed to succeed where he had failed.[23] This was one touted example of the Eskimo's incredible eye for detail and mechanical adaptability.

One of the first sequences that Flaherty worked on was the walrus hunt. Perhaps no other sequence better illustrated how the subjects of the film, the Eskimos, became an integral part of the film-making process. Flaherty had filmed a walrus hunting sequence on his fourth expedition, though some accounts credit Nanook with the suggestion of filming the hunt. Nanook suggested that they go to Walrus Island, and after three days there, they encountered a walrus herd. Flaherty described the scene as follows:

> With harpoon set and a stout seal line carefully coiled,
> and my motion picture camera and film retorts in hand,
> off we crawled for the walrus ground. The herd lay
> sleeping--twenty great hulks guarded by two big bulls.
> At about minute intervals they raised their heads over
> the snorting and swinishly grunting herd and slowly
> looked around, then sank to sleep again. Slowly I
> snaked up to the sheltering screen of a big boulder,
> and Nanook, the end of his harpoon line lashed around
> the boulder, snaked more slowly still out toward them.
> Once in the open he could only move when the sentinels
> seemed satisfied; their heads dropped in sleep once
> more. Now only a dozen feet intervened; quickly
> Nanook closed in. As I signalled he rose upon his
> feet, and with his harpoon held high, like lightning
> he struck down at the nearest bull. A bellow and a
> roar, and twenty great walrus rolled with incredible
> speed down the wave-washed slope of the rocks to the
> sea.[24]

Flaherty returned to the post, developed and printed the negative,
and showed his rushes to the Eskimo audience. They stared at the
beam of light, they stared at Nanook in person, and, as if by magic,
they stared in amazement at Nanook on the screen. "Ivuik, Ivuik!"
the walrus, they shouted. "Be sure of your harpoon! Be sure of your
harpoon! Hold him! Hold him!" they cried, as the hunters and harpooned beast engaged in a life and death tug of war. But inch by
inch the walrus was pulled in, and the Eskimo cheers rocked the house.
Now they understood Falherty's film project. The fame of the film,
Flaherty said, spread up and down the coast, and the new Eskimos who
came to the post begged him to show the "ivuik aggie," the walrus
film.[25]

The building of the igloo sequence demonstrated early in
Flaherty's film career that improvisation was necessary in order to
express and capture the reality of a particular situation. Probably
no better daily task demonstrated the mechanical ability of the
Eskimo than building an igloo. The average igloo, about twelve feet
in diameter, was too small to permit adequate lighting for interior
photography. In addition, the film stock speed was too slow. So,
Flaherty had Nanook and his friends build an igloo of twice the average size. This structure proved to be unwieldy until they began icing
the walls very early during construction. Even so, the light from the
blocks of translucent ice was still insufficient for photography.
Finally, half the dome had to be cut away, but this was not shown in
frame, thus giving the appearance that the camera had been placed
inside. Nanook and his family, as it were, had to sleep out of
doors.[26]

In January 1921 Flaherty, Nanook, and the others set off on an
abortive bear hunt for more major shooting. Unfortunately they

could not find a single bear. They ran short of food and had no oil
for lamps. They even had to burn film strips to boil water for tea.
After 600 miles and eight weeks of traveling they returned to the post
only to learn that in less than a day's travel from there a she-bear
with two cubs had been recently cornered by two huskies. But it was
too late to film. If nothing else was gained during this trip,
Nanook at least related the story of Comock of Kovik, a thrilling
tale of survival that Flaherty was to make note of and exploit much
later in his life.[27]

Nanook, according to Flaherty, tried to talk him into shooting
other scenes of Eskimo life. But by August 1921 Flaherty felt as
though he had enough footage to complete his film. (The money probably had run out by this point.) Nanook, Flaherty wrote, "never quite
understood why I should have gone to all the fuss and bother of making
the 'big aggie' of him--the hunting, yes--but surely everyone knew
the Eskimo, and could anything be more common than dogs and sledges
and snow houses?" Nanook believed that the Eskimos and traders he
knew represented the whole population of the world. It was hard to
comprehend the thousands, the millions outside, who would see him on
the screen. Nanook, waving goodbye, followed Flaherty's ship in his
kayak. Flaherty himself was never to venture North again. Two years
later Flaherty received word by the once-a-year mail from the North
that Nanook was dead. They said he had starved to death on a deer
hunt, but that was probably just speculation.[28] By the time of his
death Nanook was already immortalized in the film which bears his
name, and the news of his death flashed around the world.

Flaherty returned to New York to put his film together. He worked
with Charles Gelb on the editing and Carl Stearns Clancy on the titles. Without any training in the film grammar of the times he was
able to anticipate the close ups, medium shots, and wide angle shots
needed to create a sense of logical continuity. He worked on editing
aspects of the film during the winter of 1921-22.[29] Then followed
the most difficult job of all; finding a distributor. Unable to
recognize Nanook of the North as a film genre with a commercial formula, the major American distributors dismissed it out of hand. One
distributor even felt sorry Flaherty had gone through all the hardship in the North to make a film that the public would never see.
Another did not even answer his phone calls after previewing the film.
Flaherty had to learn a lesson that would serve him for the other
films he was to make. He had to sell interest in his films, he had
to promote them in the trade and to the public at large. Showmanship,
to a great extent, became a necessary part of the Flaherty method.

Because it was so totally different from the films of the times,
distributors did not know how to judge its commercial potential.
Nanook of the North fit none of the box office formulas, such as the
silent comedies of Mack Sennett or Charlie Chaplin or the risque ro-
mances of Cecil B. DeMille. The distributors assumed audiences wanted
to be thrilled and entertained in a fantasy world of laughter, romance,

and melodrama. They did not want to risk experimentation with a
film that was edifying, uplifting, and educational as well as
artistic.

Finally, thanks to his sponsor Revillon Frères, Flaherty was able
to secure distribution through another French-owned company, Pathé
Frères. They at first wanted to split Nanook of the North into separate episodes for a series of educational shorts, but better judgment
prevailed.[30] Securing a showcase theater was almost as difficult.
Pathé solved the problem by block-booking Nanook with the comercially-
hot Grandma's Boy, starring Harold Lloyd. So Pathé made a deal with
Samuel Rothafel of the Capitol Theater in New York, where Nanook premiered on 11 June 1922. Although Flaherty was told that Eskimos did
not interest the public, the returns showed otherwise.[31] The double-
bill grossed $43,000 in one week; though there was no way to distin-
guish between the public's interest in Harold Lloyd and Nanook.
Within six weeks of its opening Flaherty and Revillon Frères sold
Nanook for distribution in England where it ran in London for three
months. It also played in Siam, China, and Moscow. By September
1926 it had grossed about $251,000; but, because the foreign rights
had been sold too cheaply, Flaherty and Revillon Frères had only
received a profit of $36,000. The film had cost about $55,000, which
included $15,000 overbudget, also to become a Flaherty trademark.[32]

Nanook of the North opened to rave reviews and was almost immediately considered one of the greatest films of all times. Criticizing the typical feature film of the day, the New York Times
(12 June 1922) said, "Beside this film the usual photoplay, the so-
called 'dramatic' work of the screen, becomes as thin and blank as
the celluloid on which it is printed...." Robert E. Sherwood, one
of the first important film critics, chose it as one of the best pictures of the year, "literally in a class by itself." No one, however,
called it a documentary. That had to wait for the appearance of
Flaherty's next film, Moana.[33]

Meanwhile, Flaherty was able to exploit the success of his film
by writing for publication. He prepared a photographic essay entitled "Indomitable Children of the North" for Travel magazine showing
Eskimo life during the making of Nanook. For The World's Work magazine he prepared a series of articles on the origin and making of the
film as well as on his Belcher Island exploration and on tales of
survival. Finally, before the next film project absorbed all his
interest, he and his wife Frances collaborated on his first book,
My Eskimo Friends (1924) which in rich detail described his four expeditions to the Hudson Bay area and his fifth trip for the purpose
of making Nanook of the North.[34] Although Flaherty received income
from these publications, they were, in a way, part of the showmanship
he used to promote his films.

MOANA

Attracted by the commercial success of <u>Nanook of the North</u>, Jesse Lasky, Paramount executive and also a self-confessed outdoorsman, offered Flaherty another chance to make a film. Paramount had turned down <u>Nanook</u> for distribution. Now he said to Flaherty: "I want you to go off somewhere and make me another <u>Nanook</u>. Go where you will, do what you like—I'll foot the bills. The world's your oyster."[35] Whether he used these words is quite beside the point. Paramount, at least, was now interested in the commercial possibilities of the naturalist cinema as it was being carved out by Flaherty. Several months later Paramount also commissioned a similar film under Merian C. Cooper and Ernest B. Schoedsack. Released in 1925 as <u>Grass</u>, it traced the migration of the Bakhtiari tribes over the Zardeh Kuh Mountains of Turkey and Persia.[36] By 20 February 1923, Flaherty had decided to shoot his next film in Samoa. He signed a contract on that date with Paramount for the production of a film "which shall artisticly [sic] and dramatically present upon the screen the customs, life and conditions of the natives of the said Islands of Samoa or any of them which the Producer may select with such plot or other form of construction...."[37]

The idea of going to Samoa stemmed from Flaherty's friendship with Frederick O'Brien, whose book <u>White Shadows in the South Seas</u>, had gone through several editions since its appearance in 1919. O'Brien, and other friends who had just returned from Samoa, convinced Flaherty that Samoa contained one of the purest forms of Polynesian culture. They convinced him that the Samoans had preserved their old customs and habits, and had been least influenced by white culture. They even named a specific island, Savaii, and particular village, Safune, as the perfect site for his film.[38]

O'Brien must not be given sole credit for inspiring this project. Flaherty had already decided that his next film would be set outside modern civilization, in an indigenous culture endangered by assimilation or by stricter forms of cultural domination such as colonial rule. It was a mere accident of time and place that Flaherty chose Samoa. Other geographical locations would have done just as well.

Flaherty, accompanied by his wife, three daughters, his brother, and their Irish nursemaid, arrived in Samoa in April 1923. They went directly to the village of Safune on the westerly island of Savaii. They met the local czar, a trader named Felix David, made the acquaintance of the village chiefs, and went about securing accommodations for the long period Flaherty required to make a film.

White colonialism had already taken a firm root, much more so than Flaherty had expected. It detracted from the Polynesian culture and its representatives actively opposed the making of a film. For one thing the prestige and leadership role that Flaherty assumed in the eyes of the Samoans interfered with the private rule of Felix

David. David had been in the South Pacific for thirty-six years and his word was law in Safune where he was the only white man. According to David Flaherty, he exploited the islanders financially, socially and sexually. Felix David accused Flaherty of faking scenes, saying that he did not wish to see the natives misrepresented. He said Flaherty was ruining the natives with high wages and interfering with the copra-cutting industry. In short, he was a continual source of propaganda against Flaherty and the film project. Moreover, he had the support of the equally corrupt New Zealand Resident Commissioner, an alcoholic charged with enforcing the new prohibition laws. Felix David and the commissioner were finally exposed; the former was banished by the local authorities and the latter committed suicide.[39]

Frances Flaherty felt as though Polynesian life was changing so rapidly that she could see the end. Christianity had already forced the Samoans to clip their shoulder length hair, forced them to change from loin cloths to printed dresses and shirts. Western dress was the reality, but for purposes of the film the Flahertys required the Samoans to appear in their native siapos, harking back to an earlier time.

There was a certain feeling of condescension that delayed if not prevented the Flahertys' understanding and appreciation of Samoan culture. On the one hand, Frances Flaherty praised the Samoans for the way they accepted Christianity with more brotherly love than the missionaries themselves and for the way they enriched the songs, ritual, and gospel of their new religion. On the other, she described their child-like qualities and their lack of thought and intellect. "They have not tasted of the Tree of Knowledge," she wrote. "Existence for them is a beautiful plain, sun blessed, fertile, flower-spread, balm kissed, where life runs in and out and in and out like an unending repetition of song."[40] She and her husband did not understand that what appears outwardly as a simple, primitive society, can be just as complicated and ritualistic with similar demands and anxieties as any modern day civilization.

Since Robert Flaherty came to Samoa with no experience in the South Seas, with little or no knowledge of Polynesian culture, and no scenario or script, the theme of the film was not readily apparent. What the Flahertys brought with them instead was a preconceived notion about the element of struggle for survival modeled on Nanook of the North. They thought that this element could be found in the Samoans' relationship to the sea. That struggle, however, did not exist on land; food was abundant and housing needs in the warm climate were minimal. The sea held out the only hope for building a dramatic theme. So as late as November 1923, seven months after their arrival, Flaherty was still writing to Lasky that the sea was the answer for drama.[41] But Flaherty found no giant octopus or killer shark, only sea turtles and robber crabs. The theme lay elsewhere.

The rituals and hospitality of the Samoans were obstacles when the Flahertys were looking for sea monsters, but the months of residence and first-hand observation of and contact with the Samoan people changed their minds. "We had determined," Frances Flaherty wrote, "that we would make our picture simply of things fa'a-Samoa--that is, of the every day life of the village, which, after all, in its natural loveliness and simplicity and beauty, was theme enough for a South Sea Island film." What had seemed to them "trivial, unrelated and lacking in pattern" ultimately became the object of their scrutiny. Everyday work, such as making cloth, gathering food and baking it over hot stones, expressed its own beauty. The mass village dances became seas of grace and rhythm.

From June to October they did not make a foot of permanent film. They worked out technical problems of photography. They also tried to recruit the central characters around which they would structure their film. One "star" walked out on them, another cut her hair in the middle of production. They deliberately looked for physical beauty. If there were defects, they tried to hide them or not emphasize them.[42]

While shooting Moana Flaherty experimented with long-focus lenses. He found that lenses of focal lengths greater than six inches were widespread in still photography but little used in motion pictures. Although he used a telephoto lens in Nanook of the North, it was in Moana that he learned its true value. Strangely, it was in intimate scenes and portraits that he found it most useful. "I began," he wrote, "using them to take close ups in order to obviate self-consciousness on the part of my subjects. The Samoans, I found, acted much more naturally with the camera thirty or forty feet away than when I was cranking right under their noses...." When projected, the shots appeared better than wide angle shots. The figures, Flaherty said, had a roundness, a stereoscopic reality and beauty. Almost all of Moana was shot with lenses of six inches or more. The shots of a Samoan boy in the high coconut tree were made with a twelve-inch lens seventy-five feet below. In middle distance outdoors, long focus lenses also seemed superior. The Samoan dancers were "alive and real, the shadows softer, and the breadfruit trees seemed like living things rather than a flat background."[43]

The most important innovative photographic discovery--or perhaps application is a better word--was the use of panchromatic film stock. Up to this point in the history of the motion picture industry, the use of orthochromatic stock had been widespread. This stock was fine for working with whites and blacks and shades of gray, but it was fairly insensitive to color; thus, reds for example would appear black. The rich colors of Samoan vegetation and the Samoans themselves did not photograph well enough to meet the Flahertys' requirements. Flaherty had brought with him a Prizma color camera and panchromatic stock, a black-and-white, color sensitive film that had to be developed in complete darkness. Eastman Kodak, the manufacturer,

said it was tricky and should be used mainly for cloud effects.[44]
"It was an experimental use of this film," Frances Flaherty wrote,
"with our ordinary black and white camera (Akeley) that threw the
first gleam of light on our difficulty. We found that panchromatic
film, used in direct sunlight, gave an extraordinary stereoscopic
effect. The figures jumped right out of the screen. They had a
roundness and modeling and looked alive, and because of the color
correction, retained their full beauty and texture."[45] Although
Moana was not the first film entirely made on panchromatic stock
(that honor belonged to The Headless Horseman [1922]), it was the
first film to attract serious attention to the production possibilities of this film type. The film industry soon followed Flaherty's
example.

Another distinctive feature about Flaherty's photography was that
most of the footage was deliberately shot when the sun was either
rising or setting, when shadows were longest, thus increasing the
stereoscopic effect. He also shot in direct sunlight, establishing
a basic pattern in black and white; the grays looked after themselves.
All in all, Flaherty shot some 240,000 feet which was considered
rather extravagant for one director and cameraman on essentially one
location.[46]

The problems associated with developing of negatives caused a
serious setback to the Flaherty team. As in Canada, Flaherty brought
with him equipment to develop and print his film. He trained two
young Samoan men to help in the laboratory work. More than a year
after they had been in Safune they noticed dark flashes on the film,
seeming to substantiate Kodak's claim that panchromatic film was not
reliable. Even the negatives that they had shipped to the United
States further deteriorated in transit. Finally, they traced their
problem to the natural pool water which they had been using in the
laboratory cave. It seems that the silver nitrate, instead of wash-
ing away with the tides, accumulated and tainted the negative.
Finally, after changing pools they solved the problem but not before
discarding almost everything previously shot. The silver nitrate was
also discovered as the cause of Robert Flaherty's rather serious ill-
ness since he had made it a practice to drink the cave water.[47]

Since nature was so benign in Samoa--at least according to the
picture the Flahertys painted--it was difficult to find the element
of conflict that the Flahertys learned instinctively was the core of
documentary film. They chose not to develop the dichotomy of white,
western civilization and brown, Polynesian society. Man against man
as a theme was eliminated at the outset; so too, through gradual experience on the island, man against the sea; and, if you will, man
against the jungle. The only element of conflict they selected for
the screen was the process of tattooing.

The conflict in tattooing was the painful ordeal that Ta'avale
(Moana) had to undergo in order to be tattooed. It represented

14

Ta'avale's coming of age in Samoan society, his acceptance into the
society of men. This rite of passage would make a fitting conclusion
for the film. The Flahertys had seen two persons tattooed previously.
Although tattooing was officially discouraged, others have said the
practice was widespread. The Flahertys believed it was one of those
aspects of Samoan culture that was going to disappear, and so they
would capture it on film. The process itself was very painful.
Needle points of bone, impregnated with dye, are tapped into the
skin, a little at a time, with frequent moments of rest so the subject can endure the pain. Ta'avale's tattooing actually took six
weeks, and when finished, he was tattooed from the upper parts of his
body to his knees. One is tempted to say that he was permanently dis-
figured. But Frances Flaherty explained it as "the beautification of
the body by a race who, without metals, without clay, express their
feeling for beauty in the perfection of their own glorious bodies.
Deeper than that, however, is its spring in a common human need, the
need for struggle, for some test of endurance, some supreme mark of
individual worth and proof of the quality of man."[48]

If Flaherty did not film the social problems on Savaii, he did so
by choice, for he was certainly aware of them. We have already described the situation with trader Felix David and the New Zealand
Resident Commissioner. The latter's name became synonymous with
homosexuality, which was relatively unknown to native Samoans.
Newton Rowe, an island agriculture official, extensively described
the problems that beset this small community. For example, in 1924
when Flaherty was there, the colonial government embarked on a policy
of abolishing communal land ownership on a people who had no concept
of private property. They imposed legal marriage ceremonies when
the custom was marriage--and divorce--by consent. Rowe concluded:
"The administration of justice in Savaii during 1923 and 1924 amounted
to a scandal I should think without modern parallel in a British pos-
session." In many ways, the story resembled the treatment of the
American Indians in the United States. The efforts to eliminate
tribal customs, evangelize Indians, and absorb them into the mainstream of society were the same. The maladministration of the islands was so widespread that it culminated on 28 December 1929, in
the machine gunning of the island High Chief and ten others.[49]

Moana required a year and ten months to make, about three times
as long as the average Hollywood feature film in 1925. Flaherty said
in September that the cost was $153,000, again over budget, to the
tune of $53,000.[50] Griffith said Moana had earned a modest profit on
a modest investment, but in a royalty statement from Paramount dated
28 March 1931, the film costs had totalled $260,621, and although
Flaherty was to get 40% of the net profit, Paramount reported a loss
of $43,875.[51] If Moana earned any profit at all, it was only after
many years.

Paramount officials were somewhat impressed by a long rough cut
of Moana, but by the time Flaherty edited the film down to its

finished form their enthusiasm had waned. Without the sensationalism
of sea monsters or a love interest, they were perplexed on how to exploit or advertise the film. They were even tempted to shelve it.
Finally, it was previewed in six select towns where it did relatively
well. But Flaherty had to promote the film through mailing lists for
special interest groups. It opened in New York on 7 February 1926,
under the utterly misleading advertisement from Paramount "The Love-
Life of a South Sea Siren." Unlike the six-town preview, there was
no special promotion of the film.

So began a string of bad experiences between Flaherty and Hollywood, anticipated somewhat by its refusal to distribute Nanook when
he first offered it. Hugh Gray said that Paramount cut up the original negative of Moana to release it as "The Love Life of A South Sea
Siren." "Not only did they hack it to pieces," he said, "they were
so completely fed up with it that they even destroyed the negatives.
So all you can get now is a duplicate copy." Despite all the prestige, Hollywood concluded there was no money in Flaherty; and he concluded that Hollywood would not support films on the basis of artistic
integrity alone. Once he told Gray that "Going through Hollywood was
like going through a sewer in a glass-bottom boat."[52]

During the making of Moana Robert Flaherty established a life
partnership in film production with his wife Frances. She became at
once his critic, confidant, spokeswoman, and publicist. An accomplished photographer herself, as the Moana stills illustrate, Frances
could advise on photographic problems in addition to thematic ones.
The producer credits on the final version of Moana gave Robert and
Frances equal importance, and in a similar capacity she assisted in
all her husband's feature-length projects. The credits also indicate
that Julian Johnson did the editing and titles. David Flaherty, however, said Johnson did neither; they were done by Robert and Frances.[53]

Although Moana failed at the box office and with the public at
large, it attracted substantial critical attention, almost all of
which was extremely favorable. In retrospect, probably the most important single piece of critical discussion was the review written
by John Grierson under the signature of "The Moviegoer" in the New
York Sun of 8 February 1926. Here for the first time in English a
critic used the word "documentary" to describe the film, though the
French had used it ("documentaire") in reference to films of travel
and exploration. That the film prompted Grierson to begin thinking
about the theoretical foundations of this new genre was of more lasting significance.

TWO EXPERIMENTS

While waiting for the release of Moana, Flaherty made a short,
experimental film entitled The Potterymaker (1925), sponsored by the
New York Metropolitan Museum of Art, under a grant from the actress

Maude Adams. The film is notable only for a piece of trivia: the old woman in the film is the widow of General George Custer. Otherwise, it is not well thought out and ends rather abruptly with the vase in the brick oven. It did foreshadow a subject that Flaherty was to treat in more detail in Industrial Britain (1933).[54]

Another relatively small film project that occupied Flaherty's time was Twenty-Four Dollar Island (1927).[55] This is a film in which New York is the central character, principally its skyscrapers and the incessant activity in its harbor. Flaherty used this opportunity to experiment with long focus lenses. "I think I made shots," he said, "from the tops of every skyscraper in Manhattan, looking down into the canyons of streets with their antlike human life. I remember shooting from the roof of the Telephone Building across to the Jersey shore with an 8-inch lens and even at that distance, obtaining a stereoscopic effect that seemed magical. It was like drawing a veil from beyond, revealing life scarcely visible to the naked eye."[56]

In another vein, it is important to recall that Flaherty had spent most of his life in the wilderness, far away from modern urban civilization. When confronted with a film about New York it was not the people that interested him, not the achievements of individuals, but the overwhelming achievement of a civilization symbolized by its architecture. Again the film was financed outside the normal channels of the film industry. Flaherty shot some 30,000 feet, but the final cut was only two reels. It was used as a backdrop for a stage show, presumably with dancing girls, at the Roxy Theater in December 1927, and in the following January it was given a limited run at a New York art house.[57]

WHITE SHADOWS IN THE SOUTH SEAS AND TABU

In 1928 Flaherty had a bout with Hollywood that resulted in disaster. Irving Thalberg of MGM had acquired the film rights to O'Brien's book, White Shadows in the South Seas. O'Brien and Flaherty were good friends, and Flaherty had gained a good deal of experience in the South Seas during the making of Moana. Thalberg invited Flaherty to co-direct the film with action director W. S. Van Dyke. Now Flaherty had the opportunity to make a film about the exploitation of Polynesian people, and it seemed as though Thalberg had come up with yet another marvelous idea.

Flaherty, however, became very disillusioned early in the project. He and Laurence Stallings, the playwright brought in to work on the script, tried to convince Thalberg that Herman Melville's Typee would make a much better film on the same subject matter. Stallings quit (or was fired) and Ray Dole and Jack Cunningham were enlisted to finish the writing. When Flaherty arrived on Tahiti he was appalled by the production crew's indifference to Tahitian culture. None of the literature gives any details of Flaherty's relationship with

Van Dyke, though one can safely assume it was strained. Flaherty, in the end, lost interest in the project and returned to the States, with his worst suspicions of Hollywood still unchanged.[58]

Flaherty's personal feelings toward the Hollywood industry did not prevent him from taking the next studio offer that came along. In 1928 William Fox offered him a chance to make a feature film about the Acoma Indians of New Mexico. Flaherty wrote a scenario based on a story by Randall H. Faye. In the scenario, a brave Acoma warrior named Lone Wolf captures Wild Deer, an Indian maiden from the Navajos, the hereditary enemies of the Acoma. To save Wild Deer from death at the hands of the Acoma villagers, Lone Wolf must hunt the silver-tipped grizzly and bring back its coveted skin within thirty days. In one ending Lone Wolf was to be killed off in an encounter with the Navajos. In the alternative ending he was to return alive, and the lovers would be reunited. Much of the action was to be seen through the eyes of Lone Wolf's little brother, and one suspects that if Flaherty had shot the film, he would have made maximum use of Indian actors plus the dramatic natural setting. Calder-Marshall, based on the Rotha and Wright manuscript, gives the impression that Flaherty left the project because of the love story interjected by Fox. However, the basis for the love story had existed in the scenario prepared by Flaherty. The problem was not the story so much as the two white actors whom Fox hired to play the leads. Flaherty chose for the five months he was there to work with the Indian boy and other Indian actors. Then Flaherty received a better offer and left a situation that violated what he considered to be his integrity as a film-maker.[59]

Flaherty received a better offer from F. W. Murnau, the famous German director of The Last Laugh (1924) who had emigrated to Hollywood. Now Flaherty believed he would get the chance to make a film of the South Seas that White Shadows could never have been. To produce and finance the film outside the Hollywood establishment Murnau and Flaherty formed their own company and signed a contract with an independent studio called Colorart. This studio reneged or went bankrupt during the production, and the result was that Murnau had to finance the film himself, making it a rather one-sided affair and ultimately leading to Flaherty's withdrawal from the film Tabu.

The impact of western civilization upon primitive cultures as a theme still preoccupied Flaherty. From his experience in Canada, Samoa, and Tahiti he felt that white and nonwhite cultures were degraded in the colonial experience. Flaherty and Murnau wrote two original stories based upon this theme. In the first one, "Turia," a young pearl diver named Tino dives in dangerous waters for giant pearls. Tino is handsome and admirable in every way. But traders and merchants exploit his innocence. His half-caste woman, Turia, pawns his pearls to a Chinese trader one by one until they are gone. She asks Tino to dive one more time. He dies.[60]

18

In the second story, "Tabu," the protagonist is still exploited by traders in the same way but the focus of good and evil was shifted to Reri and Matahi, who represent all that is beautiful and romantic, and the priest Hitu who mercilessly enforces the _tabu_ that was placed on Reri for the high chief of the islands. Griffith said that "Turia" was closer to Flaherty's conception but he signed the second story as well.[61]

There were aesthetic disagreements between the two strong-willed directors. Since Murnau held the purse strings, he got his way. In addition, David Flaherty who was hired on the production crew, pointed out that his brother was a prodigious spender while Murnau was quite frugal, thus adding to their difficulty.[62] In September 1929 after three months on location in Tahiti, Robert Flaherty sold his share in the film to Murnau and left.

Rotha and Wright concluded that there was not much of Flaherty's work in the film. Similarly, Lotte Eisner concluded that Murnau completely dominated the film. But she does recall seeing some rushes that were identified as Flaherty's.[63] Some of Flaherty's influence, however, does show through when _Tabu_ is compared with _Moana_. Both films aroused an empathy for a noble race of innocents. Yet while they shared this purpose, Murnau and Flaherty's approaches to direction could not have been more antagonistic. Murnau planned and worked out details to the letter. Flaherty's temperament was loose by comparison. He reacted to the material, improvised, and experimented.

As a feature film _Tabu_ was highly acclaimed, made a good profit, and won an Academy Award for Floyd Crosby's camerawork. But the ill-fated Murnau did not live long enough to enjoy his success, for he died under somewhat disreputable circumstances at almost the same time the film premiered in March 1931. Flaherty could chalk off another distasteful experience with the contrivance and artificiality of the commercial cinema. As distressful as the _Tabu_ project was, it was neither Flaherty's last attempt at co-direction nor his last fling with the feature. _Elephant Boy_ was still to come. The _Tabu_ project suggested that Flaherty did not consider himself exclusively a documentarian. He felt the art cinema could draw upon his talents. But _Tabu_ helped further alienate him from the studio feature film and win many friends who shared his alienation.

Before leaving the American phase of Flaherty's life, a mention should be made of a small but significant chapter which his biographers have omitted. The correspondence, published by Erik Barnouw in 1972, between his father and Robert Flaherty revealed that Flaherty had intended to make a film on the island of Bali before the Flaherty-Murnau collaboration. Flaherty asked Adriaan J. Barnouw, a professor of Dutch history, language, and literature of Columbia University, to intercede on his behalf with the Dutch East India officials who administered Bali. In a letter to Barnouw Flaherty said:

19

> I should like nothing better than to undertake a film
> in the Dutch East Indies, particularly in the island of
> Bali of which I have heard such wonderful accounts, es-
> pecially from yourself and Maurice Stern, the painter,
> who lived there for two years. Because Bali is alto-
> gether unknown in the world--at least in this part of
> the world--the revelation in film form of the beauty
> and culture of the Balinese would, I am sure, command
> widespread attention. Another thing that particularly
> interested me was your statement that no missionaries
> are allowed on the island; this should obviate our work-
> ing for months, as we did in Samoa, to get beneath the
> veneer of missionary civilization.[64]

In March 1929, almost three years later, Flaherty was still interested
in the Bali project, with Murnau's collaboration. "Our idea,"
Flaherty wrote to Barnouw, "as regards making this picture is to go
there with no preconceived story of any kind, but to live there a
year and during that time develop and make our picture. In the picture there is going to be no concession to any box-office. Mrs.
Flaherty and I believe that it is the greatest opportunity we have
ever had to carry out our ideas since Murnau's great reputation and
name will have the effect of making producers take a more serious
view toward the kind of thing we want to do." By May 1929 Flaherty
told Barnouw that he and Murnau were first going to make a film in
the South Seas for "certain economic reasons." But "this Bali is the
Ultima Thule of our desires."[65]

FLAHERTY IN EXILE

The European phase of Flaherty's career began in December 1930
when he traveled to pre-Nazi Germany to meet his wife and family who
had been there for some time. One of his objectives was the negotia-
tion for publishing a book on his Samoan experiences. The book,
entitled Samoa, was published in German by R. Hobbing of Berlin in
1932. Calder-Marshall wrote that Flaherty was "deeply shocked" by
the open sexuality of Berlin during these late years of the Weimar
Republic. The experience struck a puritanical streak in Flaherty,
also suggested by the omission of sex in his films. In Germany,
though, he was able to meet important European directors such as
Joris Ivens from Holland and Eisenstein and Pudovkin from Russia who
admired his work and who, like Flaherty, represented more or less the
antithesis of Hollywood filmmaking. For several months Flaherty
negotiated futilely with the Soviet Trade Mission in Berlin over the
possibility of making a film about a remote tribe in Central Asia.[66]

From Germany Flaherty went to England, which served as his base
of operations for almost the entire decade of the 1930s. According
to Paul Rotha, a member of the inner circle of documentary filmmakers in England, it was Frances Flaherty who telephoned John

Grierson from Berlin soliciting a job for her husband. As head of the film unit of the Empire Marketing Board and an enthusiastic supporter of Flaherty's work, Grierson recognized his chance to elevate the stature of his film unit. The Empire Marketing Board was charged with making productions to promote British industry. But despite whatever justification Grierson may have offered to his superiors, Rotha claims that Grierson's principal objective in hiring Flaherty was to let his crew see something first hand of Flaherty's "instinctive handling of the film camera and of his wonderful powers of observation."[67]

Flaherty was not hired just as a teacher, however. He was hired to make a specific film about the personal craftsmanship of workers that was obscured by the smoke, steam, and grimy appearance of British industry. Flaherty was given the assignment at an unheard of budget of 2500 pounds, which Grierson managed to wrangle from the bureaucracy.

Some difficulty emerged over Flaherty's characteristic refusal to write a script. Grierson needed one to satisfy the demands of government officials. One frequently told anecdote involves the discord over the script for Industrial Britain. When Grierson threatened to withhold money if no script was forthcoming, Flaherty sequestered himself in a hotel for three days. He then emerged with a wad of paper. The top sheet, written in a heavy hand, said: "INDUSTRIAL BRITAIN, A Film About Craftsmen, by Robert J. Flaherty." The next was: "A Scenario: Scenes of Industrial Britain." The other pages were completely blank.[68] The point was well taken.

Flaherty did not write a script, nor did he approach this new project in his usual manner by slowly absorbing his surroundings, letting the drama reveal itself before his camera. Persons who accompanied him described his desire to shoot almost anything that attracted his interest, so prodigiously that he used almost the film's entire allocation of raw stock on what he considered "tests." But everyone was impressed with his power of observation, the deep concentration he brought to his subject matter, such as glass-blowing or pottery making, and his anticipation of movement. During this work he was introduced to the spring-driven Newman Sinclair camera with quickly interchangeable magazines and a wide range of lenses, and also a gyroheaded tripod from Gaumont British.

Although Grierson admired the craftsmanship of Flaherty's rushes, there was no unified theme to the shooting. Grierson, Basil Wright and Arthur Elton had to do additional shooting. Grierson himself edited the film with Edgar Anstey's assistance. Flaherty had no part in the editing, nor in writing the commentary.[69]

Grierson, no thanks to Flaherty, was able to bring the film in under budget. Once edited, it was shelved for about a year until Gaumont British put up some money to add a sound track. Finally

Industrial Britain was released in 1933 with a package of Empire Marketing Board films with great success as a promotional film and a landmark in the history of documentary film. Several short films were made from the Flaherty outtake footage.

To sum up the Industrial Britain experience, Flaherty found that the difficulties of working for a sponsor could be just as great as those Hollywood offered. Secondly, this film together with Twenty-Four Dollar Island represented his only film experiences in an urban and industrial milieu. Thirdly, it demonstrated a consistent perform-ance of extravagant shooting oblivious to any story or script demands. Finally, the Industrial Britain project provided a convenient if not necessary jumping off point for further film work in the Aran Islands.

MAN OF ARAN

During the time Flaherty spent in Germany and England he had an idea in the corner of his mind about making the man-against-the-sea drama which could not be realized in Moana. The idea was revived on a trans-Atlantic crossing when he fell into a conversation with a young Irishman from Cork. On discussing the depression, the young man said: "You don't know what hard times are. Let me tell you of the Aran Islands (Ireland), where I have been. These islands are barren rocks, without trees. Before people can grow their potatoes--almost the only food they can win from the land--they have to make the soil to grow them in! For the rest of their food they have to go to sea in a little canvas boat, unbelievably primitive. And this sea they have to brave in these cockleshells is one of the worst in the world."[70] As in the Moana project, too much importance should not be given to suggestions like this one, because in the long run they are but mere accidents of time and place. The perimeters of Flaherty's interest had already been well established, and the Aran Islands met those conditions. Calder-Marshall reported that John Grierson ad-vised Flaherty to read J. M. Synge's play Riders to the Sea and his book The Aran Islands. Later on, Flaherty said that he and his wife began background research quite on their own, including the words of Synge.[71]

Grierson, nevertheless, was instrumental in putting Flaherty in touch with Gaumont British, the largest company in the British film industry. After outlining his intended film, Flaherty secured the enthusiastic support of Michael Balcon, head producer at the studio, and an agreement was arranged. So, after another try at the spon-sored film represented by Industrial Britain Flaherty returned to commercial cinema. Gaumont British backed Flaherty, whose only com-mercial success so far had been Nanook of the North, because the British industry wanted to assert its own independence from Hollywood, and because of a growing critical demand in Britain for more natural-istic films.[72]

The Aran Islands are situated some thirty miles due west from the port city of Galway, Ireland. They consist of three principal islands: Inishmore, Inishmaan, and Inisheer. The largest is Inishmore, approximately nine miles long and only one and one-half miles at its widest point. The terrain slopes upward from the northeastern shore into rolling hills, bordered by stone walls and sparsely dotted by whitewashed cottages with thatched roofs. The hills end abruptly on the southwestern shore facing the Atlantic. Cliffs several hundred feet high loom over the Atlantic Ocean whose waves roll in unhindered from the open sea. Standing there on the cliffs one senses this western outpost of Europe.

The preponderance of rocks suggests the hard life which the islanders endure. Rocks stacked high mark off the pitifully small plots of land. Rocks along the coast glisten in the afternoon sun. Steep fields of stone surround the ancient fort Dun Aengus on the high cliff, an arduous climb for ancient as well as modern man. The limestone fields are amazingly flat and sheer, carved smooth by the ice age, as though nature intended them for the foundations of homes or churches. Between the rocks and crevices, lean cows search for grass.

Synge went to the Aran Islands near the turn of the century to study the Gaelic language and observe the customs of the isolated people who lived there. Aran was one of the few places in Ireland where Gaelic survived as the prevalent tongue. And Synge like other writers of his generation tried to seek out the traditional language and culture that had all but been destroyed by the Anglicization of Ireland. His book The Aran Islands (1907) described a close society of fisher folk, wary of strangers, full of mythology and superstition. The book anticipated the problems Flaherty would encounter in making his film Man of Aran. Though a resident for several years and though he learned to speak the language, Synge felt a stranger isolated from the people who surrounded him. Flaherty was also a victim of this insularity though he never admitted it. More importantly, however, Synge provided a clear literary expression of some aspects of Aran life that became parts of the film such as the gathering of seaweed and growing food from the impoverished soil. Synge's one-act play Riders to the Sea (1904), set in the Aran Islands, vividly dramatized in dialogue the life and death struggle between man and the sea that Flaherty hoped to create in images. Flaherty said: "I have never anywhere in the world seen men so brave who would undertake such risks with the sea, and yet the Aran Islander can't swim a stroke. If he touches the water he gives up, and he'll go down like a stone. And not only that, but the sea to the Aran Islander is the terror of his life, as Synge has brought out so well and so poignantly and dramatically in his wonderful play Riders to the Sea. But brave as the Aran Islander is, if one of his fellows is drowning he will not make a move to save him. For to him the sea is a monster. The sea must never be denied its victim, otherwise it will claim the rescuer, too, for its own. It must have its victim."[73] Said with some exaggeration,

it contains a core of truth. The point, however, is the clear literary relationship between Synge's work and the origin of Flaherty's
film.

On their first excursion to the islands, the Flahertys met Pat
Mullen, a native-born islander who had lived in the United States and
had returned to his homeland. Mullen served as Flaherty's assistant
director on location and was his main instrument for dealing with the
suspicious natives. Mullen's book, <u>Man of Aran</u>, is the classic account of the making of the film and it is also rich in Aran folklore.
Meeting Flaherty for the first time, Mullen described him as a "great
giant-bodied man, white-haired and blue eyed."[74] Actually Flaherty's
build made him appear taller than he really was (5 feet, 8 inches),
but it is interesting to note that he had gone completely white at
47 years of age. Since both Flaherty and Mullen were independent
characters, the relationship between them had its difficult moments.
Mullen felt as though he never quite understood Flaherty.

When the Flaherty family returned to Aran to stay in January 1932
they rented a house on the main island of Inishmore in the tiny hamlet
of Kilmurvey facing a cove of white sandy beaches. In a routine that
was familiar by now, they built a studio and laboratory facilities
and set about their first task. "We select," Flaherty wrote, "a
group of the most attractive and appealing characters we can find,
to represent a family, and through them tell our story. It is always
a long and difficult process, this type finding, for it is surprising
how few faces stand the test of the camera."[75]

Flaherty had much difficulty at first securing the cooperation of
the islanders due in part to their suspicion of strangers. Although
Flaherty was a common name on Aran and in the western Ireland, he was
a Protestant and people recalled tales of the Protestant evangelists
who came during the famine trading a piece of bread or a cup of soup
for the islanders' Catholicism. Mullen himself had something of a
shadowy reputation as a political radical which did not fare well
with some of the locals. And Flaherty was a wealthy man to these
impoverished people and therefore automatically suspect.

Through Mullen's resourcefulness and tact Flaherty was able to
obtain his "cast" of characters to play out their natural roles of
island life. He secured Michael Dillane, who was young enough not
to fear hanging over the edge of cliffs. He secured Maggie Dirrane
to play the role of Mother, rescuing her for a short time from her
destitute life with a crippled husband and four children. For the
role of the husband Flaherty chose "Tiger King." While Maggie and
Michael played roles which approximated their own lives. Tiger King,
who was to play the "Man," was a blacksmith by trade. So Flaherty
created an artificial family based on how well they photographed and
made Tiger King over into a fisherman for the purposes of the film.[76]

What Flaherty had failed to discover in Samoa he found quite
evident in Aran. The struggle of man against the sea was the drama
inherent in the daily lives of the islanders. Synge had already
brought out this underlying philosophy. Flaherty tried to bring it
to full visualization. To do so required some exaggeration and some
falsity in the name of artistic truth. How he filmed the boating
sequences and later the shark hunt illustrates this point.

Because of their unprotected location on the open Atlantic, the
Aran Islands are lashed by some of the highest seas in the world.
Yet the fisherman of Aran braved the seas in a fragile, oar-driven
craft called a "curragh," a canoe-like structure made of wooden ribs,
covered with tarred canvas. (Happily, they use more substantial
motor-driven trawlers today.) Staying afloat and landing were tricky
affairs that required strength, timing, quick intelligence, and team-
work. To be caught in the wrong position by a giant breaker meant
the end, for the islanders were notoriously poor swimmers and, besides, had a fatalistic attitude toward drowning. The crew hired for
the film took chances that they probably avoided in their normal
lives. Flaherty paid them to do it, and the greater the risk the
more he paid.[77]

Flaherty shot several storm and landing sequences to form a single composite sequence for the end of his film. Mullen describes the
countless times that the crew went out, with Flaherty and his brother
filming over and over from the shore until he got the shots he wanted.
Flaherty had them try a landing in a storm-tossed channel where even
a good swimmer would not have a chance. So at great risk to their
lives, Flaherty got the crew to perform in front of his cameras. After
some particularly tense moments, Mullen wrote, "The curragh had come
through the worst of the passage and now as this monster sea came
raging towards them there was a chance to fight it, and this Patcheen
and his men, with superhuman effort, prepared to do. I shall never
forget the thrill it gave me, when I saw Big Patcheen with a left-
hand stroke, his men timing their strokes instinctively with his,
get ready to meet the crest of the wave...." And later, "as the
curragh swung around, those rocky fangs came up dripping white and
seemed to reach out for her, but death missed Patcheen and his crew
by a foot; with superhuman strength and uncanny skill they had managed to hold the curragh about a foot from the cruel toothed rock as
she met the sea bows on, while the next breakers came foaming in; she
was turned in again in the flash of an eye, and was now running
straight for the shore." Mullen convinced them to go out in this
weather. But he watched, more sensibly, from the shore, cheering
the men on.[78]

The exaggeration of the curragh's landing in a storm represented
part of the poetic license that Flaherty felt was necessary to his
technique. By adding the basking shark sequence he stretched this
license to portray the islanders not as he found them but as they
might have existed 100 years prior.

The selection of the basking shark as a major subject in the Aran
film was not preplanned but one of those on location discoveries that
reshaped the entire project. It did so for two principal reasons.
First, it represented a former way of life that Flaherty hoped to
record before the camera, only in this case he had to reconstruct it
even to the point of teaching the islanders to hunt the basking shark
since their generation had never known how. Secondly, it coincided
with Flaherty's desire to find at least one sensational element of
danger which he hoped would excite audiences and make the film a
commercial success.

The importance of getting these shark hunting scenes is borne out
by the fact that it caused Flaherty to extend his stay on Aran for
almost another year. He wrote to Gainsborough Studios that "I expect
to complete my shark sequence during the months of February, March,
and April (1933). That is why I have set the completion date at the
end of April; because it is pretty hard to tell just when these
sharks, within that broad limit of time, will appear."[79] Actually
the shark scene filming ran well on into the summer of 1933.

Flaherty was excited by his discovery that the basking shark was
larger than scientific records and accounts had seemed to indicate,
that is, forty feet as compared to upwards of 60 feet in maximum
length. "I believe," he wrote, "the biggest selling point for the
film will be the shark sequence. It is hardly known to anyone anywhere that this shark is the <u>largest fish in the world</u>!" (his
emphasis).[80]

There can be no doubt of how seriously he considered the commercial exploitation angle. "Perhaps this all sounds dry as dust to
you," he wrote, "but it is not so dry when you realize that it is
perfectly feasible for us to bring a mounted specimen for theatrical
display in London. That, and the largest fish in the world idea,
ought to mean something to any showman.... It is vital that no word
leak out about what I have told you about this shark, especially the
line: Largest Fish in the World. This goes for your Gaumont British
News as well. What I mean is, I want no one to come over here and
get anything on the shark before we have the film done."[81]

According to Mullen, the unofficial historian of the Aran Islands,
shark hunting was a "big moneymaking industry on the west coast of
Ireland about a hundred years ago." The sharks were hunted for their
giant livers that rendered a very fine oil principally used for
lighting. This was later supplanted by paraffin. The hunt was part
of their folklore and mythology, including tales of boats being towed
into the sunset by a harpooned shark never to be seen again. For
some years the spring migration ceased, and it was thought that the
species had died out. All that remained of the industry were a few
rusted harpoons and the faded memories of old men. Mullen liked to
claim credit for the background research on the shark hunt, and
actually he did scavenge some information from old-timers, but

Flaherty also went to more authoritative sources like the National Museum in Dublin and the Boston Society of Natural History.[82] To his credit, however, Mullen wrote a highly colorful account of the numerous shark expeditions that Flaherty outfitted, including the use of a trawler and gun harpoon in the event the men on the curragh should miss their shot. Flaherty filmed several such expeditions from the trawler, gathering more than enough footage to edit the single sequence he wanted.

Even in Aran's primitive isolation, Flaherty managed to make himself comfortably at home. The idea that Flaherty was off in these exotic corners of the world with all the discomfort that that implied was patently absurd, except for making Nanook of the North. Harry Watt, himself a key figure in British documentary, would recall many years later: "The extraordinary thing was that Flaherty always lived like a king in these primitive places." On Aran he rented a summer house from a wealthy woman and he imported a cordon bleu cook; the Irish on Aran or elsewhere have little taste for gourmet cuisine. "And I never lived so well in my life," he continued. "We had two grown men just to put the peat on the fire. I'd gone out a skinny youth, and they used to give me barrels and buckets of Guinness and I had the easiest time of my life. I stayed there about a year, came back as fat as a pig. I never got thin again. That made me fat."[83] The same picture of opulence also held true for Flaherty's experiences in India and Louisiana later on.

Watt also recalled that he suggested to Flaherty that he should film one of the major events of the year in Aran, the seasonal towing of cattle to the steamer behind the curraghs, which resembled something of a rodeo and was for the islanders a rather grand occasion. Synge also described this event in great detail in his book on the Aran Islands. But for some unfathomable reasons Flaherty chose not to include it in the film. Of course many other aspects of Aran life, such as religion, were omitted from the film as the critics were to point out. Such omissions demonstrated the highly selective process of Flaherty's technique. The structure of his films relied on a few key scenes which he improvised on the spot but from which he would not wander.

While shooting Man of Aran, Flaherty pursued his experimentation with long-focus lenses, which so marked his camera style. He even used an enormously long 17-inch lens, which in other hands, would have resulted in unsteady images. Flaherty believed that some of his best seascapes in Man of Aran were shot with this lens, notably the shot near the end where the sea curls up a high cliff and over the land. The camera was two miles away. He felt that such shots with the aid of filters did not suffer in tone. "In brief, I owe almost everything to long-focus lenses. Here are some of the shots in Man of Aran which would have been impossible without them: The seascapes. The shark scenes. These scenes were shot mostly from the deck of a trawler, at distances of from a hundred yards to half a mile, often in a rough sea. The scenes of the canoe coming in during the storm. The camera was on shore, a quarter of a mile to half a mile from the canoe."[84]

Flaherty continued his profligacy with camera footage, trying to accomplish in the camera what other filmmakers would have done in the editing room. John Goldman described one "pointless" pan shot of the cliffs over two minutes long. "His feeling," Goldman said, "was always for the camera. This wanting to do it all in and through the camera was one of the main causes of his great expenditure of film-- so often he was trying to do what could not in fact be done."[85] Flaherty was defensive about this; the smoothness of the gyro-headed tripod just encouraged him.

Goldman, the editor on the film, saw that some basic shots were needed for continuity, and this is where Flaherty and he fell into disagreement. Goldman himself, under the recent influence of Soviet filmmakers, said that Flaherty had no sense of the rhythm of film, that is, the timing of shots in a particular sequence, their duration on the screen, and their cumulative effect. Flaherty's delight, as Goldman pointed out, was in the shot per se; this was consistently true for almost all of Flaherty's work.[86]

Man of Aran was shot as a silent film, because in part the Flahertys resisted the arrival of sound and had to be convinced of its usefulness. The cast was brought to London to record the inter- mittent and asynchronous dialogue and snatches of words used on the sound tracks. The sound effects were all post-recorded and dubbed in.

From approximately 37 hours of original negative, Man of Aran emerged as a 76-minute film. At a cost of 30,000 pounds, it grossed over 80,000 pounds within twelve months of its London premiere, 25 April 1934. This was not spectacular as films go, and Flaherty earned nothing but the weekly salary he drew during production. It was a prestigious coup for Gaumont. Nevertheless, after its initial earnings the distributor was prepared to let the film die a natural death. Once again Flaherty took to the road to drum up publicity and interest for his film.

Flaherty's Man of Aran was well received by the overwhelming majority of newspaper reviewers in the United States and Europe. In Italy it won Mussolini's Grand Prix of the Second Venice Film Festival. For some writers this award only confirmed the view that Flaherty's documentary was reactionary and supported the causes of fascism. The popular success of Flaherty's film challenged the docu- mentary movement to reappraise its own techniques and objectives. In this manner Man of Aran precipitated the most important critical de- bate in Flaherty's life and showed clearly where he stood in relation- ship to the documentary movement of the 1930s. This issue is discussed in some detail in Chapter II.

ELEPHANT BOY

Flaherty tackled the commercial feature film one more time in his life in spite of his past experiences that had resulted in failure. He signed a contract with Alexander Korda to direct Elephant Boy in India, based on Rudyard Kipling's children's story, "Toomai of the Elephants."

The roots of this film go back to the Acoma Indian film project when Robert and Frances Flaherty learned of an actual incident in Mexico in which a famous fighting bull was pardoned by public acclaim because of his bravery. In 1929 they wrote a short story called "Bonito the Bull" depicting the incident through the eyes of a Spanish boy who had cared for the bull and loved him dearly. The Flahertys planned all along to use a native cast. "We found what good actors native children can be," Frances Flaherty wrote, "and how appealing they unfailingly are to an audience. So we had this idea; why, if we wrote a film story around extraordinary adventures that a native boy might have in his native environment, wouldn't it be possible to 'star' that boy himself in the film?... We set about to write a story that might film. This was not very congenial practice for us. We usually worked from the barest outlines, preferring to 'find' the story in our material."[87] They had doubts, however, about being able to show a lovable bull on the screen convincingly. They had already made up their minds that it should be an elephant instead and that the location should be switched to India. It was Frances Flaherty's distinct impression that Korda remembered the Kipling story and suggested it as the basis for the film.[88] Korda, then riding the crest of success after his film The Private Life of Henry VIII (1933), purchased the film rights for "Toomai of the Elephants" from the Kipling estate for $25,000, and had every intention of producing a big spectacle with professional actors.

The Flaherty family departed for India at different intervals in the winter of 1935, leaving two daughters in school in England. Flaherty went to the province of Mysore in Southern India about 800 miles from Bombay. The publicity that preceded the production crew's arrival generated a great deal of interest in the project in a country that had already become film conscious. Newspapers announced that Flaherty was coming and he was beseiged by job-seekers to appear in the film.

Except for building their own laboratory, not much reminded them of their experiences on the other films. There were numerous people to handle every detail; cameramen, electricians, carpenters, tailors, bearers, sweepers, mahouts, animal trainers, clerks, accountants, and interpreters. There were loads of equipment and luxurious quarters.

One of the most pleasant discoveries on the trip was finding the young boy Sabu to play the role of Toomai. Frances felt uncanny about how Sabu fitted so closely into the role they conceived for their

story. Sabu's own childhood experiences among a family that lived
and worked with elephants closely paralleled the incidents portrayed
in the film. Sabu's obvious charm and familiarity with elephants
easily displaced others for the leading role. Frances Flaherty wrote
a short book about Sabu, who later went to England at her husband's
suggestion and became a popular star to the delight of movie audiences
all over the world.[89]

She described her fascination with Indian life, the photographic
adventures of working with elephants, and all the effort that went
into the construction of an elephant stockade and the big drive that
climaxed the film. She revealed very few of her husband's personal
thoughts on the filming and gave no intimation that something had
gone awry. In fact she stated just the opposite: "So now that our
script is beyond the preadventure of further change, we can go ahead
with our work as fast as possible."[90]

Actually as many as three scripts were being used simultaneously
and all being shot by different camera units. Flaherty had shot,
with subordinate cameramen, over 55 hours worth of film in running
time. But this was not enough. Korda felt there was not enough of
a story line. Major script changes were decided upon after the completion of location shooting. Zoltan Korda, the producer's brother,
directed the studio footage shot in London Denham studios. White
movie actors with Oxford accents dressed as Hindus acted out a whole
new script, replacing the fragments of dialogue that Flaherty had
intended with a detailed narrative.

Griffith describes one script change that illustrates the two
contrary lines of thought. Flaherty had the elephant Kala Nag go
mad at the death of his master, following the Kipling story. The
Kordas, evidently, felt that a more melodramatic motivation was
necessary, and so they introduced a wicked mahout who chainwhips the
grieving elephant.[91] His introduction caused still further changes
and additional scenes because the mahout's evil act required
retribution.

Unlike the other commercial features which Flaherty left in mid-
stream, he hung on to the end, this time collecting a handsome salary,
but with diminished enthusiasm. He felt a responsibility for seeing
it through, and even participated in the film's promotional aspects,
in which he had much experience. He and Zoltan Korda received credit
as co-directors. A rough distinction is that the outdoor footage was
shot under Flaherty's direction and the studio material under Korda's.

TWO ADVENTURE STORIES

As the industrialized nations of the world moved closer and
closer to war, Flaherty's film options ran out. His wife Frances
published two books in 1937, <u>Elephant Dance</u> and <u>Sabu</u>. Robert also

resumed his writing and in the next two years published two novels based on his experiences in the North, The Captain's Chair and White Master.[92]

The Captain's Chair paralleled Flaherty's experience as an explorer in the Hudson Bay region. An account of one long journey in first person narrative, it is held together by descriptions and anecdotes, and stories within stories. Because he witnessed things first hand, he was able to write with feeling and authenticity:

> At Cape Jones the Indian country came to an end. Before us lay a wide panorama of ice and snow. They were the barrens of the Eskimos. The coast now ran to the north and east until it was lost in the blue. In the soft light of the low sun the vast white blanket spread over land and sea like satin. Its wrinkles were blurred by snow smoke, the usual drift no matter how low the wind; for the snow of the barrens is as fine as flour, and the least wind disturbs it.

But Flaherty was foremost a raconteur, not a writer; anecdotes appear throughout, reduced to the written word. He tells an amusing one, to cite an example, something on the tune of grabbing the bull by the horns. On a particularly difficult sledge journey he told his Eskimo companions, "Then we are up against it, like the hunter who caught Nanook the bear by the tail." They didn't understand. "Well, you see," he said, "the hunter did not want to hold on to the tail of Nanook the bear, but he couldn't let go, could he?" They were still confused, and at the next rest they were paralyzed with laughter, and now Flaherty did not understand. "Holding Nanook by the tail?" they replied. "Nanook has no tail!" And they all rocked with laughter.

In a separate chapter entitled "The Story of Comock," the Eskimo described how he had led his family, two wives, and another Eskimo family on a search for an island in the bay. Parting ice drifts cut their igloo in half causing the loss of life, equipment, and food supplies. They drifted on broken ice and had to eat dog meat. Comock had to kill his friend who had gone mad. Comock finally made it back to the post after ten years. This story turned out to be a great success, having been printed several times and even was narrated by Flaherty himself on a BBC radio broadcast in 1950.

Although Flaherty used the novel form, the book has no plot except for his long episodic journey. Characters are introduced and then disappear; he had a flare for description but not characterization; the captain remained an elusive figure. The book's primary virtue is its masterful description of landscape, walrus and seal hunting, building an igloo, and Eskimo customs.

His second novel, White Master, again demonstrated his good eye for detail, gained through years of experience in a savage land. But its narrative structure seemed even more awkward than the one in The Captain's Chair. An historical novel, set in the Hudson Bay area in the late 19th century, the narrator tells the story of a young Englishman named Kendall who falls in love with the daughter of a trader, but the girl is reserved for the boss of the fur post. The young man, therefore, loses no time in earning the enmity of his employer. The Factor sends him off on an impossible journey. Kendall's survival experiences are related in letters and manuscripts. Long given up for dead, he returns to the post to seek revenge. The Factor, interestingly, is portrayed as a paternal figure who exploits the poverty-stricken Indians. None of the characters, however, stood out. This was Flaherty's last attempt at writing novels.

THE LAND

In the summer months just before Germany's invasion of Poland, Flaherty was induced to return to the United States to make a film for the United States Government.

The fledgling growth of documentary film in the United States and Flaherty's own declining career seemed to coincide. While Flaherty's options abroad and in Hollywood had ceased, Pare Lorentz was building an American documentary movement. His films, The Plow That Broke The Plains (1936) and The River (1937), addressed themselves to the problems of the Great Depression and dealt with public policy toward their solution. A former movie critic, like Grierson, Lorentz made these films for theatrical distribution under the sponsorship of the U.S. Department of Agriculture; and based on his success, he attempted to institutionalize public policy documentaries in the government through the establishment of a United States Film Service. Lorentz convinced President Franklin Roosevelt of the wisdom of such an agency and was himself appointed to its directorship. Lorentz's contribution can be described not only in terms of his films but also in the talent that he attracted and the creativity he inspired. He was an originator of The City (1939), whose credits read like a "Who's Who" in American documentary and which proved to be the culminating documentary experience of the decade. But Lorentz was more of a filmmaker than an administrator and was less like Grierson that his administrative assistant, Arch Mercey, who for all practical purposes ran the Film Service and found time to write and lecture about the relationship between documentary film and public policy.

Flaherty was glad to return to his native land after so many years of self-imposed exile. In an earlier meeting with Lorentz in April 1938 he told him: "I left America because of Herbert Hoover, but now I'm tired of the understatement of the British Empire and would like to work for the U. S. Government, if they're allowing people to do such things as The River." Lorentz told Flaherty that he would hire him to direct a film for the government if the opportunity arose.[93]

R. M. Evans, head of the Agricultural Adjustment Administration, believed that Lorentz would direct the film, although Lorentz had just begun a new film project in Chicago entitled The Fight for Life. As a public official, Evans was most concerned about having an approved script beforehand, naturally an anathema to Flaherty. Mercey wrote a basic outline script. In Mercey's opinion "The task becomes not one of doing an educational film for the AAA, but that of doing an exciting picture which will have theatrical use followed by field use in farm meetings throughout the country."[94] On the basis of the outline, the AAA approved the film project for $40,000. Russell Lord, a well known writer on rural America, was hired to develop the script in detail. A book he had recently published described mistreatment of the land, a theme common to The Plow That Broke The Plains, The River, and The Land.[95] Under Lorentz's direction the U.S. Film Service undertook a film project for the AAA to deal with the problems of rural Americans displaced by drought, erosion, poor soil management and overproduction. The film was intended for theatrical release and was to be of the same caliber as The Plow That Broke The Plains and The River.

During the summer of 1939 a new outline script was prepared detailing shot sequences and naming specific locations for filming. In August and September Flaherty met with the government officials and Russell Lord to discuss the script. The promised collaboration with Lorentz did not materialize because of his other film commitment. Lorentz, who by now had several years experience in dealing with bureaucrats, might have provided the buffer that Flaherty needed. Further complicating matters was the shifting of the film from one government agency to another. The U.S. Film Service's life ended when Congress refused to allocate funds for what some considered to be a propaganda device for the New Deal. The AAA agreed to supervise Flaherty's production. Flaherty, already shooting in Iowa since the end of August, met a few weeks later with AAA information official Wayne Darrow who represented the Agency's interests in the production. Concerning the script, Darrow said there was no meeting of minds. "He listened but didn't know what we were talking about. He knew little of America and nothing of Agriculture. He said let him loose with a camera and he'd find the story. Without plan or script we set Bob Flaherty adrift in rural America."[96]

Flaherty set out to rediscover his own country in the midst of poverty and devastation, on the one hand, and abundance and great wealth, on the other. His crew consisted of cameramen on the U.S. payroll, including Irving Lerner who was associated with several important American documentaries. Flaherty intended to follow past practices, to absorb slowly his surroundings, and find the drama inherent in his subject matter. On this peripatetic journey through America's heartland, there would be no actors, no cast, and no laboratory.

He shot film like mad, within a month cutting deeply into the budget. As always he preferred to shoot in the morning or late after-noon sun. On his first field trip he had gone to Iowa in August and shot granaries, boats, and railyards bursting with harvests. He turned South and filmed poverty and squalor. In the West he followed the migrants, the homeless, the "Okies." "They told him their sto-ries," Russell Lord wrote, "and his anger and compassion knew no bounds."[97]

George Gercke, a member of the film crew, reported directly to Lorentz on the aimlessness that he sensed in Flaherty's wandering. Others said the same thing during his shooting on Industrial Britain. Gercke objected to the lack of a story or shooting line and felt that Lord should be on location with them since he had the agricultural knowledge and story sense and could mediate between Flaherty, the artist, and the agricultural experts. Flaherty, he felt, had no story. In addition, he reported that Flaherty was being distracted by the war. David, his brother, and friends still lived in England, and the war news terribly upset him, and he rarely spoke of anything else.[98]

As the film stood in February 1940, already a month past the deadline, it did not meet the objectives of the AAA. Mercey arranged a meeting in New York with Flaherty, Lorentz, and another AAA infor-mation officer. Lorentz gave Flaherty a choice of editing the foot-age in partnership or taking over the project himself directly under AAA. If he chose the latter course, Lorentz believed that Flaherty could develop his own ideas for organizing the footage without being tied down to the original script.[99] In March the film was put under AAA, and Flaherty completed it in the Department of Agriculture mo-tion picture facilities.

Flaherty once described a motion picture "as the longest distance between two given points," and so it seemed trying to edit the mass of 75,000 feet shot over a 20,000-mile journey. Flaherty's strength was in shooting a camera and directing; he never made claims to being an editor, though he did edit out of necessity. Clearly Flaherty had to be rescued from his predicament; he enlisted the aid of one of the best documentary film editors in the business, Helen Van Dongen. She had received her training during years of work with Joris Ivens, the Dutch filmmaker who directed such films as The New Earth, The Spanish Earth, and The Four Hundred Million. In the interests of improving the caliber of government films, Lorentz had also invited Ivens to make Power and the Land for the Rural Electrification Administration, part of the U.S. Department of Agriculture.

Van Dongen confirmed Flaherty's obsession with the war. "I thought," she wrote, "it unusual that a man engaged in the making of a film on such complex social and economic issues could set aside his thoughts so completely when most filmmakers could not have stopped talking about their problems and frustrations. I found Flaherty's disengagement extraordinary." He used to spend several hours each day on the war.[100] Joris Ivens advised her "Observe, look, and listen." Gradually from his monologues about the war, the waste of human lives, the destructive influence of civilization and mechanization, she began to make a connection to the footage and to see things from Flaherty's viewpoint.

Van Dongen, an expert in spotting staged scenes, recognized an element of falsity about the shot in which an old Negro man living in a ruined mansion dusts off a bell. When she asked Flaherty about it, he left the room. All the other scenes were real, and therefore according to Van Dongen's strict concept, The Land was Flaherty's only true documentary among his full-length films.[101]

The scenes of stark reality impressed her. She knew they were real because there was no backup materials, no extra takes that are sure signs of rehearsed action. Scenes of the young boy asleep, picking peas in his sleep, of the young woman aged before her time, were starkly real, crying out exploitation and resentment, hunger, poverty, and abuse.

It was Van Dongen who persuaded Flaherty to narrate his own film. There was an obvious precedent, though she has not mentioned this in her articles. Ernest Hemingway wrote and spoke the narration for The Spanish Earth (1937), also edited by Van Dongen. Neither he nor Flaherty were professional narrators, but their untrained voices were virtues and they shared the same roughness, inflection, cadence, and feeling for their subjects. Flaherty, resistant at first, in the end spoke a narration that no professional could improve upon without destroying its emotional value.

In later years Flaherty never discussed the film with Van Dongen. Unlike his other film experiences, there were no funny stories. Flaherty tried to avoid, according to Van Dongen, what was ugly in the world. Some sequences are emotion packed; others bad, empty, and contradictory. "The film," she wrote, "is no more than a record of a journey, putting most of the blame for the plight of the migratory workers on 'the Machine'—a simplification of cause and effect. The film takes no position." More recently, she has said: "I don't think The Land has anything which is particularly mine. There are certain indications of my style, but the film scatters over too many things to have time to develop."[102]

The finished film had difficulty finding an audience. At a government showing in June 1941 the film was poorly received. Several AAA regional directors ridiculed it. The war in Europe was quickly absorbing farm surpluses, and defense measures were taking care of the excess labor pool. The film seemed behind events.

After the Japanese attack on Pearl Harbor, Flaherty argued that the film had value as a morale builder. A few top officials at the

White House saw it, and said it would not do.[103] Lord dreamed up
another approach to get the film into circulation. He proposed filming an introduction by Secretary Henry Wallace to two films: Tanks
and The Land. The introduction would make clear the relationship
between tanks and land. "By the grace of our tanks, our planes and
our ships, peace will again be ours. But in winning the war with
machines, we must also win a peace which will make machines the ser-
vants of men. That is why I am asking you now to look at a motion
picture called The Land. Bob Flaherty, in making this picture, has
told a story of the land which does not forgive misuses, either by
machines or men."[104] Lowell Mellet helped edit the introduction, and
Wallace himself even worked on it. There is no evidence, however,
that the introduction was ever filmed. But it does indicate the
willingness of top Agriculture officials to get the film into distribution. But the will of the White House prevailed, and films like
The River, The Plow That Broke The Plains, and The Land were with-
drawn from wartime circulation, lest in the wrong hands they be used
as anti-American propaganda. A premiere showing of The Land was
arranged on 7 April 1942 at the Museum of Modern Art in New York. A
film which in the final tally cost the taxpayer $80,000 (uninflated
dollars!) was never used for the purpose for which it was intended.

As Rotha and Wright have pointed out, it seems ironic that the
one film in which Flaherty had faced up to sociological and technological problems was rarely seen.[105] Griffith, in a position to know,
said that Flaherty always continued to hope that The Land would one
day find its audience. He sincerely felt involved in this social
problem, and he believed that the imaginative use of machines was
the answer.[106]

Lord deserves the major credit for scripting The Land. His
writings, especially Behold Our Land, were the major source for the
commentary. Flaherty played an important part in refining it, re-
ducing it to bare essentials in order to let the images speak for
themselves. Lord kept up with Secretary Wallace's policy pronounce-
ments, and tried to interest Flaherty in them. Despite the changes
in American agriculture due to the war in Europe, Wallace was still
concerned about problems that lingered on. In his statement to the
Senate Civil Liberties Committee of 2 May 1940 he explained the
problem of migrant labor. The principal cause remained: waste and
exhaustion of the soil, ruinous farm practices, disappearance of
foreign markets, an unsound system of land tenure, farm tenancy, un-
suitable agriculture, growing farm population, and agribusiness. Lord
incorporated such ideas into the script, but a full working script
was not available until 15 September 1940, after the principal shooting. The final revised copy is dated 13 October 1941.[107] Griffith
says Flaherty discarded the script (p. 140). Actually he discarded
the outline scenario due to his past practices. These scenarios or
treatments bemused him, especially inasmuch as AAA was still pushing
a policy that bore little relationship to events.

36

Even after the film was completed Flaherty maintained the fiction in a New York Times interview that he was not given a story. "They gave me a camera and threw me out into the field to make a film about the land and the people that live by it. I was fresh and had no pre-conceptions whatever; I was so sensitive you could hear me change my mind. So I merely groped my way along, photographing what seemed to me significant; it was only later that we began to see the pattern. The film is different from my others. It isn't a romance. It hasn't any specific solution for what the camera sees, but it is often crit-ical. And that perhaps is the most amazing thing about it, that it could be made at all. It shows without flinching." And what it showed was often grim. Naively, he posed the machine at the root of the problem. "It is incredible," he said. "With one foot in Utopia where the machine can free us all, we have yet to dominate it." Per-haps precipitously, the reporter asked: "Did we say Mr. Flaherty was a romantic?"[108]

The hiring of Robert Flaherty to make The Land was an admirable step in that it represented a sincere desire to elevate government documentaries from mediocrity and obscurity and to treat important national issues dramatically and artistically in order to reach the widest possible audience. In fact, however, Flaherty was a poor choice. The decision revealed sheer ignorance of Flaherty's working methods and indifference to his artistic sensibilities. The subject matter of The Land was too complicated, broad, and amorphous for him. Moreover, the conditions he encountered seemed out of touch with events on an international scale. Flaherty found it difficult if not impossible to apply his knowledge and past experiences. The federal officials neither understood, nor appreciated his temperament, and he could not readily turn their policy statements into a film. That any film as sensitive and moving as The Land should come out of such inauspicious circumstances was remarkable.

AN INTERLUDE

In 1941 a New York Times reporter described Flaherty as "Friar Tuck--a great tumbling man with massive red cheeks, brilliant blue eyes, and the sharp profile of an eagle. His size was matched only by the exuberance of his wit; he tossed ideas like an agile bull lifts the matador. A born raconteur, he talked fabulously out of a memory shot full of colorful, bawdy, and heroic reminiscences of all the places he had ever been....He talked like a man who had just finished a long grueling job."[109]

In 1942 with the war in full force Flaherty seemed finished, an anachronism, no place to fit in a world rushing helter-skelter into destruction and mass slaughter. The predominant use of film was for propaganda, some of it helpful, informative; and much racist and hateful. He was 58 now, an age when few men care to risk changing their lives. His wife asked him to retire to their farm in

Brattleboro, Vermont. But asking a man like Flaherty to give up his art and vocation was like asking a farmer to give up his land. Flaherty would make films as long as someone would sponsor him. He did not need moments of rest; they were only forced upon him.

America's output of film propaganda (in its broad generic sense) was dominated by the United States Government, and it was bizarre and ironic in at least one major respect. The principal responsibility for producing documentary films with propagandistic intent was given not to documentary filmmakers but to Hollywood producers, directors, and writers. It was given to the Fords, Capras, and Wylers; they were awarded commissions in the War and Navy Departments. There were occasional exceptions like Louis de Rochemont who was schooled in The March of Time (not really a documentary series). But Pare Lorentz, on the other hand, was shunted off to the Air Transport Command, with his talented cameraman, Floyd Crosby.

The men who had grown up with documentary film during the 1930s, like Willard Van Dyke, Henwar Rodakiewicz, Irving Lerner, Lowell Mellet, and Arch Mercey, uniformly went to work for the U.S. Office of War Information. Flaherty would have fit better in the OWI where they made quiet, understated films about American life to present to the Allies abroad. Flaherty expressed an interest in working for OWI, but it is not known if he pursued it. Surely they would have hired him.

But the irony of war required that the "father of documentary film" be hired by Frank Capra, an entertainment film director during the 1930s who had never made a documentary and even regarded it with professional disdain before the war. In May 1942 Flaherty enlisted in the war effort by going to work for Capra's Army orientation film unit. Capra had been given responsibility for producing the major ideological films for the War Department. At the same time Capra was working on his highly popular "Why We Fight" series, Flaherty was assigned to a newsreel-like project, called "State of the Nation," originally suggested by Eric Knight. He worked through the summer, travelling up and down the eastern United States. But the footage that he shot would not fit into a story; it bewildered the Army editors. The whole idea of quickly shooting a brief story to be sent back and edited by someone else went against the Flaherty grain. It was absurd to have put him in this situation.

Capra had assigned fifteen men to work with Flaherty, men with ranks from private on up; they expected to be ordered around, but Flaherty had no orders for them. One of the cameramen told Capra "Frank, we're just sitting down here drinking beer all day. We're just wasting our time." Flaherty appeared to be relieved when the project was cancelled and he was let go.[110]

The Sugar Research Foundation and the U.S. Office of Price Administration hired Flaherty to make films on sugar and the war's impact on the industry. Three films were made in 1944-45. What's Happened to Sugar? carried Flaherty's name as producer. But all three were actually made by his brother David, under Robert Flaherty's general supervision.[111]

About one year later Robert Flaherty began another project, far removed from his earlier work. He intended to make a film on calligraphy, as written and told by John Howard Benson of the Rhode Island School of Design. The foreword to the film was to have read: "the purpose of this film is to show how the letters we use came to be what they are. It tries to accomplish that end by showing how good letters are the inevitable result of simple tools and materials when used with understanding and skill." Flaherty and Benson had a falling out and the project was abandoned.

LOUISIANA STORY

A portrait of Flaherty, photographed by Henri Cartier-Bresson in 1946, showed a hulk of a man in rumpled clothing, with enormous hands covering his knees. He was 62 and looked his years. He was overweight and his once broad shoulders were starting to hunch. The remaining hair on the sides of his head had turned completely white. It was the portrait of an unhappy man with the weight of the world upon him. The look of grim determination as he stared off into a corner showed a private vision, a preoccupation that would be realized in yet another film.

Robert Flaherty's last major film project and for many, his most sublime work, was Louisiana Story. While the world seemed to pass him by, leaving him no niche, he wrangled a film contract that every independent filmmaker would yearn for. And he secured a theme that would resolve the unsettling relationship between man and machine as portrayed in The Land. In Louisiana Story he found the perfect balance.

While on a forced vacation at his farm in Vermont, Flaherty received a note from a friend at Standard Oil of New Jersey asking if he would "be interested in making a film which would project the difficulties and risk of getting oil out of the ground—admittedly an industrial film, yet one which would have enough story and entertainment value to play in standard motion picture houses at an admission price?"[112] He and his wife Frances took off for the Southwest, agreeing to make a three-month exploratory trip. In the Bayou country of Louisiana they saw an oil rig being towed up a river. It became "movement and rhythm," in a word, a motion picture. They also became enchanted by the Cajun people who lived there. These people had a superstitious attitude toward the Bayou that the Flahertys found delightful.

According to Frances Flaherty, Standard Oil wanted "A classic, permanent, and artistic record of the contribution which the oil industry has made to civilization...a film that would present the story of oil with the dignity and epic sweep it deserved and assure this story a lasting place on the highest plane in the literature of the screen. The film would also be such an absorbing human story that it would stand on its own feet as entertainment anywhere; because of its entertainment value it would be distributed theatrically through the regular motion-picture houses both in America and abroad."[113] The film project was admittedly a publicity gesture for Standard Oil, but the terms of the agreement went beyond generosity. Flaherty was to have complete artistic control and would not have to submit a script for approval, always a sore point. The sponsor would not be mentioned in the film credits. Flaherty would retain all exhibition rights. The company advanced $175,000 in January 1946 for the film, and later added about $83,000. Not since the days of William Mackenzie in Canada had any sponsor shown such faith in Flaherty.

Flaherty moved his film crew to an old mansion in Abbeville, Louisiana. Among others, the crew included Robert and Frances, Richard Leacock as cameraman, who was to become a documentary filmmaker in his own right, and Helen Van Dongen as editor, this time almost from the start. Leacock and Van Dongen worked in an associate producer capacity as well.

The mansion, already in decline, was inhabited by the principal members of the film crew; the cast lived elsewhere. Many visitors were drawn to Flaherty during the shooting. Van Dongen observed that there was a certain distance between Flaherty and the local people and that in the long run the film crew remained outsiders.[114]

They searched for a "cast" to portray the typical Cajun family. But most importantly they searched for a Cajun boy, for through his eyes the film would be presented to the audience. Frances Flaherty has said that in the making of Louisiana Story her husband was remembering his childhood with his father, and in this sense the film was autobiographical.[115] For his hero, then, Flaherty dreamed up a half-wild Cajun boy. Frances Flaherty and Leacock found Joseph Boudreaux to play him, and in the film he was given the unlikely but poetic name Alexander Napoleon Ulysses Latour. "I spend perhaps more time on this aspect of picture making than any other," Flaherty wrote, "for I believe that the secret of success in making this type of film lies in finding the right people."[116]

The first part of the story dealt with the boy's life in the swamps and bayous. Flaherty attempted to recreate a child's fascination with the bayou wilderness, the mystery of its appearance, and his relationship to the creatures that lived there. Alexander's companion, the pet raccoon, fitted perfectly into the story though it was not anticipated in the beginning. Flaherty always had to allow for these discoveries that were key parts of his creativity. The alligator as a symbol of unknown danger figured prominently in his thinking, and now it could be played off against the raccoon in a dramatic ritual which Flaherty needed.

If Flaherty worked with no "preconception," he also worked by trial and error. The oil drilling sequence is an example. He shot the oil drilling in daylight, and neither Flaherty nor Leacock were terribly pleased with the results. The footage was competently shot, but neither interesting nor exciting. Then Flaherty suggested going back and shooting the same scenes at night. "At night," Flaherty wrote, "with the derrick lights dancing and flickering on the dark surface of the water, the excitement that is the very essence of drilling for oil became visual." Leacock, recalling the shooting some years later, said: "It eliminated all the cruddy details that were distracting, that were carrying your eye away from the central action. But we didn't know that. We had to find out the hard way."[117]

Since Flaherty felt the film was a fantasy, he had more reason to stage scenes as he had done in his other films. This was the case for the "blow-out" of the oil well. Actually it had happened some sixty miles away. They went out and shot the footage, filmed the oil and mud spouting in a fury, and cut it into the narrative as though it had happened at Abbeville. Something similar occurred in the sequence showing the boy and the alligator in deadly tug of war. Two cameras on this scene were not sufficient. They went to a wildlife refuge and shot footage of a professional alligator hunt. The additional footage undoubtedly enhanced the excitement of the scene but it was to a great extent faked, though not inconsistent with the way Flaherty had made Man of Aran or Nanook of the North. Van Dongen pointed out that the tonal values of each group of shots were distinctly different.[118]

To the last, Flaherty remained at heart a silent filmmaker. As an editor, however, Van Dongen was highly conscious of the interplay of sound and image. Since there was no sound editing equipment on location, she had a relatively free hand in putting the two together when she returned to New York. In the by now celebrated oil drilling sequence, it was Van Dongen who ordered the placement of microphones for disc transcription of sound effects and also who edited them into a veritable symphonic score of atonal bangs, crashes, and screeches. Flaherty was suspicious of this aspect of production because he had to relinquish control.[119]

For the first time Flaherty had to work with synchronized speech. Louisiana Story, essentially a silent film with a "music and effects" track, had a few scenes where the "actors" spoke a dialogue that Flaherty had written. He listened to the patois speech of the Cajuns, wrote a dialogue script, fed it to his actors, and had them say it over and over until it sounded like their own words. It was difficult for these untrained "actors" to remember their lines, or to avoid sounding stultified. The retakes were never quite the same, and many a shot had to be salvaged by cutting away at the proper moment. Whereas Rotha said that Flaherty had a "magical veracity" with natural speech, Van Dongen makes a convincing argument that these scenes were carried by her editing.[120]

In Van Dongen, Flaherty had no mere technician; she had a sophisticated understanding of the theories of editing. After all she had worked with Ivens, and her own News Review No. 2 (1943) for the State Department was considered something of a milestone in compilation. She could verbalize and write about such things as rhythm, spatial movement, and tonalities, aspects of editing to which Flaherty paid little attention. Flaherty, she thought, seemed to resist organizing scenes into a logical order. He was content shooting. According to Van Dongen, he would have been happy shooting record footage of a way of life, leaving it in unedited form for storage in archives. But this was not the way to earn a living. Flaherty jealously guarded his rushes and on a daily basis asked to see everything that Van Dongen had assembled. While Flaherty called her stubborn, a "Dutch mule," her impression was that he wanted no interference and distrusted her independence. Flaherty and Van Dongen had a working relationship, albeit a strained one. In fact, she felt that he would never ask her to work for him again.

Despite everything, she was able to discover Flaherty's intention and edit with a style and balance that conformed to the director's design. In the opening sequence, Van Dongen and Flaherty brought their troubled collaboration to near perfection. "We are deep in the Bayou country of lower Louisiana," the narrator (Flaherty) says. "It is the high water time of the year--the country is half drowned. We move through a forest of bearded trees. There are wild fowl everywhere, in flight and swimming on the water. We are spellbound by all this wildlife and the mystery of the wilderness that lies ahead." An enormous amount of footage was shot to cover this sequence. (The overall ratio for shooting was 25 to 1.) Shots of fearsome alligators, magnificent birds, floating lily ponds, slithering snakes, and other wildlife, flora and fauna, were given unity and continuity. A graceful movement brought them together in a sequence that is often imitated but never equalled.

Flaherty frequently digressed in his shooting, for example, to shoot a water snake or an alligator attacking an egret. At one point Flaherty even wanted to shoot footage on the making of a pirogue but Van Dongen persuaded him against it.[121] The two dominant personalities counterbalanced one another.

It is interesting to note that despite Van Dongen's enormous contribution to the effectiveness of the opening sequence, her name is never mentioned by Leacock and Frances Flaherty during the two-hour discussion on the making of this sequence contained in A Film Study of Robert Flaherty's Louisiana Story (entry 355). Robert Flaherty himself never tried to belittle her contribution.

42

Van Dongen came away from the Louisiana project with mixed emotions. She did not lose respect for Flaherty, and in the end they remained friends. Although others referred to Flaherty as naive and innocent, she recognized that "it takes great sophistication to portray a world of one's own making, then to display it seen by a child. His mind was not as innocent as a child's, nor was he naive. He had a penetrating mind and acute powers of observation."[122] Yet she felt Flaherty was essentially very lonely, possessive, and lived by his own rules which one had to follow in order to enter his world. To Van Dongen, Flaherty was not a documentarian because "he makes it all up." He uses a documentary style and background to tell a story, and he would turn back the clock one hundred years if it suited him. "They are Flaherty-films, but I do hesitate to call them documentaries."[123]

Actually most of the footage called Flaherty's was shot under his direction by Richard Leacock. Flaherty did some camerawork but depended largely on Leacock. Like Van Dongen, Leacock was chosen because of his skill, and the making of the film was a learning experience that served him later on. Leacock has left his account of the making of the film not so much in writing but in the sound track of the Louisiana Story Study Film where he and Frances Flaherty are the two discussants. He recounted how one artistically bankrupt film company wanted him to reshoot the opening sequence of Louisiana Story for another production. He was staggered by the idea. These shots are what Flaherty discovered often by accident and luck. Leacock, too, was bothered by Flaherty's apparent lack of discipline. His digressions and distractions did not seem to relate to the work at hand. One day, for example, when the Cajun boy was present and all dressed for shooting, Flaherty had Leacock shoot a spider's web and that is what ended up being used in the film from that day's shooting. Filming animals and water took a great deal of time because they could not control conditions of lighting and movement. They had to respond to what was there or not get the shot at all.

Flaherty was still interested in portability and mobility. He had two cameras set up on a floating platform. Flaherty also used Arriflexes, at a time when they were regarded with suspicion by filmmakers. Their relative lightness impressed him, and also he wanted the versatility of reflex viewing through the lens.

Louisiana Story was a success because of the collaboration of talented people, and this was no less true of the music score by Virgil Thomson, the eminent American composer and critic. Flaherty, as always, had exhausted the original budget before final completion. One of the tasks left to last was the musical score, because it had to be locked into an edited film. Standard Oil at first did not want to spend any more money for music until their public opinion experts said otherwise. Thomson, who had worked with Lorentz on The River and The Plow That Broke The Plains, was an ideal choice because of his background in American folk music. Although adaptations for

Mendelssohn and Debussy were used to accompany images of natural scenery, he composed Acadian waltzes and square dances and songs into a vivid and colorful musical score that was essential for creating atmosphere and continuity. Thomson was also impressed by Van Dongen's sound accompaniment for the oil drilling machinery which he found more interesting than tonal compositions for other industrial films.[124]

Louisiana Story was shown at the Edinburgh Festival in August and premiered in September 1948 in New York where it opened to immediate acclaim. The Saturday Review said "he has produced a poetic vision and lasting human document which will bring pleasure and understanding to audiences for years to come."[125] Flaherty received a telegram of congratulations which read, "Just saw your magnificent film. Do it again and you will be immortal and excommunicated from Hollywood, which is a good fate." Congratulations: Oona and Charlie Chaplin, Esta and Dudley Nichols, Dido and Jean Renoir.[126] Also in September, Louisiana Story won the 9th Italian International Film Festival along with John Ford's The Fugitive. It was ironical that even in the documentary's moment of glory it had to share the honor with a feature film.

It is hard to say when a man goes into decline. At the age of 64, Flaherty seemed to recapture freshness, youth, and poetry, a fitting close to a long career. But he was always looking over the next horizon. While reaping the laurels of his latest film he said he was regarding television with great interest.[127]

THE LAST YEARS

The last three years of Flaherty's life are filled with minor film projects that pale into insignificance compared to his earlier work. Despite failing health and advancing age he was not to be put out to pasture, nor to Brattleboro. In 1949 a major series of New Yorker profile articles by Robert Lewis Taylor attempted to portray his colorful life and highlight the making of his films from Nanook of the North to Louisiana Story. Taylor described him as a benevolent Sydney Greenstreet in a Panama hat, "a round, jovial, gregarious man. His face, conditioned by tropic suns and arctic blasts, has a cherubic ruddiness, and his head is circled by a fringe of silky white hair."[128] Taylor, who conducted lengthy interviews with him, said that Flaherty was still planning film projects although his wife Frances wanted him to settle on the farm. And even at 65 years of age he was still saying: "I sympathize with Frances's feeling, but I'm primarily an explorer and only incidentally a moviemaker." Similarly, Willard van Dyke recalled a party at his home attended by a lot of filmmakers. Suddenly he became aware that Flaherty's wonderful presence was missing; he found Flaherty in the nursery, down on the floor, with his son, playing with his electric train and having a tremendous time. Flaherty, he observed, was not really interested in film.[129]

In the spring of 1949 Flaherty attempted a film analysis of
Picasso's famous mural of Guernica, utilizing a film graphic technique. It was a photographer's experimental impression of a painting,
shot in the Museum of Modern Art in New York, but it remained uncom-
pleted at the time of his death.

Also in 1949, as a direct result of his interest in "Guernica,"
Flaherty lent his name to the production of a film on the life of
Michelangelo entitled The Titan. A group of film entrepreneurs purchased the rights of a seized German film from the Office of Alien
Property Custodian, Curt Ortel's Michelangelo: The Life of a Titan,
and re-edited it, laying over a new sound track narrated by Frederic
March. The film is an excellent recreation of the political and religious influences on Michelangelo's life; it uses painting, sculptures,
and architecture to tell the story, and the imaginative way they were
filmed gave these objects a graceful sense of movement that in other
hands would have been lost in the motion picture frame. But the work
is basically Ortel's, not of the group that exploited it. Flaherty's
name only lent credibility and prestige to their undertaking.

He also lent his name to other projects that were actually carried out by his brother David Flaherty. These included The Gift of
Green for the New York Botanical Society, and Green Mountain Land
for the Vermont Historical Society. He visited Europe where he was
greeted with great recognition. He appeared on the BBC which did
broadcasts of his reminiscences, and he even paid a nostalgic visit
to the Aran Islands, which had not changed since the old days. Also,
the State Department sent him to the American zone of Germany on a
goodwill visit. After Flaherty had returned to the United States,
the University of Michigan, in the state of his birth, awarded him
the honorary degree of Doctor of Fine Arts.

As always, Flaherty attempted to find a sponsor for his films.
He negotiated unsuccessfully for the production of a State Department
film on the amalgamation of races in Hawaii in the context of Western
democracy, but an agreement could not be finalized. He still could
not find a sponsor despite all the accolades.

On his final project he became associated with producer Mike Todd
and narrator Lowell Thomas to work in the new film medium of
"Cinerama." Flaherty was to film General MacArthur's dramatic return
from Korea, followed by a grandiose world tour for something called
"Film Symphony" which was to utilize the Cinerama process. Herman
Weinberg, who recalled a last social gathering with Flaherty, said
his heart wasn't in it, and well it was not, for it clashed sharply
with all that his life had been.[130]

At the age of 67 Flaherty suffered from severe arthritis and
shingles, requiring morphine to ease the pain. Hospitalized for a
time in New York, Flaherty seemed to make a slight recovery and his
wife brought him back to Vermont. He died on 23 July 1951. The

official cause of death was listed as cerebral thrombosis. His body was cremated and his ashes were buried on the side of Black Mountain in Vermont. Robert Joseph Flaherty had come home to final rest but this was not his home.

NOTES

1. Robert Flaherty, in his radio broadcast, "Aran and Some of Its People." BBC (December 1949).
2. Arthur Calder-Marshall, The Innocent Eye: The Life of Robert J. Flaherty. Based on research material by Paul Rotha and Basil Wright. Baltimore: Penguin Books, 1970 (first published 1963), pp. 15-16.
3. David Flaherty, quoted in Russell and Kate Lord's (eds. and illus.), Forever the Land: A Country Chronicle and Anthology. New York: Harper and Brothers, 1950, pp. 23-24.
4. This account of his school days is based on Robert Lewis Taylor's The Running Pianist. Garden City, New York: Doubleday, 1950, which contains a chapter entitled "Flaherty--Education for Wanderlust," pp. 116-164. Reprinted from his New Yorker articles.
5. Paul Rotha and Basil Wright, "Flaherty Biography." Unpublished manuscript, 1959, pp. 9-10.
6. Robert Flaherty, My Eskimo Friends. Garden City, New York: Doubleday, 1924. See also Terry Ramsaye, "Flaherty, Great Adventurer." Photoplay Magazine 33, No. 6 (May 1928) 58, 123-126, reprinted in George Pratt's Spellbound in Darkness. Greenwich, Conn.: New York Graphic Society, 1973 rev. ed., pp. 351-352.
7. Robert J. Flaherty, "Two Traverses Across the Ungava Peninsula, Labrador." Geographical Review, 6, No. 2 (August 1918), 116-132.
8. Taylor, p. 130. Flaherty, "The Belcher Islands of Hudson Bay: Their Discovery and Exploration." Geographical Review, 5, No. 66 (1918), 433-458.
9. Quoted in Calder-Marshall, p. 55.
10. Quoted from the "Flaherty Papers," Columbia University, Box 59, by Erik Barnouw, Documentary Film: A History of the Non-Fiction Film. New York: Oxford University Press, 1974, p. 33.
11. Richard Griffith, The World of Robert Flaherty. New York and Boston: Duell, Sloan & Pearce, 1953, p. 36.
12. Flaherty, My Eskimo Friends, p. 119.
13. Ibid., pp. 123-124.
14. Ibid., p. 126.
15. Barnouw, p. 35, quotes Frances Flaherty diary entry, 15 February 1915.
16. Calder-Marshall indicates 17 1/2 hours, and 70,000 feet, p. 74. Rotha and Wright, p. 26, indicate 70,000 feet. However, Flaherty himself had said 30,000 feet. Cf. Robert E. Sherwood, "Robert Flaherty's Nanook of the North," in his The Best Moving Pictures of 1922-23. Boston: Small, Maynard, 1923, pp. 3-8.
17. Note: Taylor, p. 131, says he was editing the film when the fire took place. If that had been true, the work print would have been destroyed as well.
18. Quoted in Griffith, p. xiv.
19. Ibid., pp. xv and 36.
20. Later published as Anerca: Drawings of Enooesweetok, edited by Edmund Carpenter. Toronto: J. M. Dent & Sons, 1959. The drawings and carvings have been donated to the Royal Ontario Museum.

21. Barnouw, p. 36.
22. Robert Flaherty, "Robert Flaherty Talking," in The Cinema 1950, edited by Roger Manvell. Middlesex: Harmondsworth, 1950, pp. 11-29.
23. Flaherty, My Eskimo Friends, p. 140.
24. For some curious reason this passage is omitted from Flaherty's My Eskimo Friends, during his description of the walrus hunt (see pp. 38-39). Also omitted from Calder-Marshall's lengthy quotation, pp. 80-82. But it is quoted in Griffith, p. 39.
25. Flaherty, My Eskimo Friends, pp. 135-136.
26. Ibid., pp. 139-140.
27. Ibid., pp. 145-165.
28. Ibid., p. 170. Flaherty wrote "Less than two years later, I received word by the once-a-year mail that comes out of the north that Nanook was dead. Poor old Nanook!" Quoted in Griffith, p. 43, Flaherty wrote, "He had ventured into the interior hoping for deer. The herds did not come his way, and he starved to death. Poor old Nanook!" A diary entry cited by Barnouw, p. 43, notes that one night Nanook coughed up splotches of blood on the igloo wall. One can also speculate that he knowingly went off to die. The Taylor interview, p. 137, indicated that Nanook got caught on an ice drift.
29. Calder-Marshall, p. 91, indicates winter of "1922-3," which I must assume is a typographical error since he notes the correct release date later on.
30. Taylor, p. 138.
31. Sherwood reprinted in Jacobs, p. 18.
32. Letter from Flaherty to Adriaan Barnouw, dated 29 September 1926, reprinted in Erik Barnouw's "Robert Flaherty (Barnouw's File)," Film Culture, 53-55 (Spring 1972), p. 164.
33. A discussion of the film's critical reception, as with the other Flaherty films, is contained in Section II.
34. Travel, Vol. 39, No. 4 (August 1922), 16-20; "How I Filmed Nanook of the North." The World's Work (September 1922), pp. 553-560; "Life Among the Eskimos," Ibid. (October 1922), pp. 632-640; "Wetalltook's Islands," Ibid. (January 1923), pp. 324-336.
35. Quoted by Griffith, p. 50; Taylor, p. 138; and Calder-Marshall, p. 98.
36. Merian C. Cooper, The Epic of a People's Fight For Life. New York: Putnam, 1925; and his "Grass: A Persian Epic of Migration." Asia (February 1925), pp. 118 ff. Cooper and Schoedsack went on to make King Kong (1933).
37. Copy of contract in "Flaherty Papers," Box 27, Butler Library, Columbia University.
38. Griffith, p. 50; Calder-Marshall, p. 99. See also Robert J. Flaherty, Samoa. Berlin: Reimar Hobbing, 1932, p. 11.
39. David Flaherty, "Serpents in Eden." Asia (October 1925), pp. 858-869, 895-898. David Flaherty refers to Felix David as "Hermann Bauer" in this article, probably to avoid libel and slander suits.
40. Frances Flaherty, "Fa' A-Samoa." Asia (December 1925), p. 1085.
41. Flaherty to Lasky, 28 November 1923, "Flaherty Papers," Box 25.
42. Frances Flaherty, "Behind the Scenes with our Samoan Stars." Asia (September 1925), p. 747.

43. Robert Flaherty, "Filming Real People." Movie Makers (December 1934), reprinted in Lewis Jacobs (comp.), The Documentary Tradition: From Nanook to Woodstock. New York: Hopkinson and Blake, 1971, pp. 97-99.

44. Robert J. Flaherty, "Picture Making in the South Seas." Film Daily Yearbook, 1924, pp. 9-13; Rotha and Wright, p. 85.

45. Frances Flaherty quoted in Griffith, p. 62.

46. Rotha and Wright, p. 86. Also, John Grierson, "Flaherty as Innovator." Sight and Sound, 21, No. 2 (October-December 1951), 64.

47. Frances Flaherty, "Fa' A-Samoa," pp. 1088-1096: Calder-Marshall, p. 111, credits David Flaherty with making the silver nitrate discovery.

48. Quoted in Griffith, p. 69.

49. Newton Rowe, Samoa Under the Sailing Gods. London and New York: Putnam, 1930, pp. 108, 181-182.

50. Flaherty to Adriaan Barnouw, 29 September 1926, published in Erik Barnouw, "Robert Flaherty (Barnouw's File)," p. 176.

51. Cf. Griffith, p. 74; Paramount royalty statement, "Flaherty Papers," Box 27.

52. Hugh Gray interviewed in Donald E. Staples (ed.), The American Cinema (Voice of America Forum Series). Washington, D.C.: U.S. Information Agency, 1973, p. 199. Flaherty frequently said the original negative had been destroyed.

53. In a letter to Rotha and Wright, p. 97.

54. Calder-Marshall, p. 121, says it was made in 1926, but the study print available at the Museum of Modern Art is dated 1925. Cf. also Rotha and Wright, p. 116, and Frances Flaherty, The Odyssey of a Film-Maker; Robert Flaherty's Story. Urbana, Illinois: Beta Phi Mu, 1960, p. 44.

55. Calder-Marshall, p. 122, indicates 1926; and Frances Flaherty, The Odyssey of a Film-Maker, p. 44, indicates 1925. However, the contract for the film is dated 29 February 1927, "Flaherty Papers," Box 29.

56. Flaherty, "Filming Real People," in Jacobs, p. 98.

57. Donald H. Clarke, "Producer of Nanook Joins Metro-Goldwyn." New York Times (26 June 1927), reprinted in Pratt, p. 348. John D. Pearmain, Twenty Four Dollar Island, unpublished introduction, "Flaherty Papers"; Rotha and Wright, p. 84; Pratt, p. 347. Note: The two-reel version no longer exists. The Museum of Modern Art has only a one-reel version.

58. Rotha and Wright, p. 121, indicates that Flaherty was given a screen credit with Ray Dole for the "original story." The usually authoritative, The American Film Institute Catalog of Motion Pictures Produced in the United States: Feature Films 1921-1930, New York and London: R. R. Bowker, 1971, gives an "Additional Directing" credit to Flaherty with scenario by Jack Cunningham and adaptation by Ray Dole. Griffith concludes that perhaps a dozen shots in the final cut were by Flaherty, p. 76. However, in the print I viewed distributed by Films, Inc., the production credits make no mention of Flaherty.

59. Robert Flaherty, "Acoma." Unpublished scenario, 17 pp., "Flaherty Papers," Box 29; Rotha and Wright, p. 124; Calder-Marshall, p. 125; Griffith, p. 76; and Taylor, pp. 149-150. It has also been suggested that Fox called off the film because Flaherty had not begun to shoot the story and that they did not want to invest any more money in a silent when they were switching over to Movietone sound film.

60. For text of story see F. W. Murnau and Robert J. Flaherty, "Turia, An Original Story." Film Culture, No. 20 (1959), pp. 17-26.

61. Richard Griffith, "Flaherty and Tabu." Film Culture, No. 20 (1959), p. 13. For the text of the story see F. W. Murnau and Robert J. Flaherty, "Tabu, A Story of the South Seas." Film Culture, No. 20 (1959), pp. 27-38.

62. David Flaherty, "A Few Reminiscences." Film Culture, No. 20 (1959), p. 16.

63. Eisner, Murnau. Berkeley: University of California Press, 1973, p. 218.

64. Flaherty to Barnouw, 29 September 1926, published in Erik Barnouw's "Robert Flaherty (Barnouw's File)," p. 177.

65. Letters dated 8 March and 14 May 1929, Ibid.

66. Fred Zinnemann, "Remembering Robert Flaherty." Action (May-June 1976), pp. 25-27. Zinnemann, later to become a successful direc-tor in his own right, was hired by Flaherty as a production assistant for the intended film in the Soviet Union.

67. Paul Rotha, Documentary Diary: An Informal History of the British Documentary, 1928-1939. New York: Hill and Wang, 1973, p. 50.

68. Ibid., pp. 52 ff.

69. Grierson in Forsyth Hardy (ed. and comp.), Grierson on Docu-mentary. New York: Praeger, 1966 rev. ed., pp. 69-70. Also, Grierson interviewed in Elizabeth Sussex, The Rise and Fall of British Documentary...Berkeley: University of California Press, 1975, pp. 24-26.

70. As recalled by Flaherty in his "Account of Making the Film (Man of Aran)." Typescript, p. 1, "Flaherty Papers," Box 31. Also quoted in Griffith, p. 83.

71. Calder-Marshall, based on Rotha and Wright, p. 142; both say The Aran Islanders [sic]. Robert Flaherty, "Aran and Some of its People." BBC Radio Broadcast, recorded 17-18 December 1929; tran-script, "Flaherty Papers," Box 31.

72. Calder-Marshall made this observation, p. 142. See also John Grierson's "Summary and Survey: 1935." The Arts Today, re-printed in Hardy, p. 176.

73. Flaherty. "Aran and Some of its People." Ibid. Synge, The Aran Islands. London: George Allen & Unwin Ltd., 1907, and his Riders to the Sea, in A Treasury of the Theatre, edited by John Gassner. New York: Simon and Schuster, 1960 ed., pp. 628-632.

74. Pat Mullen, Man of Aran. Cambridge, Massachusetts and London: The M.I.T. Press, 1970 (orig. ed. 1935), p. 60.

75. Flaherty, "Account of the Making of the Film (Man of Aran)," p. 3. Also quoted in Griffith, p. 84.

76. Hugh Gray said in an interview that King was not even an islander but a "strange wandering character." Later, he joined the Garda, the Irish police force. He was not in the boat for the storm sequence. "They had three of their absolute experts to do that." Interviewed in Donald E. Staples (ed.), p. 208.

77. Taylor, p. 157.

78. Mullen, pp. 268 and 274, respectively.

79. Flaherty to Edward Black, dated 29 December 1932, "Flaherty Papers," Box 30.

80. Ibid.; also, Flaherty to Mr. Boxall, Gainsborough, dated 28 February 1933.

81. Ibid.

82. Dr. A. Mahr to Dr. Allen, dated 7 June 1933, "Flaherty Papers," Box 30.

83. Harry Watt interviewed in Elizabeth Sussex's The Rise and Fall of British Documentary: The Story of the Film Movement Founded by John Grierson. Berkeley: University of California Press, 1975, p. 29.

84. Flaherty, "Filming Real People." Movie Makers (December 1934). Reprinted in Jacobs, The Documentary Tradition, p. 99.

85. Goldman quoted in Calder-Marshall, p. 151.

86. Calder-Marshall, pp. 156-157; Gray quoted in Staples, p. 204.

87. Frances Flaherty, Elephant Dance. New York: Scribners, 1937, p. 14.

88. Ibid., p. 15.

89. Frances Flaherty, Sabu: The Elephant Boy. New York: Oxford University Press, 1937.

90. Elephant Dance, p. 134.

91. Griffith, p. 134.

92. The Captain's Chair: A Story of the North. London: Hodder & Stoughton; New York: Scribner's, 1938. White Master. London: Routledge, 1939.

93. Letter from Lorentz to Robert Snyder, 5 April 1962, quoted in Snyder's Lorentz and the Documentary Film.

94. Mercey to Lorentz, 15 May 1939, quoted by Snyder, p. 132-133.

95. Behold Our Land. Boston: Houghton Mifflin, 1938.

96. Wayne Darrow, "The Land," unpublished memorandum, dated 8 October 1971. Official AAA records in the custody of the National Archives contain virtually no significant references to the problems involved in the production of The Land. Records at the Division of Information level were not saved; unfortunately they probably contained the documentation relating to Flaherty. The Administrator's central file contains only marginal references, suggesting that AAA's top officer, "Spike" Evans, was not involved in the day-to-day problems of dealing with Flaherty.

97. Russell and Kate Lord (eds.), Forever the Land: A Country Chronicle and Anthology. New York: Harper Brothers, 1950, p. 26.

98. Gercke to Lorentz, 3 September 1939, quoted in Snyder, pp. 136-137.

99.   Lorentz to Snyder, 5 April 1962, in Snyder, pp. 139-140.
100.   Helen Van Dongen, "Robert J. Flaherty, 1884-1951." Film Quarterly, 18, No. 4 (Summer 1965), 2-14. Reprinted in Richard Barsam (ed.), Nonfiction Film: Theory and Criticism. New York: E. P. Dutton, 1976, pp. 212-229.
101.   Professor David Culbert brought to my attention that at least one other sequence was staged for the benefit of the cameras. At Mercey's request, Charles Herbert of Livingston, Montana, photographed "fields of grain" footage to be cut into The Land. He had to take several liberties with the harvesting operation to do so, to get proper equipment in one scene. Correspondence between Herbert and Lorentz and Mercey, filed in records of Office of War Information, "Charles W. Herbert" folder, Washington National Records Center, Suitland, Md. Entry 265, Box 1449, Record Group 208.
102.   Ben Achtenberg, "Helen van Dongen: An Interview." Film Quarterly, 30, No. 2 (Winter 1976-1977), 54.
103.   Darrow memorandum.
104.   "Introduction to the Land," Flaherty Papers, Box 42. Also Lord to Flaherty, 13 January 1942.
105.   Rotha and Wright, p. 309.
106.   Griffith, p. 142.
107.   Flaherty Papers, Box 42.
108.   Theodore Strauss, "The Giant Shinnies Down the Beanstalk: Flaherty's The Land." New York Times (12 October 1941).
109.   Strauss, p. 197.
110.   Telephone interview with Frank Capra, conducted by Professor David Culbert, 18 January 1977. "State of the Nation" was revived soon thereafter as "Army-Navy Screen Magazine," which became very popular with the troops.
111.   What's Happened to Sugar? was produced for the U.S. Office of Price Administration; copies are in the National Archives.
112.   Robert Flaherty, "Making a Film in the Louisiana Bayous." Travel, 92, No. 5 (May 1949), 13.
113.   Frances Flaherty, Odyssey of a Film Maker, p. 34.
114.   Van Dongen, "Robert J. Flaherty, 1885-1951," reprinted in Barsam, p. 226.
115.   Frances Flaherty, Odyssey of a Film Maker, p. 38.
116.   Flaherty quoted in Griffith, p. 150.
117.   Leacock interviewed in G. Roy Levin, Documentary Explorations. Garden City, New York: Doubleday, 1971, p. 211.
118.   Van Dongen, "Three Hundred and Fifty Cans of Film," in Cinema 1951, edited by Roger Manvell. London: Penguin Books, 1951, pp. 59-60.
119.   Actenberg, p. 51.
120.   Cf. Paul Rotha, Documentary Film. In Collaboration with Sinclair Road. Richard Griffith. New York: Hastings House Publishers, 1952 ed., p. 321; Van Dongen, "Robert Flaherty" in Barsam (ed.), pp. 64-65.
121.   Arnold Eagle, "Looking Back...at the Pirogue Maker, Louisiana Story and The Flaherty Way." Film Library Quarterly, 9, No. 1 (1976), 28-37. Eagle went on to make the film on his own.

122. "Robert J. Flaherty, 1884–1951," in Barsam (ed.), p. 227.
123. Van Dongen interviewed in Actenberg, pp. 50–51.
124. Virgil Thomson, Virgil Thomson. London: Weidenfeld and Nicolson, 1967, pp. 393–394; Frederick Sternfeld, Louisiana Story. Film Music Notes, 7, No. 1 (September–October 1948); and Roger Manvell and John Huntley, The Techniques of Film Music. London and New York: Focal Press, 1957, pp. 99–109. Thomson was nominated for an Academy Award for the sound track but lost, presumably because it was "un-professional." He was, however, awarded a Pulitzer prize for the film score, the first one ever given in this category.
125. 9 October 1948, pp. 61–63.
126. Quoted in Taylor, p. 117.
127. Time (20 Sept. 1948), pp. 94–96.
128. "Profile of Flaherty," New Yorker (11, 18, and 25 June 1949). Reprinted in Taylor's chapter "Flaherty—Education for Wanderlust," in his The Running Pianist. Garden City, New York: Doubleday, 1950, pp. 116–164. Quote from pp. 118–119.
129. Van Dyke interviewed by Harrison Engle, "Thirty Years of Social Inquiry," Film Comment (Spring 1965), reprinted in Jacobs, The Documentary Tradition, p. 358.
130. Herman Weinberg, "A Farewell to Flaherty." Films in Review, 2 (October 1951), pp. 14–16. Reprinted in his Saint Cinema: Selected Writings 1929–1970. DBS Publications, 1970, pp. 109–112.

Critical Survey of Oeuvre

When Robert Flaherty's Nanook of the North appeared in 1922 it overwhelmed reviewers and critics, taking them completely by surprise. The New York Times (12 June 1922), for example, said: "Beside this film the usual photoplay, the so-called 'dramatic' work of the screen becomes as thin and blank as the celluloid on which it is printed." Further on, the Times said: the film was "far more interesting, far more compelling purely as entertainment than any except the rare exception among photoplays." In London reviewers were equally unreserved. The Daily Graphic said: "Nanook of the North is a motion picture unexampled in the history of the screen." The Sunday Express: "It is the most remarkable film ever shown in London. If you never see another film you must see Nanook." And so on.

The critical impact of Nanook of the North of course relied on the film's merits, which were many, but to a great extent it was also the result of viewer sensibilities and their perception of nonfiction cinema in 1922. As a documentary Nanook was unlike other films that had been shown before. It told a story of people who acted out their own everyday roles in their own world, and the story conveyed a high level of emotional involvement. If this was a documentary, as we recognize it today, an academic framework let alone a popular conception did not even exist. To be sure, movie audiences had been treated to actualities on the screen from the days of Edison and Lumiere and the early Pathe newsreels. But the scenes they contained were so brief that they could hardly convey a sense of narrative, neither in film terms nor journalistically.

The feature-length actualities of the Great War such as America's Answer (1918) and Pershing's Crusaders (1918), produced by the U.S. Committee on Public Information, were equally primitive in as much as they failed to utilize the shot as the basic element of film editing, relying instead on long shot after long shot occasionally interrupted by a title. These first government-sponsored propaganda filmmakers learned nothing from D. W. Griffith whose culminating work, Birth of a Nation (1915), had appeared before America's entry into the war. Once popular, the CPI films were cast into the dustbin of history after the war was over.

Nanook of the North was not the first feature-length actuality film, nor was it the first real-life film set in exotic lands. Travel-adventure films such as Paul J. Rainey's African Hunt (1912), Martin Johnson's Jungle Adventures (1921) and his Head Hunters of the South Seas (1922), and Burton Holmes's film lectures (1921) were widely shown, and even Flaherty had seen a few of them. Their numerous long shots of strange and exotic scenes barely sustained a narrative.[1] And by no stretch of the imagination could they be considered works of art with emotive content.

Nor did film criticism exist as it is known today through magazines, journals, and advanced film theory taught in graduate schools. Nevertheless, one of the first important film critics, Robert E. Sherwood, chose Nanook of the North for inclusion in his book The Best Moving Pictures of 1922-23. There had been many "fine travel pictures with gorgeous scenery," he rightly stated, but Nanook stood "literally in a class by itself." The grounds upon which he praised Flaherty's film debut included: the logical and consistent arrangement of scenes; the realism, that is the reflection of the Eskimo's emotions, philosophy, and endless privations; and the achievement that it was essentially a one-man film, where previous films had represented the combined talents of many. Thematically, he emphasized the simple conflict or struggle between Nanook and his environment.[2]

Despite the relative simplicity of film criticism in the early twenties, Nanook received a surprisingly perceptive review by Frances Taylor Patterson, a professor at Columbia University. The reviewer hit upon some of the key elements of documentary film without defining it as such. "Here are natural scenery," she wrote in The New Republic, "natural actors, the unembellished conte of a portion of life in Ungava. The 'stars' are the native esquimaux. The 'extras' are the polar bear [sic], the seals and the walrus that wander about the country. The 'sets' are the frozen vastness of the North. For drama there is the struggle of Nanook, the hunter, to wrest sustenance from barren waste of snow." The film had heroism, drama, and suspense. Like Sherwood, Patterson stressed the difference between this film and travel exotica. The film did not wander from one island to another, or from one jungle to another, showing glimpses of life here and there. Instead it showed one location and one hunter in order to represent an entire culture. Nanook, also, was educational in that one learned a great deal about Eskimo life. But to Patterson, Nanook's greatest appeal was its pictorial beauty. Through images Flaherty created a mood, a spirit of loneliness and desolation, a naturalness achieved through the camera. Patterson even ventured to pronounce Nanook of the North as the first photoplay of the natural school of cinematography.[3]

After the initial excitement had passed some negative criticism began to appear, centered more or less on the questionable authenticity of events portrayed in the film. Iris Barry, who published one of the first books of film criticism in 1926, made a direct challenge to Nanook's authenticity. She put forward the claim that Nanook was actually made in the latitude of Edinburgh and acted by extremely sophisticated Eskimos. She was right on the former to a degree, though the climates were entirely different, and absolutely wrong on the other point.[4]

According to the writer and explorer Vilhjalmur Stefansson, once Barry's employer, the film's picture of Eskimo life was most inexact. First of all, he said, the Eskimos had guns for generations but the film gave the impression that they only hunted with primitive weapons. Secondly, he debunked the seal hunting scene in which Nanook pulls a noticeably dead seal through a hole in the ice: "nor do I think a seal could be killed by that method unless he were a defective." Flaherty did not fool Stefansson who was certain that audiences realized the seal was "still and dead." Stefansson pursued another incidence of fakery in connection with an igloo scene. He realized that Flaherty had to cut away one of the walls to obtain sufficient lighting for photography but he objected to the innocent lie on a title to the effect that the reason Nanook's family shivered and that their breath was visible was because the igloo walls and roof had to be kept freezing inside to prevent thawing. Nor did the temperature average 35°F degrees below zero in the Hudson Bay region as another title indicated. These inaccuracies and incidences of fakery destroyed for him the value of the film. They were but examples of myths and half-truths accepted as "Knowledge," the theme of his peculiar book, The Standardization of Error.[5] In both Barry and Stefansson's attack, authenticity was the sole criterion for measuring the film's value. Both writers ignored art and creativity. It could have been the most beautiful film ever made, but if it distorted the truth, they seemed to say, it was worthless.

A rather confused Gilbert Seldes, writing in 1924, lamented the decline of the "large, spectacular films," and to prove this state of affairs he naively described Nanook of the North as "a spectacle to which the producer and artistic director contributed nothing—for it was a picture of actualities, made according to rumour, in the interest of a fur-trading company." This is further evidence that "Something wrong has crept into the spectacle film." Presumably actualities were a bad thing![6]

Another criticism by virtual omission was Terry Ramsaye's A Million and One Nights, first published in 1926 and still a classic history of the silent cinema through 1925. Giving Nanook less than a sentence, he described it as "propaganda for Revillon Frères." Later Ramsaye tried to make up for slighting Flaherty by writing a biographical article which promoted the image of Flaherty as a great explorer in the 17th-century tradition.[7]

It remained for a Frenchman (evidently of Italian origin) to elevate Nanook to the status of Aeschylus's tragedies. "Here,"

Ricciotto Canudo wrote in 1927, "'reportage' and 'documentary' have ventured so far into space and into reality that a true tragedy has spontaneously taken shape with the magic of celluloid. And the Every day Tragedy of polar man spreads out into the emotions of the entire world, more moving, more 'direct' than all the most pathetic plot complications that the poets have ever imagined." For Canudo, Nanook represented the eternal struggle of humanity. The subtitle given the film in France, "Man of Primitive Times," was phony. "Nanook is not primitive man nor polar man. He is Man, in all his truth." Canudo continued with a persuasive reading of the film's symbolism. It is not explained, however, as Flaherty's vision or as an expression of his inner feelings, so crucial to the auteruist school of criticism, but rather as the import and meaning of human life reduced to its essential terms in the barren north.[8]

Flaherty's biographer, Richard Griffith, also believed that Nanook "elicited from life itself," that Flaherty himself sought the spirit of man in the "secret places of the earth." Griffith, however, related the film to Flaherty's own personality, his temperament and character, and to his own experiences in life, particularly his boyhood. But the film's major critical achievement, he argued, was the portrayal of Eskimos from their own outlook on life. For the Eskimos of those days believed that they were the Innuit, which meant "We, the people." No other civilization existed outside of their sparse numbers. The white man and the Indian, their closest contact with the outside, were almost another species. Flaherty penetrated the psyche of Eskimo culture and could present it on its own terms. And what he found impressed him so much it became his basis for judging others for the rest of his life. "To him," Griffith explained, "the Eskimos were we the people, as we should be."[9]

In reviewing Griffith's biography of Flaherty, the famous photographer Walker Evans stated precisely the visual power of the film: "No one will ever forget the stunning freshness of Nanook of the North. The mere sight of a few stills from the production has the power to bring it all back....Add to this the sheer line of that particular photograph (Nanook launching his harpoon): the diagonal shaft of the weapon, the sweep of the cord looping to Nanook's raised hand, then the coiling in black calligraphy against the sky."[10]

Paul Rotha's initial assessment of Nanook of the North was published in his seminal Documentary Film (1935). Rotha, avoiding the grandiose and philosophic, emphasized only a few specific points limited to the simplicity of the film's statement, excellent photography, and an imaginative use of the camera. As Rotha saw the film, "It brought alive the fundamental issue of life in the sub-arctic—the struggle for food—with such imaginatively chosen shots and with such a sincere feeling for the community interest of these people, that it suggested far greater powers of observation than the plain description offered by other naturalistic photographers." So he praised Nanook not only for what it had accomplished but for the

potential it offered others. Always the social filmmaker, Rotha saw
a purpose in the film, namely, "the progress of civilization depends
upon Man's growing ability to make Nature serve a purpose, and by his
own skill to bend natural resources to his own needs."[11]

Writing many years later, in collaboration with Basil Wright,
Rotha lifted his restraint. For example, "Out of the tangled wilderness of Northern Canada and out of the barren ice of the Hudson Bay
had come a man who, on the one side, challenged the whole art of the
cinema as it had been gropingly developed up till then, and on the
other struggled against the whole industrially organized machinery of
the film trade. It is impossible to overrate the magnitude of this
challenge and the courage of the man who made it." For the first
time, as they pointed out, the camera did more than record what was
in front of the lens. Additionally, they related Flaherty's success
to his knowledge of the land and its people which he knew through
many years of experience.[12]

They raised one critical problem which is pertinent to any discussion of Flaherty films: Did Flaherty intend an accurate picture
of Eskimo life as he filmed it or as it used to be? Flaherty did not
date his films; he intended timeless documents. But Rotha and Wright
believed that Flaherty gave the impression that he filmed life as he
found it. Properly, this is an important question for each film.
However, it is well known from the written accounts of the making of
Nanook of the North that Flaherty took certain liberties to express
essential reality of Eskimo life, a standard procedure in the
Flaherty method.

Edmund Carpenter, an authority on Eskimo culture, made an important contribution to the critical history of Nanook of the North in
particular and to Flaherty's art in general by constructing a direct
relationship between Eskimo art and the way he made his films. Paul
Rotha, Basil Wright, Arthur Calder-Marshall, and Frances Flaherty
have all endorsed Carpenter's analysis in one form or another.

Carpenter attempted to gauge the effects of Flaherty's years of
exploration in the North, a time in which Flaherty became himself an
aficionado of Eskimo art, a collector of carvings and drawings. The
latter were published in a book by Flaherty as early as 1915.[13] With
life in the North reduced to its bare essentials, Carpenter wrote,
art and poetry turn up among them. To the Eskimo the creation of art
is "an act of seeing and expressing life's values; it's a ritual of
discovery by which patterns of nature, and of human nature are revealed by man." Carpenter went on to use the tusk of ivory as an
example. Ostensibly formless, the Eskimo artist discovers the tusk's
hidden form and perfects its lines, for example, into the shape of a
seal. Man has only released the form through a process of discovery.
Carpenter saw the same process at work in Eskimo language, again revealing form from a universe of disorder. Flaherty's years in the
barren wilderness and his close association with Eskimos gave him

their uncanny power of observation, and this power, together with the concept of letting the material shape its own meaning, formed the basis of Flaherty's art.[14]

Influenced by the writings of Claude Levi-Strauss, French critics have recognized the modernity, that is to say the classicism, of the "pensée sauvage." And as true auteurists, they argued that the film represented the director's philosophical outlook and his particular manner of filmmaking. Nanook under such interpretation becomes less of a film about a tribe and more of one about human life reduced to its elementary "dynamisme," to survive or die, to draw subsistence from an unrelenting nature. Flaherty, therefore, worked with the exterior of a people only to discover the true spirit of man.[15]

French writers rather consistently have defended Flaherty's avoidance of social problems in his films. Nanook figures in this though it was more of an issue in relation to Man of Aran. The problem of exploitation was avoided in Nanook. One argument advanced by Marcel Martin was that Flaherty could not deal with complex social problems because it conflicted with his style of pure imagery. His editing, unaffected by the Russians or French avant gardistes of the same era, was dictated by clarity and continuity of movement. Flaherty rejected montage and a dialectic vision of the world, but his art in its own way was aesthetic, intellectual, revolutionary, and militant. Martin rejected the perjorative label "innocent eye," concluding: "Flaherty was essentially a painter of the world busy dying, the poet of last fragments of earthly paradise subsisting on the surface of our world in full transformation, the poet of eternal moral values and of man who is at the same time Prometheus and Sisyphus."[16]

The making of Nanook of the North has become a standard part of all recent histories of documentary film or nonfiction film;[17] certainly Lewis Jacobs recognized the significance of Nanook. Evidently following Carpenter, he wrote: "The drama of Nanook was not imposed, but derived from the material itself, arranged into a loose narrative to express what the filmmaker had learned and experienced from living with his subject and what he wanted the viewer to know and feel about these people and their way of life." Further on he said: "The singular treatment of reality in Nanook was the fullest expression up to that time of the film of fact. It brought the nonfiction film to a new level of achievement. Discovering the essential drama with the material itself became the method which created the prototype of documentary film and established its tradition." Flaherty carried perception beyond the eye, beyond the camera. On the other hand, statements such as: "Scenes are full of minute observation, with no false gestures, no artificiality; the Eskimos play themselves, but they do not act; everything seems true" are clearly incorrect.[18]

In his history of nonfiction film, Barsam's interpretation of Nanook is also derivative from Carpenter's influential analysis. Hence, "From the Eskimos, Flaherty learned that art is more than

just an expression of life's values, that art enables man to understand his relationship to life, and that art is also artifact, a
utilitarian record of the moment. The Eskimo sees life clearly and
simply, in terms of existence and action, and from the wastes of snow
and ice, he makes his statement as an act of conquest and affirmation.
In his carvings, he reveals form so that he might protest against the
formlessness of his environment. The Eskimo's approach is to explore,
conquer, and record; for Flaherty, too, filmmaking was an act of exploration first, and affirmation second."[19] Barsam begs the question
whether Nanook is a documentary and comes up on the negative side on
the grounds that it offers no help for these people living under conditions of hardship, nor does it have any immediate social value.
Rather, "Its value is the value of any work of art that illuminates
man's nobility."[20]

In Erik Barnouw's general survey of documentary film, by now a
standard text, his chapter on Flaherty concentrates largely on biographical data and the physical details of the film's making, but
does add to the critical literature. In the first place Barnouw
points out that Flaherty had "apparently mastered--unlike previous
documentaries--the 'grammar' of film as it had evolved in the fiction
film." This is true only in a limited sense, because Flaherty never
mastered the art of editing which "grammar" implies, even toward the
end of his career. Editing was never his forte.

Barnouw felt that the sense of shared discovery that Flaherty
imparted was among the film's most important achievements. The titles
never over explained. The audience discovered for itself that a
square cut in an igloo wall became a window, that one block of ice
became a window pane and another a reflector to catch the low sun.
Similarly, the unseen seal at the end of Nanook's harpoon line allowed
the audience to participate in another discovery.

Barnouw does not pursue Carpenter's theme of the relationship
between Flaherty film and Eskimo art. More a humanist that aestheti-
cian, the theme of cultural conflict and exploitation interests him
more. He saw the film as a valid expression of the Flaherty personality, an expression of an inner personal conflict acquired through
his years of contact with primitive societies. Flaherty saw the
gradual deterioration of Indian and Eskimo life under the advance
guard of Western industrialization. So Flaherty hoped to record
before the camera a vanishing culture in its last throes. He hoped
to record the Eskimos as they saw themselves in their traditional
past, not as he saw it and not as he found it.[21]

Although Flaherty's concern with cultural conflict does not
materialize in the film itself, it was a genuine concern and a continuous theme in his life. It almost found expression on the screen
in his collaboration in White Shadows of the South Seas (1928) and
Tabu (1931), both dealing with the theme of exploitation of Polynesian
societies, which Flaherty had come to know since his experience in

making Moana. Both collaborative efforts ended in failure and in
Flaherty's withdrawal.

As it turned out, Flaherty unwittingly was a pioneer of the ethnographic film technique. He immersed himself in each culture, most
of all in Eskimo life. He tried to make his film specific enough so
that valid generalization could follow. He saw the family as the
basic unit. And whether by accident or design he involved people before the camera in the filmmaking process. The use of reconstructions
and staged action, however, detracted from the ethnographic value.
But for many years Flaherty films were the only ones available for
use in anthropology courses, and they still remain favorites.[22]

Luc de Heusch explained the ethnographic value of Nanook as an
outgrowth of Flaherty's artistic integrity. Flaherty's own "témoignage
authentique" allowed Nanook the freedom to interpret his own role. The
camera was discrete and hardly visible yet it participated in the social life of the Eskimos, provoking reactions and dialogue and posing
questions which demanded responses. De Heusch compared Nanook to a
form of "sociodrama" where Flaherty was a "metteur en scene." Because
of the artistic integrity that Flaherty brought to observation,
De Heusch argued it was necessary to accept his reconstructions for
the study of ethnography.[23]

Critics and film historians were obligated to face up to the historical value of Nanook of the North because of its primacy as the
first documentary which combined pictorial information, narrative
structure, and the filmmaker's art with its implicit emotive statement. Lacking any of these qualities would have made Nanook a museum
piece, a mummified curiosity as so many pre-documentaries are viewed
today. But it did not marshal in a new era of filmmaking, nor did it
initiate the documentary movement as such. Documentary emerged much
later from an amalgamation of sources and influences, among them the
pervasive spirit of Nanook. Nanook was an anomaly that excited the
imagination of other filmmakers like Grierson and Cavalcanti who
carried the movement forward. Nanook excited them about the possibilities of making films in a real world not for a sense of discovery
as Flaherty would have wanted, not so much even for art, but for the
cause of social justice and civic education, as Grierson began to
refine his ideas. And as films set in reality were shaped for political causes, documentary would serve the cause of social revolution.
"We Russians," Eisenstein once said, "learned more from Nanook of the
North than from any other foreign film. We wore it out studying it.
That was in a way our beginning."[24] Flaherty never used his films
for causes other than his own, but Eisenstein's statement is still a
fitting tribute.

Contemporary reviewers of Moana were generally pleased by
Flaherty's newest film. Now that they had had time to reflect upon
Nanook and compare it with Moana they could readily sense a pattern
in Flaherty's work. They could take Moana at face value, accept its

photographic realism, and its claim to art; they could apply the adulation "masterpiece" as film critics are wont to do. <u>Moana</u> also suggested to its contemporary audience that film could be a "document." This realization was to form a significant start of the documentary movement.

European reviewers of <u>Moana</u> were especially ecstatic. According to a Paramount spokesman, it "received finer press reviews in Stockholm than any picture ever released by any company in this territory."[25] The <u>London Sunday Pictorial</u> (27 June 1926) said: "It is the most beautiful revelation of Native life ever shown on the screen. Mr. Flaherty has happily refrained from introducing mere movie stuff into this picture. He has been content to show this Southern Paradise as it is, and so to make us feel that we have seen a land of marvellous beauty and met a people of extraordinary fascination. We follow Moana in the sea, in the field, in his home and in love, and it is all delightful because Mr. Flaherty has done his work so perfectly that Moana and his people never once seem to act." The tattooing sequence is singled out as "one of the most extraordinary scenes ever shown on the screen." It continued: "Moana is by far the most sensitive interpretation of the character of a people the screen has yet shown, because, in addition to beauty, it possesses a delicate emotional appeal altogether irresistible. This is a motion picture masterpiece."[26]

The playwright Austin Strong wrote to Flaherty praising the film for the picture it presented of the beauty and dignity of the Samoan people. He expressed his gratitude to Flaherty for this "human <u>document</u> of a great race so soon, alas, to vanish from the earth." "You have no protagonist," he continued, "nor have you betrayed us with a falsified story--instead, with the unerring instinct of the artist, you have weaved a pattern from Nature herself, for sky, clouds, water, trees, hills and the everyday simple acts of men, women, and children." Finally, he said, "Moana reaches the dignity of an epic poem."[27]

Flaherty was proud of such compliments, for he used them to endorse his own work. Strong, for his part, used the term "document" to praise <u>Moana</u>. It is not known whether he had read the Grierson review, but surely he valued the film for the same reason.

Robert Littell, writing in <u>The New Republic</u>, appreciated the care and patience that went into the making of <u>Moana</u>. But Littell was skeptical of the film's portrayal of paradise. "It was well enough for Samoans to be happy, lazy in the sun, but surely our own civilization would disappear if we did not struggle for life. The Heaven in the South Seas which the white man thought he had discovered for himself is not for him at all. It might have lasted for the native. In a very few corners some traces of it may still be found. Whether Mr. Flaherty found one of these corners intact, or whether we welded traces of the real thing with his imagination of it does not matter. His reconstruction remains a living reconstruction."[28]

Herbert J. Seligmann, critic for the prestigious magazine <u>The Arts</u>, analyzed the film's visual beauty, the essence of which was movement, the movement of individuals or as members of a family. "To have seen these moving shapes as Flaherty saw them," he wrote, "to invest the slightest movement of human figures with such glamor, is to give proof of an antecedent love for human beings in their dignity. It is a man's passion for seeing the thing before him that gives <u>Moana</u> its distinction...." Seligmann concluded his review by suggesting, prophetically as it turned out, that Flaherty should work closer to home. He suggested as a fitting subject the vanishing American Indian, "with their decorative sense manifest in their ceremonial dances." Just two years later Flaherty went to New Mexico to make such a film.[29]

<u>Moana</u> was important in a critical sense because it prompted Grierson to use the English word documentary in reference to a film. While in the United States studying the press and communications, Grierson occasionally acted as a guest critic for <u>The New York Sun</u>. His anonymous review appeared on 8 February 1926, under the signature of "The Moviegoer." Almost as an aside Grierson wrote: "Of course, <u>Moana</u> being a visual account of events in the daily life of a Polynesian youth and his family, has documentary value." Grierson was still not comfortable with the word documentary, for he believed that the documentary aspect was only a secondary value of the film. Nor, one should hasten to add, was he using "documentary" in the social-political sense which he advocated in the 1930s.[30]

Grierson, too, emphasized the poetic aspects of the film, adding to the chorus of critics who were by now calling Flaherty a film poet. "The film is unquestionably a great one, a poetic record of Polynesian tribal life, its ease and beauty and its salvation through a painful rite. <u>Moana</u> deserves to rank with those few works of the screen that have a right to last, to live. It could only have been produced by a man with an artistic conscience and an intense poetic feeling which, in this case, finds an outlet through nature worship." For Grierson, <u>Moana</u> achieved greatness "primarily through its poetic feeling for natural elements. It was like a poem which sung of the loveliness of sea and land and air, and of man in his primitive innocence, part of his beautiful surroundings." He believed that <u>Moana</u> showed far greater mastery of the cinema than <u>Nanook of the North</u>, in terms of photography--camera angles, composition, design, and the tonal values of the panchromatic film--and in terms of structure--that is, in following Moana's daily pursuits and culminating in his tattooing, which Grierson viewed as a necessary act of bravery that Samoan culture required for survival. To Grierson, naively, the Samoans' pain and pleasure and their way of life were statements of their innocence.[31]

It was characteristic of both Robert and Frances Flaherty to write articles and books on the making of their films. Frances Flaherty for example detailed the making of <u>Moana</u> in her travel series published in <u>Asia</u> magazine. Generally they omitted any critical discussion of film as art. This would have been much too pedantic for Robert who treasured more his anecdotes and photographic experimentation. Frances's writings stuck to the physical world, describing the day-to-day problems encountered on location. This changed after Robert's death, however, and she began to lecture and write and tried to formularize in her own mind the essence of her husband's life. Frances was in a way her husband's spokeswoman in the realm of art.

Frances wrote an article one year after the Grierson review of <u>Moana</u>; its significance was twofold. She herself, and presumably her husband, accepted and used Grierson's documentary label. Secondly, she began to develop the documentary principle even before Grierson that drama must be discovered in the subject matter of the film. The Flahertys approached the filming of <u>Moana</u> with the preconceptions of <u>Nanook of the North</u>, primarily in assuming a primeval struggle for existence. Proven wrong, this assumption confused them and caused endless delays in filming and structuring <u>Moana</u>. Hunting had little to do with life in Samoa. Samoan drama could be found, rather, in speech, movements of body, singing, dancing, feasting, ceremony, and ritual. The camera had to discover what was inherent and not imposed from without.

In 1927 the Flahertys saw Eisenstein's film <u>Potemkin</u>. Frances wrote in the same article that they had used the camera in a similar way: "an historical incident has been re-enacted, and over these re-enacted scenes the camera has been brought to play as over actual life, and the result is that same conviction of reality." She saw <u>Nanook</u>, <u>Moana</u>, and <u>Potemkin</u> as experimental in this sense: "It is this development, independent of stage, or story, or star, depending on nothing but what is in the camera itself, that I suggest to you as a destiny of the screen. I suggest it as a great destiny, because pictures made from life, of the drama inherent in life, are <u>documentary</u> and philosophic. In them the educational, the religious and the dramatic are blended into one."[32]

Only a few years later Grierson began writing that <u>Moana</u> demonstrated one of the first principles of the documentary--that the story must be taken from the location and that it should be the essential story of the location.

Paul Rotha also adopted the principle of observation in <u>Moana</u> in another way: "The material for the theme must be observed at first-hand and absorbed into the mind before the film is actually started," and "while the material used for the film is photographed from real life and is, in fact, recorded 'reality,' by the selection of images, brought about by an intimate understanding of their presence, the film becomes an interpretation, a special dramatisation of reality and not mere recorded description."[33] It can be summarized that Flaherty first demonstrated the principle of discovery, Frances

Flaherty first articulated it, Grierson recognized it as essential
for all documentary film, and Rotha explained that discovery required
artistic interpretation.

In more recent years the slight critical praise for Moana rested
more on its photographic qualities than anything else. Many believed
it was the first feature-length film entirely made on panchromatic
emulsion, so Moana showed more sensitivity to coloration than was
previously thought possible. Flaherty's caressing camera movements,
in an age when the camera had been relatively static, also drew
praise from the likes of Paul Rotha, Basil Wright, and Arthur Calder-
Marshall. Flaherty used the close-up more thoughtfully in Moana but
he continued to use the long-focus lens as his mainstay and as a
particular trademark of his camera style. Both the English and European literature on Flaherty lack major, even lengthy critical discussion of Moana. Moana has not endured in the same way as Nanook of
the North and today is looked at more with curiosity than appreciation. The same photographic qualities which Rotha, Wright, and
Calder-Marshall praised, according to one view, marked Flaherty's
transition from an artist to technician. For Richard Corliss detail
became trivialized, craftsmanship not elemental but ornamental; and
except for the tattooing, Samoan life appeared static, undramatic.[34]

And so, Moana which started out with the highest critical praise
has begun to drift lower and lower in the Flaherty oeuvre. Where
once critics and filmmakers applauded Moana for its revolutionary
stereoscopic-like photography, enhanced by color sensitive film, low
sunlight, and pronounced shadows, at least one film historian now
calls it static photography and Flaherty's camera movements crude.
If Corliss and Barsam share this point of view, then photographic
qualities are no longer a touchstone for measuring a film's success
or failure, and consequently many of Flaherty's works would fail
under such criticism because this is where he devoted his principal
creative energies. But Barsam goes further than most writers on the
subject in saying that Moana's "unimaginative attention to the facts
of local color and daily life provide none of the insights into human
strength and behaviour which made Nanook such a powerful statement."
And, "There is no conflict, no hostile elements of nature, no sex;
in fact, there is precious little to interest the moveigoer." We
have apparently come full circle to the reaction of Paramount upon
first seeing what it hath wrought.[35]

Not considered one of his major works, Twenty-Four Dollar Island
(1927), was an anomaly in Flaherty's career. Although most of his
films could be viewed as experimental, Flaherty did not view them
as experiments save perhaps for this one and Guernica. The project
gave him his first and only opportunity with an urban subject, the
metropolitan architecture of the island of Manhattan. It gave him
still another chance to work with the long-focus lenses which had
become his trademark. Critically, this film did not attract much
attention even in the major studies on Flaherty. This is perhaps

deservedly so because Twenty-Four Dollar Island compares rather unfavorably with other city films of the same era such as Ruttmann's
Berlin: The Symphony of A City (1927) and Cavalcanti's Rien Que Les
Heures (1926), two landmark documentaries on city life. In comparison Flaherty's film failed to establish a rhythm of images, so important to films of this genre. There was not enough action within the
frame to sustain continuous static long shots. Nor did the film show
the same painstaking detail and observation reflected in such films
as Joris Iven's The Bridge (1928) and Rain (1929). Twenty-Four Dollar
Island did not make a personal statement and lacked almost all the
other virtues of Flaherty's other work. Nevertheless, Marcel Martin
viewed it as an admirable poem of images upon the American metropolis,
images where the director searched to express by the structural compositions what makes the architectural genius of a city.[36] Lewis
Jacobs also wrote favorably of the "semi-abstract pictorial values of
the city," including foreshortened viewpoints, patterns of mass and
line, the contrast of sunlight and shadow."[37]

White Shadows in the South Seas (1928) was primarily the work of
action director W. S. Van Dyke and except for a few scenes is not
properly part of the Flaherty oeuvre. He received no MGM credit for
the production. Flaherty removed himself from the project owing to
differences of opinion with the film crew on the worth of Tahitian
culture. The finished film, however, shared the look of Moana in its
panchromatic photography, similarity of locale, and naturalness of
the actors. In this sense the spirit of Moana predominated. The
film's theme, although imposed by a Hollywood script, had some rele-
vance to the issue of white exploitation of the native tribes which
deeply concerned Flaherty. White Shadows strongly condemned exploitation by white traders who cheated and robbed the natives and ultimately destroyed their way of life. Flaherty seemed so determined
to make a film on this subject that he entered into a second collaboration when the opportunity arose to return to the South Seas.

Contemporary American reviews of F. W. Murnau's Tabu (1931)
assumed a greater contribution by Flaherty than was actually merited.
The film's credits led to the confusion inasmuch as equal producer
credits were given to both Murnau and Flaherty as well as script
credits. Many reviewers made the inevitable comparison with Moana,
whose visual style resembled that of Tabu's. The extent that it
differed from Moana was the touchstone for appraising Tabu's success
or failure as art.

Harry Alan Potamkin criticized Tabu because he felt the two
leads were cast to the preference of Western white audiences when
"far more convincing types, handsome Gauguinesque maidens, appear
incidentally in the film." Potamkin evidently did not realize that
Flaherty also cast his "characters" according to Western perceptions
of physical beauty. Although Potamkin appreciated the photographic
qualities of Tabu, he criticized it for not being Moana, for not
being a true picture of native life, for imposing fabricated

literary material, and for failing "to respect the experience of a people as something to draw upon seriously for theme and plot."[38]

James Shelley Hamilton, though somewhat more generous in his review, also saw Tabu as a "bit contrived and forced."[39] The New Republic (1 April 1931) called Tabu another White Shadows, with a contrived and formalized story imposed upon beautifully photographed material. The point in these contemporary reviews is that they all quite frankly yearned for a film closer to Moana that derived its structure from minute observation of its subject matter. Clearly they wanted a documentary style in the sense that Flaherty had made it understood. Even though they may have sympathized with Tabu's anti-imperialist message, they distrusted its artificiality. Moana had generated a new sensibility which these reviews reflected.

The most pervasive issue in more recent critical discussion of Tabu as it relates to both Murnau and Flaherty is the extent to which Murnau imposed his own European vision on Polynesian society. Rotha, Wright, and Calder-Marshall unfortunately offered little guidance on this issue, concluding that there was not much of Flaherty's work in Tabu. However, in Tabu there was a theme that struck at the heart of the Flaherty personality, "the first collision of two cultures resulted in the destruction of the moral fiber of both," as described by Richard Griffith.

Secondly, although the first outline story "Turia" was much closer to Flaherty's original conception, the second more romantic version was signed by both Flaherty and Murnau and with a few minor exceptions was an exact scenario for the finished film version of Tabu. Some of the footage was filmed under Flaherty's supervision, notably the pearl diving and opening sequences. The problem came in the area of motivation. Flaherty stuck to the story of the white man exploiting the native. Murnau was instrumental in shifting the focus of good and evil between native and native, between the forbidden lovers and the high priest who was charged with enforcing the tabu. Griffith described Tabu as beauty filtered through the European's imagination of the twenties, and writing years later he cited Maurice Scherer's argument that in Tabu, Murnau had revenged Western art for Gauguin's revolution against it by imposing upon Polynesia a traditional European imagery.[40] Flaherty himself told Griffith that he thought Murnau's version of the tabu legend not only romanticized but Europeanized the Polynesian custom, in both psychology and motivation. The style of lighting and photography were also more European.

Lotte Eisner in her admirable study of Murnau defends him against Flaherty's followers.[41] Just as Flaherty refused to discuss his disagreement with Murnau, who died shortly after the film premiered, Murnau left little account of his collaboration. But she asserts that the original story, "Turia," is so romantic "that it may be regarded as proof that even before 'Tabu' Flaherty had given way to Murnau." In disagreeing with Griffith's allusion to "Germanization" of the plot, she said that Murnau formed his perceptions of the islands from his readings of London, Stevenson, O'Brien (Frederick), Conrad, and Melville, none of whom obviously were German. In writing that "Murnau offers us an apotheosis of the flesh," Eisner alluded to Murnau's obsession with sex which found expression in Tabu. So she sees the film as a valid extension of Murnau's personality. Several times she wrote that Flaherty and Murnau did this or that, such as choosing to make Tabu in the style of a silent film. But Murnau did not set out to make a documentary of native customs. "He was an artist who had set out with endless European nostalgia for beauty and sun. What he sought he found. And he transformed it, and gave us a glimpse of it." In her detailed discussion of Tabu's editing, based upon an annotated script, she concludes that the scenes were edited by Murnau. She did recall seeing rushes of Tabu, some of which were marked "Take Flaherty."

Murnau's interest in achieving authenticity by filling his cast with nonprofessional actors who had never been in front of the camera before may have been at least one sign of Flaherty's influence. In fact the film crew built their own motion picture laboratory on Tahiti, trained natives as technicians, and went through the island looking for suitable people needed for the cast, all of which was reminiscent of the making of Moana. Henri Agel saw details that carried the mark of Flaherty but his judgment is purely impressionisitc. In the final analysis he concluded that the "Romantisme germanique" of Murnau prevailed over the "Sensibilité Apollinienne" of Flaherty.[42]

Industrial Britain (1933) is a film of minor critical significance in terms of Flaherty's work, but at the same time, it is a landmark for the British documentary film movement. As discussed elsewhere, Flaherty was largely responsible for the camera work which he filmed under his own direction. The film was edited and completed under the supervision of John Grierson and other members of his film unit after Flaherty's share was finished.

Grierson's comments on his own film were predictably favorable. But in addition he marvelled at Flaherty's ability to pick out the details of craftsmanship--such as the pottery making sequence--which in other hands might have appeared boring and routine. Flaherty observed his subject well enough in order to be able to anticipate movement and move his camera as "though it were the mind and spirit of the man himself."[43] Grierson wrote many years later that Industrial Britain brought together Flaherty's approach and that of his unit's, as different as they were, setting "the line for a decade of documentary film-making--here and abroad."[44] Other notables of the British documentary such as Paul Rotha and Stephen Tallents expressed similar appreciation of the sensitive photography that gave beauty and dignity to British craftsmanship.[45]

Man of Aran (1934) raised the most important critical debate in
Flaherty's life. It is not that he answered his critics' charges.
Flaherty rarely explained his films in terms of theory, nor did he
intellectualize about documentary. Nor was it for the most part a
debate with salvos going back and forth. Newspaper reviewers in
Europe and the United States praised Man of Aran. But they rarely
addressed themselves to the more fundamental issues raised by writers
who wrote for a different audience in more specialized journals and
periodicals. This is where Flaherty's Man of Aran took an enormous
beating that both bewildered and disturbed him. In due time, however, even critics like Rotha, Grierson, and Griffith modified their
initial judgments. After the Great Depression when documentary became less of a vehicle for solving the world's problems, when the
sense of urgency had passed and cynicism replaced optimism, more
sober judgments could be made.

Andre Sennwald passed favorably on Man of Aran in the New York
Times (25 October 1934) but felt the film would not succeed com-
mercially with American audiences because it was intellectually
demanding: "The film has been fashioned with such purity of theme
and economy of method that its freedom from false dramaturgical excitement is glaring." Italian newspaper reviews made Man of Aran
out to be the new masterpiece of cinema. The Corriere Dela Sera
(27 August 1934) of Milan wrote: "The persons in the film are
superbly characterized and alive, and yet they are kept sufficiently
in the middle distance to give to the film the impersonal quality of
an epic." Il Giornale D'Italia (28 August 1934) said: "Flaherty's
direction has succeeded in achieving a definite form of cinemato-
graphic poetry in his portrayal of the life of the fishermen of
Aran.... There is in this film such a wealth of poetical beauty that
one does not feel the need throughout the film of that action which
is necessary in ordinary films." Equally in La Triburna of Rome
(28 August 1934): "Man of Aran can be ranked among the classics of
the screen. It is not easy to maintain the continuity of action in
a film which in one and the same sequence is based on human actions
and the movements of nature." Similarly the Catholic Herald of
London (8 September 1934) said: "Flaherty is the one genuine artist,
who with the purest and simplest photographic techniques shows how
to forcefully direct, how to hold general attention, to move the
audience and to cause enthusiasm." Many other comparable words
could be cited from the newspapers of Britain, Germany, France, and
the United States.

Some periodical writers were content with passing judgment on
the film, favorably or unfavorably, without reference to the ideological battle over method and purpose of documentary film. James
Shelley Hamilton wrote in the National Board of Review (November 1934)
that: "The nameless man of Aran is separated from us only by the
generations that brought towns and machines and easy living to our
own kind. He even speaks a language that is not foreign to us--he
is ourselves when we had to feed ourselves, by our own hands, from

the earth and the sea." Vernon Grenville, writing in The Commonweal
(9 November 1934), said: "The art of photography has never reached a
higher point than in this beautiful film made by Robert Flaherty in
the Isle of Aran. The story is the universal one of man's battle
with the elements...." Otis Ferguson in The New Republic
(7 November 1934) qualified his praise by saying it was occasionally
dull and not as good as Synge's "Riders to The Sea" in its portrayal
of island life.

The ideological storm over Man of Aran had nothing to do with
this kind of off-the-cuff criticism. It began in England, where the
film premiered and soon found expression in the United States. Ivor
Montagu was one of the first to criticize Man of Aran for not presenting a more realistic picture of Aran life. "Man's struggle with
Nature," he wrote, "is incomplete unless it embraces the struggle of
man with man." The bareness of subsistence was not enough to please
him; rather, he seemed to want a film that dealt with more relevant
issues. "No less than Hollywood Flaherty is busy turning reality
into romance. The tragedy is that, being a poet with a poet's eye,
his lie is the greater, for he can make the romance seem real."[46]

C. A. Lejeune's review in the Observer (29 April 1934) contained
some fine words of praise, but she criticized the film's lack of a
story, concluding "Man of Aran is a sealed document, the key to which
is still in Flaherty's mind." A reader's letter prompted her to add
a few days later that the real story of Aran was the struggle against
eviction, told to her by Flaherty himself.[47]

These were only skirmishes, however, compared to the pronounce-
ments shouted from the pages of Cinema Quarterly, a principal platform for British film intellectuals of the 1930s. The summer and
autumn issues of 1934 contained two leftist criticisms of Man of Aran
that charged Flaherty with escaping from the dutiful task of docu-
mentarians to serve the social revolution. In the summer issue
Ralph Bond wrote that "Man of Aran is escapist in tendency, more so
probably, than any previous Flaherty production. Flaherty would have
us believe that there is no class struggle on Aran, despite ample
evidence to the contrary. There is a sequence in the film showing
the islanders scrapping for precious drops of soil in the rock crevices, but no mention, as Ivor Montagu said in the Daily Worker, of
the absentee landlords who sent men to tear down their huts and scat-
ter their soil in default of payment for things they made themselves."
For Bond these were the real issues of Aran, and Flaherty, to the
contrary, was "a romantic idealist striving to escape the stern and
brutal realities of life, seeking ever to discover some backwater of
civilization untouched by problems and evils affecting the greater
world outside." Bond argued, furthermore, that Flaherty's world,
however beautiful, had nothing to do with documentary. He had con-
cealed the class struggle, sought sensationalism, and ignored the
life of the island to the extent of leaving out its customs, tradi-
tions, and ceremonies.[48]

In the autumn issue the attack was resumed by David Schrire in an essay entitled "Evasive Documentary," in which he called Flaherty the "arch priest" of idyllic or evasive documentary. Schrire said that until then critics had been reluctant to attack this form of escapism because they felt that it was in the best interests of documentary in its ability to do well at the box office and attract a wide audience. But the use of natural material alone, he said, does not make a documentary. Schrire argued that it was the treatment and purpose that constituted a documentary, not the material itself, however real. His definition, which automatically excluded Flaherty's films, was that documentary "may be defined as the imaginative delineation through the medium of films employing natural material of current social struggle and conflict; the word 'social' is used in its widest sense, embracing political, economic and cultural aspects of modern life." Documentary, therefore, was a means to an end and had to serve a purpose beyond itself. Schrire described the problem as "the relationship of man with his fellow man within the existing economic structure of society, his struggle to abolish hunger and unemployment, earn a decent wage and equate distribution with production—these problems are the taut sinews of modern capitalism." Aside from the formal attributes of Flaherty's films which he admired, Schrire concluded that Flaherty's model was essentially a hindrance to the development of documentary. Flaherty, according to this view, conditioned the public toward evasive documentary and identified it with the "noble savage."[49]

Other attacks on Flaherty, frankly Marxist in origin, appeared in the United States. Brian O'Neill, writing in the New Masses, said that Flaherty's portrayal of the islanders as Neanderthals, cut off from all social relations, including modern capitalistic society, was false. The islanders were indeed affected by British imperialism, the historic struggle for land and with it, evictions and battles with the police; imperialism had caused migration. Flaherty was content with beauty, not the broad sweep of Pudovkin or Eisenstein.[50] Peter Ellis wrote a comparable piece saying that Flaherty had no use for the sociological implications of the subject matter that confronted him. The class struggle had no place in his work. The fact that Mussolini awarded Man of Aran the Gold (plated) Cup in the 1934 Venice Festival demonstrated that the film supported fascism.[51]

Grierson felt obliged to defend what Flaherty had done. In doing so he was not praising the particular merits of Man of Aran but paying a past debt for what Flaherty had contributed to documentary. Grierson's position came in the form of a direct reply to Schrire's article.[52] Grierson reiterated what he had said several times before, namely, that Flaherty had taught documentary filmmakers to create a theme out of natural observation, that his particular kind of film required the backing of commercial cinema, which Flaherty had pushed to its conceivable limits. Grierson could accept recreations and distortion. Yet it was reasonable in a documentary to distill life over a period of time and deliver only its essence. Flaherty was

born an explorer, and his films represented his own interests and
personality. It was unfair to expect more. Still Grierson could not
abandon what he himself had wrought, and so he sympathized with the
desire for a tougher documentary that dealt with social organization
rather than literary idyll. He, too, would have preferred something
on the Irish landlords.

Rotha had the most balanced judgment in his Sight and Sound review.[53] He called it the best work that Flaherty had done and "in
its particular sphere represents the furtherest lengths to which
documentary of this sort has been taken." There were moments in the
film that were so beautiful in feeling and perfect in realization
that their image to him was indelible. On the other hand, some images
though perfect in themselves tended to weaken the main shape of the
film. And after all, Flaherty was not interested in the reality that
existed on Aran but the one which he interpreted.

As Rotha prepared his book, Documentary Film, for the 1935 publication, his assessment turned much harsher, reaffirming the need
for utilizing documentary film in the social struggle. Man's battle
against nature was less important and even a diversion from the more
important struggle. Flaherty's method was an evasion devoid of social analysis, with little contemporary significance. Such statements were judiciously omitted from the Rotha and Wright manuscript
on Flaherty dated in 1959. To Rotha and Wright only the sea and its
fury remained impressive, not the shark sequences nor the struggle
for soil to grow food. They concluded: "It is the stark tragedy of
the islanders themselves which is so poignantly missing from Flaherty's
film. The sea in all its fury is there; but not the common human experience of the people."[54]

Richard Griffith's initial judgment was extremely hostile. In a
personal letter to Paul Rotha, he wrote "my dislike was inescapable.
All my criticisms of documentary apply here with double force. The
characters were non-existent as personalities. One knew they were
human beings because of their form, but nothing more...." Griffith
criticized the film because of its failure to dramatize the conflict
between men and the sea and for lacking an editorial point of view.[55]

Griffith overshot the mark when he later wrote that besides commercial stupidity and cupidity Flaherty had to contend with the criticism of his own disciples. They were more properly Grierson's
disciples, though their politics were more radical than his.
Griffith believed that such severe criticism was not justified.
"The ostracism of Flaherty's films was a major error for the documentary movement, the more so because it took place in public." The
public at least had responded to the humanism in Flaherty's films,
more so than any other documentary director, and the popularity of
documentary was made possible by Flaherty.[56]

The criticism that the sociological followers of documentary film made of Man of Aran (1934) could also have been made of Moana (1926), yet Moana encountered no such criticism at the time of its release. Samoa was rampant with problems brought on by the onslaught of Western civilization and commerce, causing the gradual deterioration of local institutions, authority, and customs. Flaherty knew well that the way of life he portrayed on the screen would soon disappear. Man of Aran's criticism, like any criticism, was a product of its time and place. For one thing, in between the release of Moana and Man of Aran the Griersonian idea of documentary had evolved. Film as art occasionally transcends the limitations of its contemporary world but film criticism is chained to a role of reflecting the tastes and value judgments of its own historicism.

The second most important influence on these critics was that of the Russian directors of the 1920s, Eisenstein, Pudovkin, Dovzhenko and Vertov who had linked film art with revolution and social change. Even Grierson was influenced by them though he was never a revolutionary. Thirdly, the Great Depression brought the social and political problems of the world to the forefront, and intellectuals who thought deeply about them were incensed at Flaherty's apparent indifference. They equated his aestheticism, which they regarded as romantic, with fascism. Kracauer argued the same relationship in regard to the romantic "mountain" films of the pre-Nazi era. Even the great Russian directors could not escape such criticism. Beginning in 1928 and into the 1930s the Soviet Communist Party rejected as formalistic and elitist the striking experimentation of earlier years. For these stolid commissars Eisenstein's artistic radicalism had become too abstract to serve the needs of the people. Before leaving Man of Aran it is worthwhile to mention one of the more modernist interpretations which Flaherty was capable of inspiring.

Henri Agel related Man of Aran to the Homeric world of the Ilyiad and the Odyssey. Flaherty, he said, decided to film a mythological past, represented by the sun fish or basking shark. His use of parallel montage was just the opposite of Eisenstein's. The slow rhythm was deliberate, forming the "leitmotiv" of certain images, which in Agel's estimation intensified the feeling of real time. This was part of the poetic structure of the film. Flaherty was sensitive to the human condition, but on a more poetic scale. This fundamental fight for sustenance gives life to the community and builds its dignity. The structure was both poetic and musical. The anxiety of the woman and child is developed exactly like the movement of a symphony of Mozart or Beethoven. He compared the film to the music of light that was admired by certain theoreticians of the 1920s. The distant participation of the family watching and the small boat tossing upon the seas formed two plastic elements that gave the impression of an allegro.[57]

Elephant Boy (1937) received mixed critical reaction. Some contemporary reviewers were impressed by the scale of the film, the

elephant stampede, and the delightful performance of Sabu. It won a
dubious Venice Film Festival award for best direction, even though in
retrospect the film lacked a directorial style. The highly regarded
British critic Graham Greene led the attack by criticizing its plot,
poor adaptation, repetitiveness, lapses in continuity, and the use of
models for the elephant dance.[58]

The studio work in an outdoor film was also apparent to Otis
Ferguson who found the actors, except for Sabu, "a group of Hamlets
in turbans with the best Oxford English." Ferguson connected the film
with others by Flaherty, in the sense that he had used forms of fiction such as faking, but not as well as Hollywood. Some of the details of production had become public knowledge, so Ferguson realized
that a story had been forced on Flaherty, but he erroneously blamed
Flaherty for the poor performance of the actors. The blame should
have been assigned to the Kordas.[59]

James Shelly Hamilton, lamenting the loss of "documentary" qualities, realized that the imposed story got in the way of those who
might have appreciated a film just of the elephants, the boy Toomai,
and glimpses of India and the jungle. Basically, he felt the story
was necessary to move the action along and that the actors obtruded
very little in the panorama. "For Flaherty has accomplished his
customary magic and recreated one of those far-off places the ordinary person can only read and dream about, and put it vividly and
beautifully." Not knowing the chaos in the studios and the extent
of Korda's interference, these reviewers ascribed more artistic control over the film to Flaherty than was merited by the facts.

In one essay Grierson used Elephant Boy as a launching pad from
which to attack the studio style of filmmaking and the mimicry of
Hollywood which it represented. He respected the elements that seem
to emerge out of Flaherty's art: the jungle setting, the magnificence
of the elephant, Toomai, dignity for the Indian People, the expecta-
tion of excitement, and a relationship between man and nature as profound as in Nanook. Actually, though, the film portrays the Indians
as servile toward their British masters and is blatantly racist and
patronizing. But Grierson, too, said in so many words that the studio camp scenes and polished voices brought the film to an artificial
plane. Reality was not achieved, and occidental motives were introduced. "The studio people," he wrote, "insist on a species of drama
more familiar and more dear to them than the fate of a native in the
jungle and the limitation of their scale of values is going to be
difficult to overcome, unless a producer comes along who can wed
studio and natural observation in a new and vital formula."[60]

Calder-Marshall criticized Flaherty for not conceiving of Elephant Boy in audiovisual terms, for making essentially a silent film
as he always had done, and thereby lending some justification to
Korda's interference and efforts to make a commercial product of
tried and proven formula (p. 184). Flaherty's original plan,

according to Griffith, was to fill the sound track "with the life of the jungle, with only snatches and fragments of dialogue supporting the essentially visual story...." (p. 134).

Elephant Boy missed being an enduring work of art by a wide margin. Still it could have been a brilliant film if Flaherty had been left to his own devices. Some of the scenes retain their magnificence, hinting at what the film might have been, among them the shots of Kala Nag and Toomai, the work in the jungle, and Toomai praying before the monolith Jain. Had shots such as these prevailed, the results would have been remarkably different. The narrative imposed on this material had few saving graces. The acting, except for Sabu, was stilted and out of step with its surroundings. Motivation and characterization were nonexistent. For Flaherty the experience signalled his final attempt to work with a studio in London or Hollywood.

Critical opinion concerning The Land (1942) falls roughly into two camps: those who favored it because it brought Flaherty into the fold of the documentary that was designed for social purposes, and those who regarded it as a failure because it did not meet their personal aesthetic standards.

Griffith's first review of The Land described it as "that new kind of documentary which other men have built on the Flaherty form, which does not merely lyrically celebrate a way of life but marshals facts about it, raises issues, dramatizes arguments pro and con." He compared it to The River in its dramatization of government data. Because The Land had to cover greater territory and more complex programs like soil conservation, parity, and farm resettlement, even Griffith felt it was not as successful. It lacked the "wholeness and gradual building toward a climax" of other Flaherty films. His concluding comment alluded to the central issue of social criticism: "...this film is important and perhaps great because it means that Flaherty in the fullness of his years has come back into the modern world, to work alongside the rest of us...."[61]

Writing another assessment a few years later Griffith had not changed his mind. "Looked at today, it remains that epic poem of the land which perceptive observers saw in it at the time of its making. Unlike other Flaherty films in material and structure, it turned constantly from the generalized problem of agriculture to some brief personal story, some chance encounter, which brought into the foreground the consequences of waste and greed." Flaherty brought back the "unvarnished truth." What Griffith criticized was the confusion in the theme, partially caused by Flaherty's personal enthusiasm for the machine as a solution for rural poverty.[62]

By 1943 Richard Griffith had become the leading American writer on documentary film and had chosen Flaherty as his champion, defending him at every turn. What was bad about The Land, he wrote, was

its simplified exegesis of the government's agricultural program.
Actually this was not really an issue. What was good about it was
that it showed how some Americans got shut out of American life, left
to fend for themselves in tragic conditions. It said this, with such
eloquence, he continued, "that its sponsors seem to have decided
against giving it full distribution," on the grounds that with the
"onslaught of war, Americans must not be further shocked by the
sight of their countrymen in distress." Here it should be reiterated
that its original sponsors did not decide this but the White House.
Griffith believed that more films of this type would help not hinder
the war effort.[63]

Calder-Marshall did not agree with the judgment of Grierson,
Rotha, Wright, and Griffith about Flaherty "fully facing up to the
sociological, technological and economic problems of our time." It
did not go far enough for him; it avoided mention of the economic
system, including "greed and under-capitalization" and the snatch-
crop farming in the style of the pioneers that plundered the land.[64]

This was an impossible criticism if only because it failed to
take into account the relationship between sponsor and filmmaker.
Flaherty had no authority, nor inclination, to portray an interpretive history of American agriculture. It seems fairly naive to expect a dominant institution to sponsor a film criticizing the
existing economic order that it is pledged to maintain. Neither The
Plow That Broke The Plains nor Power and The Land made this kind of
fundamental criticism. Additionally, the type of film that Calder-
Marshall seemed to want could only have been made with a great deal
of staged material with an analysis read over a sound track.

Kracauer saw obvious weaknesses in The Land, among them its lack
of precision, its failure to grab hold of the problem it attacks,
and a certain incoherence. The beauty and honesty of its images
outweighed these, however. Kracauer also used the word "naivete" to
define Flaherty's sensibility, to explain why Flaherty said what he
felt. "The secret of these pictures is to include time. They re-
semble fragments of a lost epic song that celebrated the immense
life of the land; nothing is omitted, and each episode is full of
significance. Among them that with the old Negro slowly wiping then
ringing the bell belongs to the unforgettable scenes on the screen."[65]

The Land has received little or no attention in recent writing on
documentary film, and therefore remains fairly low in estimation. It
was cherished more by the social filmmakers like Rotha, Wright,
Grierson, and Griffith, who put their thoughts into writing.

In his "reappraisal" of Flaherty's films, Richard Corliss went
out on a tenuous limb when he wrote that "Flaherty's refusal to
absolve the New Deal with a fast shuffle made The Land a failure as
propaganda...." This was not at all the issue. The Department of
Agriculture wanted a hard-hitting, dramatic film comparable to The

Plow That Broke The Plains and The River. Had the film been completed
in 1939 its reception would have been entirely different. Even so,
there is evidence to demonstrate that The Land was supported at the
highest level in the Department of Agriculture. But the presidential
advisors had the final say in its use. Corliss had to admire, however, its images of America's dispossessed which "helped make it a
great document." He too observed that the lack of cohesion was a
problem too overwhelming for the film's constraints, and concluded
like Griffith, Rotha, and Wright, from the very start, that "The Land
is Flaherty's belated attempt to come to terms with the twentieth
century."[66]

The Land was an about-face for Flaherty. The Griersons and the
Rothas had every right to feel pleased by it because, superficially
at least, it seemed to bear out their advocacy of the 1930s. That
Flaherty took this project in response to the social-political criticism of Man of Aran was unlikely. Such criticism did not prevent him
from working on Elephant Boy, an even more outrageous example of
British imperialism. The Land was Flaherty's best film opportunity
at the time owing to the circumstances of events. Flaherty did not
accept the project in order to demonstrate he could work within the
Griersonian school. Flaherty confronted the problem of poverty in
rural America not by choice but by necessity. Aside from certain
camera techniques he could not bring any of his old devices into
play; he could not immerse himself in his material; it was too broad
in scope for that. He could not "cast" characters or choose a single
family to typify the daily lives of rural outcasts. Only fragments
of the earlier Flaherty approach are shown. The Land revealed
Flaherty's natural sympathy for a people in a desperate situation,
and he tried to present their case as truthfully and dramatically as
his talents and temperament permitted.

In 1948 Louisiana Story was hailed as a crowning achievement to
a long career, though over the long run it did not provoke much critical debate. Among the many phrases of adulation, Mary Losey wrote
in the Saturday Review that Flaherty "has produced a poetic vision
and lasting human document which will bring pleasure and understanding for the years to come."[67] "Poetry" seemed to be the most popular
association that these reviewers could make.

Similarly, Harold Clurman in one of the better contemporary
reviews wrote,

> "The greater part of Louisiana Story is a photographic
> poem which relates it to the best of Flaherty's work.
> Flaherty's genius lies in his effort to rediscover
> nature, so to speak, at its source. This does not
> imply softness or sentimentality. Struggle and pain
> are always present in nature and Flaherty observes
> these with just as patient and loving an eye as its
> more smiling aspects. In all Flaherty's films nature

is shown in its fathomless loveliness, mystery, and
grandeur, together with people toiling to live within
the pull of its fierce dialectics.... In the opening
sequence of Louisiana Story, the camera flows through
the inlet and describes its intimacies of strange
foliage, delicate wild life, wondrous gestation,
beautiful efflorescence of nature's joyous and tender
secrets together with the ominous presence of the
monster that is as much a part of all this glory as
the rest."

Clurman concludes with such words as "pure vision" and "simplicity"
as the hallmarks of the Flaherty style. It is worth noting that the
theme of industry and nature confused the otherwise perceptive reviewer, who couldn't decide whether the coming of the oil industry
to the bayou country was supposed to represent a "boon or a bane."
The alligator appeared more a threat to life than the oil machinery.[68]

Robert Hatch, writing in The New Republic, was also perplexed by
the theme and purpose of Louisiana Story, and went further than most
in his negative criticism. To him the boy's antics seemed invented
for the camera; he recognized that the alligator sequence was carefully staged. For him the film's prettiness did not substitute for
"documentation." He even referred to the fast cutting as "over-
edited." Oil drillers change the world they find in reality, he
said, and, "as it stands, 'Louisiana Story' is neither a satisfactory
lyric nor a convincing documentation of progress and change."[69]

Richard Griffith, ecstatic over Flaherty's film, wrote, "It is
time to put an end to the perennial attempt to force Flaherty into
the mould of social criticism, or alternatively to cast him out into
darkness as an irrelevant reactionary. Both alternatives are false
because they do not relate to the record. The record shows that
Flaherty's role has been that of proclaiming to the world what a
marvel the movie-camera can be when it is turned on real life." The
film's dialogue for him had a magical veracity. But Flaherty "succeeded best when the camera did the narrating and speech fulfilled
the function of revealing emotion, character, psychology, coming from
the people as their own expression."[70]

In addition to a personal interpretation of the film's symbols
Rotha and Wright criticized its slow rhythm and failure to dissect
its subject. Flaherty simply revealed, by contrasting images of
swamp and machine. They concluded that the figure of the mother was
not clearly drawn, the dialogue seemed stilted and halting, and the
acting scenes were not effective.[71]

Calder-Marshall endorsed the view of Iaian Hamilton in the
Manchester Guardian: "Flaherty has pitched away the last mechanics
of prose, and the result is pure poetry...." Hamilton attributed to
Flaherty the "clear, true vision of a child." His art seemed

inadequate for the word "documentary." Hamilton added: "The actions of these people, as Virginia Woolf once wrote of Homeric characters, 'seem laden with beauty because they do not know they are beautiful.'" Finally, he called it the very essence of romanticism, "the master light of our seeing."[72]

Calder-Marshall called Louisiana Story, Flaherty's "greatest film achievement," evidently on the grounds of its symbolism. "Drilling," from the boy's viewpoint, "was dangerous because it was a violation of the forces hidden beneath the earth, more dangerous, more powerful than those found on the surface." The blow-out is nature's revenge, which can only be satiated by magic. The oil itself is a form of ancient prehistory. He offers other examples of symbols such as the boy's rusty rifle and his pet raccoon, but does not carry them very far.

French critics have always been interested in Flaherty's films. Louisiana Story was of special interest because it portrayed the life of a French ethnic group in the United States. The French people saw a different version from the one released in the United States. The principal difference was in the overcrowded sound track which explained the action in facetious detail as in the 1947 sound version of Nanook of the North. In the English version the commentary was laconic and dialogue limited to a few brief exchanges.

Henri Agel described Louisiana Story as an "audio-visual symphony upon the screen." The opening sequence was akin to an overture. And the film itself was constructed like a symphony. The music added to the enchanted universe of imagery. Agel, too, went to some length to explain the symbolism in the film. The alligator, for example, represented the permanent menace which corresponds to the subterranean force with which the derrick workers play. The interruption of oil prospectors seemed like a disturbance, an alteration of this Eden-like world. Agel felt that the plastic order dominated over the psychological viewpoint of the boy, imagery over attitude and state of mind. Through a series of discoveries the boy's attitude and world change. Nature is changed. "Les yeux pantheistes de Flaherty nous font sentir dans les mouvements de la machine le battement d'un coeur, la respiration d'une immense et mysterieuse totalité animée vie abyssale." Agel saw the two themes as the magic of nature and that of industry, as represented by the juxtaposition of the two dramatic episodes of the fight with the alligator and the eruption of gas and water in the oil well. While not parallel montage, he observed the analogic character of these two key events.[73]

Claude Mauriac pursued the analogy of a poet describing an enchanting ambience. To him the film was not about the search for oil but an illustration of the imagination of a poet. The Cajun people in the film represented the "bon sauvage a la Rousseau," a fundamental preconception for Flaherty. The story was only a pretext for Flaherty to find what would illustrate his personal humanism; it was not the documentation that he sought but the poetry, the basics of life, everywhere different, and everywhere the same.[74]

Recent histories of documentary film recognize the importance of Louisiana Story. Barsam called it Flaherty's "masterpiece," noting its exquisite sensitivity, dreamlike quality, an autobiography by a "romantic whose eyes at the age of sixty-two, were still filled with the wonder of a boy as he explores the world around him."[75]

Barnouw saw the role of industry as the principal difference between Louisiana Story and Flaherty's other films. In Nanook of the North, Man of Aran and Moana the industrial world is the intruder left off stage, to be sure, but sealing the fate of a doomed way of life. In Louisiana Story industry was not only the intruding force but the sponsor of the film. "The pattern of Louisiana Story became a strategy for resolving this conflict...Flaherty thus imposed, on the documentary substance of Louisiana Story, a fable-like framework related to his own experience and conflicts." Writing in a era much more conscious of industrial intrusion in natural environments, Barnouw was more sensitive to the propaganda content of the film. It is true that the film did not advertise Standard Oil per se, but it lent credence to the oil industry's argument that unspoiled wilderness was safe; the anonymous sponsorship was not merely generosity.[76]

It was John Grierson who first associated Robert Flaherty with the world of documentary by his famous review of Moana. He brought him into the fold of a movement which had yet to be initiated. It began more properly in England with Grierson's production of Drifters (1929) for the Empire Marketing Board. Grierson, in addition to being a filmmaker, was an articulate spokesman for a movement which he had hoped would become a new channel of communication for improving society's understanding of the industrial order and democratic government, hopefully with an eye toward progress and change. His body of writings more than his films served as the philosophical basis for understanding documentary film as it developed in Western-styled democracy. Grierson used Flaherty's films to sharpen and refine his own concepts of the documentary. Although Grierson's purpose differed drastically from Flaherty's, it is important to understand how Grierson built upon Flaherty's work and how his ideas evolved into a new form of documentary.

To begin with, Grierson categorized Flaherty in the naturalist tradition, a label that Rotha also applied and which stuck to Flaherty's reputation thereafter. He saw in Flaherty a basic sympathy with Britain's position in the film world. Although technically an American, Flaherty spent a good part of his life working on or near the fringes of the British Empire in Canada, Samoa, India and the Aran Islands. And he saw in Flaherty's difficulties with Hollywood, a natural ally for British documentary. He felt also that Flaherty had a sympathy for the British people, for their landscape, their craftsmanship, and for the many people he worked with during the making of <u>Industrial Britain</u>. Writing this in 1931, Grierson may have been trying to justify his undertaking of putting Flaherty on the royal payroll. But it is entirely veracious that Flaherty developed into an Anglophile.

To be sure, Grierson had doubts about the application of Flaherty's romanticism to the depression-ridden British economy. But Flaherty's approach "ensured that the raw material from which we work is the raw material most proper to the screen." Grierson had already become infatuated with the magic of the camera, a sentiment that Flaherty had expressed on many occasions. It was also clear that Grierson shared Flaherty's sense of discovery; the camera gave emphasis where one might not think emphasis existed. The camera could see more intimately than the human eye. Grierson and Flaherty shared the same mystical faith of the motion picture camera to reveal reality.

Flaherty created a film language, Grierson seemed to say, like D. W. Griffith and the Russian directors to whom he alluded, that language needed only to be applied to English life. But it was Flaherty's method rather than substance that Grierson exhorted others to follow, to absorb fully their material before giving it form. The more practical Grierson admonished, however, that British filmmakers could not afford to immerse themselves years on end and that they should work from a pre-conceived idea, meaning no doubt a script. Grierson asked that greater attention be paid to everyday life in England rather than the exotica for which English writers and filmmakers were famous. Whereas Flaherty could work well with primitives, Grierson, the supreme propagandist, urged that "men must accept the environment in which they live, with its smoke and its steel and its mechanical aids, even with its rain." Flaherty suggested to him numerous possibilities of films within the empire, so long as there was freedom for discovery. Grierson agreed above all that the story must come from the location, another Flaherty dictum set by example.[77]

Where Flaherty and Grierson began to part company was not so much as in method, but in choice of subject and philosophy. Grierson recognized Flaherty's work as exceptional, but he did not exactly persuade others to follow in Flaherty's inimitable footsteps near the far corners of civilization. For Flaherty was the poet who avoided coming to grips with his present, a form of escapism or "Neo-Rousseauism," to use Grierson's characterization. Other writers have tended to exaggerate the difference between Grierson's sociological-propagandist approach to documentary and Flaherty's own unique style. Such misplaced emphasis has obscured the real and valuable contribution Robert Flaherty made to the documentary. Grierson after all built upon Flaherty's foundation. Grierson states rather unequivocably that: "Flaherty illustrates better than anyone the first principles of documentary."

Differences in philosophy were of course significant. Grierson cast much doubt on the ability of the heroic individual to transcend the economic forces that governed his life. Other filmmakers emphasized the political forces in the same manner. Grierson obviously preferred to stress "the essentially co-operative or mass nature of society: Leaving the individual to find his honours in the swoop of creative social forces."

In comparison to Flaherty's romantic documentary, the realist documentary, as he termed it, had a much more difficult task. Beauty and poetry with respect to the "noble savage" had been articulated by generations of writers. To find the equivalent in the markets, slums, and factories required a greater challenge. The formalism of Berlin and Rien Que Les Heures had not succeeded in meeting this challenge. Grierson, patting himself on the back, offered his film Drifters as a better example. From Flaherty's world it borrowed something of the noble savage and the theme of man against nature but placed it in the context of modern industry.

When Grierson elucidated his first principles of documentary in 1932 their origin in Flaherty's example could clearly be seen.[78] The three basic principles, as Grierson stated, were: that documentary represented a new and vital art form for observing and selecting from life itself, heretofore largely ignored by the studio films; that real persons playing their own roles in life were preferred over actors imposed from the outside; and that the materials and stories taken from real life could give a greater power of interpretation than anything conjured up in a studio. Grierson added that "documentary can achieve an intimacy of knowledge and effect impossible to the shim-sham mechanics of the studio, and the lily-fingered interpretations of the metropolitan actor." It is important to note that none of these principles written in 1932 excluded any of Flaherty's work. To the contrary, they were almost exact descriptions of what Flaherty had done. As of 1932 Flaherty, according to Grierson, had not diverged from the British documentary but from Hollywood, which was the villain of the piece. Grierson used the making of Moana to illustrate how Hollywood intended to impose an artificial reality over the raw material. Hollywood failed in the case of Moana but succeeded in White Shadows and, through Murnau, in Tabu.

Over the years Grierson continued to acknowledge the documentary's debt to Flaherty. Writing in 1937 and somewhat relaxing his definition of what constituted realism, he said that Nanook of the North among its contemporaries alone stood the test of time. Concerning Man of Aran, Grierson defended Flaherty by reiterating that Flaherty taught documentary to create a theme out of natural observation; also, he marvelled at Flaherty's ability to succeed in creating drama out of reality in spite of the needs of a commercial studio which backed the project. Grierson even admired the "realism" of Elephant Boy which other serious critics had rejected out of hand.

In a 1945 article on the historical development of documentary film Grierson wrote: "The history of the documentary film so far as I personally have been concerned with it has derived in part from my own theoretical deviation from Flaherty; but I ought also to add that we have been closest friends for twenty years and that no difference of opinion has affected our complete dependence on each other. In the profoundest kind of way we live and prosper, each of us, by denouncing the other." "Derivation" would have been a better choice of words over "deviation," and "denounced" was perhaps too strong a word, for Grierson was more gentle in his criticism, and Flaherty never criticized Grierson in writing. Nevertheless, he still portrayed Flaherty as a filmmaker in revolt against the studio system. Hollywood was the bête noire.

Flaherty led the way for bringing the camera out of the studio and drawing the story from real life. "All this, of course," Grierson wrote, "was very sensible and exercised an enormous influence on those of us who were thinking our way to the film of reality.... No eye was clearer, nor for that matter, more innocent." He called Flaherty one of the "great film teachers of our day," who enriched filmmakers by his example. Grierson was asking that Flaherty's principles be used in a different way, to make drama out of the present day reality, to sort out patterns of modern politics and society, to act not as an individual artist pursuing a personal obsession but as a group interested in the public good.[79]

When Flaherty died in 1951 Grierson naturally took upon himself the task of summing up a remarkable man and career. His writings at this time must be viewed in the context of a eulogy. He said that Flaherty's unique contribution was the visual beauty he brought to the cinema. His essays are filled with effusive phrases such as Flaherty "was the first to seize upon the enormous powers of the motion picture camera to observe nature and the natural"; "it was Flaherty who was the first to take up in film the essential task of painter and poet"; and, "It was Flaherty, too, who first taught how uniquely and significantly the camera could be made to illumine the spontaneous movement of natural emotion and ritual which time had worn smooth."[80]

Grierson, perhaps more than anyone, propitiated the image of Flaherty's innocence. The child as the constant motif in Flaherty's films represented his detachment from the problems of the world. In this he was a faithful disciple of Rousseau. The British documentary went off in a different direction, motivated by the problems that its filmmakers confronted daily. Grierson admitted that they were propagandists, helping the working man to understand the technological society, to improve it in John Stuart Mill's words for utilitarian benefit. This path was taken up by governments and other institutions, each with their own objectives. "And yet and yet," Grierson mused, "I look (at) it all today and think with the gentler half of my head that Flaherty's path was right and the other wrong."[81]

Next to Grierson, the second most important theoretician of documentary film is Paul Rotha, also a filmmaker as well as film scholar. In his encyclopedic Film Till Now, first published in 1930 and dealing for the most part with the commercial cinema, Flaherty was just barely mentioned. At the time he preferred Moana to Nanook of the North, on the grounds of its having a spiritual intimacy that was missing in Nanook. Although he rejected White Shadows in the South Seas, because of its essentially false imposition of plot and actors, he credited Flaherty with inspiring a "new movement in the American cinema that later gave rise to such films as Grass, Chang, Stark Love, White Gold, White Shadows, and Trader Horn."

Later, in his Documentary Film (1935), he placed Flaherty's work in what he termed the "naturalist (romantic) tradition," one of the four basic approaches to documentary; the other three consisting of the realist (continental) tradition, the newsreel tradition, and the propagandist tradition. Flaherty's work met Rotha's criteria for relating the story to the natural environment, for discovering the story inherent in the environment. Nanook, for example, visualized the fundamental struggle for survival in the sub-arctic. This applied to Rotha's need to show how documentary could serve the community interests. Moana was still a better example because it was more the work of a poet steeped in the natural and because of its photographic achievements. Rotha agreed precisely with Grierson regarding the Flaherty method: "It became an absolute principle that the story must be taken from the location, and that it should be (what he considers) the essential story of the location." To Grierson's principle, he added that by the filmmaker's intimate understanding of his subject and by his selection of images, the film becomes an interpretation, "a special dramatisation of reality and not mere recorded description." Man of Aran was another example that Rotha used to describe the romantic school. "Here is the perfect idyllic conception of the romantic mind," Rotha wrote, "drawing on natural material and natural people for its screen interpretation." Rotha, however, was not out to endorse this school or Flaherty's work in particular, only to draw upon its methods for more socially minded purposes. He supported the propagandist dialectical aims of Grierson. But he wished to shed the movement of any romantic holdovers, of any dying generations in backwater parts of the world bound by the struggle between Man and Nature. Unemployment, poverty, and social unrest were more immediate concerns. "Our essential problem today," as Rotha wrote in the midst of an economic depression, "is to equate the needs of the individual with production, to discuss the most satisfactory economic system and to present the social relationships of mankind in their most logical and modern ordering." Man's battle against nature was of secondary interest and might even divert attention from the more important struggle.

Rotha's assessment of Flaherty in 1935 was hostile even though he credited him with the pioneering spirit that warded off the commercial interests that tried to dominate his talent. Echoing the

attacks that followed the release of Man of Aran, Rotha wrote "that
the Flaherty method is an evasion of the issues that matter most in
the modern world, is devoid of any attempt at serious social analysis,"
and "that his understanding of actuality is a sentimental reaction
towards the past, an escape into a world that has little contemporary
significance, a placing of sentimentalism above the more urgent claims
of materialism."

The negative criticism of Flaherty never reached the same tumul-
tuous heights in the years following the great depression. Actually,
among those writers and critics who were more interested in the
aesthetic side of documentary, Flaherty's reputation increased. Lewis
Jacobs' classic survey, The Rise of The American Film (1939), explained Flaherty's influence on the commercial feature in this manner:
"Flaherty brought to movies an interest in the contemporary drama of
man's struggles with forces of nature, a feeling for the significant
facts, an objective approach to contemporary life and a new kind of
realism. More and more in recent years, owing to profound social
changes that are taking place, these contributions have taken on
increased value and have become criteria for the fictional as well
as thematic film. If Flaherty's works are not in themselves great
filmic accomplishments, they nevertheless broadened the scope of
motion pictures and pointed the camera toward new horizons."

In the literature on documentary since 1940, one finds less of
the social criticism made of Flaherty's Man of Aran. "Simplicity,"
"timelessness," "beauty," and "poetry" became the key words for later
appreciations.

In 1943 one of the lowest points of Flaherty's life, that is
between the shelving of The Land and before he received his commis-
sion from Standard Oil to make Louisiana Story, the National Board of
Review Magazine devoted most of its January issue to Flaherty. In
its editorial it said: "It is a civilized thing to take time in
these days so crucial for humanity to salute a man whose character
and art have worked together so powerfully to reveal the fundamental
dignity of mankind. During all this core of years, the National
Board of Review has looked to Robert Flaherty as one of the foremost
justifications of its faith in the motion picture, and as an art and
as a means of communication through which the people of the world
may reach and understand one another."

Writing in the midst of the swirl of events of World War II,
Griffith pointed to the failure of the modern documentary as conceived by Robert Flaherty's critics to divert the path of history
from anything but war.[82] During the war when films preached hatred
and deception the universality of Flaherty's films must have seemed
the only hope for documentary.

Willard van Dyke, one of the deans of American documentary films,
also enlisted himself in the defense of Flaherty's romanticism and

escapism. Flaherty, he argued, was showing indirectly some of life's
contemporary problems. "The longer I look at film, and the more I
see of Flaherty's work, the more I realize that it has a profound
vision that goes beyond all this narrow terminology."[83]

Hugh Gray defended the naturalistic documentary as a "non-
theatrical film, nor purely representational, but having a dramatic
form, theme, and unity, and taking as its subject from the actual
world, some aspect of the life of man, either in a state of primitive
nature or, at least, unaffected by industrialization." He agreed
with Flaherty's dictum that one often has to distort a thing in order
to catch its true spirit. It was difficult if not impossible to draw
a line between reconstruction and reality in any art.[84]

To Ernest Callenbach, longtime editor of Film Quarterly, the
structure of Flaherty's films around conflict formed the basic appeal
of his art and still served as a model for documentary filmmakers in
any milieu. This was far more preferable to the false injection of
themes, stories, human interests and problems. Man's courage in
meeting his world applied anywhere.[85]

Flaherty's friend, critic, and colleague, Helen Van Dongen, said
that he turned from the ugliness of the real world to form one of his
own making. Invention and reconstruction did not fit her rigid conception of documentary, and therefore, she felt it was misleading to
call him a documentarian, let alone "father of documentary." His
films, she said, are not the statements of a historian; they are the
creations of a storyteller and all is fable. Yet she added it takes
more than mere simplicity to invent a world of one's own making and
make others believe in it.[86]

Frances Flaherty through her writings and lectures spent much
of her life explaining her husband's art and is partly responsible
for the sheer reverence in which he is held.[87] She shared in her
husband's discovery of the magical ability of the camera to reveal
life through motion beyond the capacity of our own eyes. Each culture has its own pattern of living, its own pulse and rhythm, its
own drama. To discover them one needed to explore and not precon-
ceive. "Nonpreconception," she often said, as a method of discovery
and as a process of filmmaking was Robert Flaherty's contribution to
the motion picture. Everything flowed from that. "Robert Flaherty
was a mystic of the modern age; in his approach to a powerful machine
he took the scientist's discipline of 'surrender to the material and
surrender to the tool' in order to come to the mystic's ecstasy and
delight, and to his wisdom."

European critics of Flaherty have remained steadily in his favor.
If we may count Siegfried Kracauer among them, he shared in their
general appreciation of the beauty, patience, and sensitivity that
went into his films, "to show the interaction between man and nature,
man and man." Even as late as 1960 he was still supporting the

argument that a story is desirable for documentary, that the story must come out of the life of a people, and not from the actions of individuals.[88] These principles were enunciated by Grierson in the early thirties but they were worth repeating.

Well up into the 1960s other European writers were still defending Flaherty against the sociological criticisms prompted by Man of Aran and the Great Depression. Such writings were largely personal and impressionistic. José Clemente, for example, wrote that with the passage of time the lesson of Flaherty has been more enduring that the other "transcendental pretensions"; he admired Flaherty's desire to be an independent artist rather than a sociologist. Clemente wrote that his use of the camera to discover emotional and spiritual movement taught men to see anew. For Clemente this is the essence of cinema.[89]

For French writers the total unity of Flaherty's work established him firmly as an auteur. Flaherty had a more rightful claim to the title of auteur, popularized by Andrew Sarris, than most directors, because he was unquestionably the principal creative force for his films. He never worked from a detailed shooting script prepared by someone else.

What Callenbach called structural conflict, Quintar described as dialectic in Flaherty's films: man and nature, man and sea, man and land, man and machine. In the last, Louisiana Story, a sort of amity is established. "The unity of Flaherty's work proceeds not only in the dialectic of its subject but also in the structure of its approach by the narrative and of the simplicity of its dramatic construction." Quintar recognized the devices of the family and the boy to show everyday life.

In his search for the timeless appeal of Flaherty's films Quintar described the roots of Flaherty's work as a kind of oriental contemplation of the elements. Flaherty described an equilibrium, man the creature in a cosmic order. Flaherty's art was a "pantheistic mysticism" in which nature represents the highest manifestation of the mystery of creation. In this sense Quintar stood in sharp disagreement with Paul Rotha's pigeonholing Flaherty into the school of naturalist cinema. Rather, his was a poetic approach dealing with the human qualities and the universal need for survival in any milieu. Flaherty was not a fantasist but a realist who searched for man without establishing a racial or social line. Quintar did not oppose the Rotha documentary that exposed the social ills; he said it was not the only way.[90]

CONCLUSION

The roots of documentary have their beginning in Flaherty's films, especially in Nanook of the North and Moana. By the early 1930s the

Russian experiment, the avant gardistes, and the British school had also made their mark. By 1934 when <u>Man of Aran</u> was released, documentary had become identified as a vehicle for solving the world's problems, and later it became an ideological weapon of war itself. Flaherty's highly individualistic approach and pursuit of personal goals divorced him from the mainstream of the documentary movement. If he has become more highly regarded in recent years, it is because the documentary has become less politicized, less an advocate. This of course is not true for societies today which are undergoing the throes of social revolution.

Yet in contrast to today's free-wheeling cinema-verité stylists Flaherty had some sense of self-discipline, an even keener sense of selection, and a desire for perfection. It is true he approached his chosen subjects without a script, lacking even a basic plan of approach, but the finished product was never haphazard, nor lacking a point of view. And his viewpoint was always the same: he ennobled his subject and shared his fascination and admiration with the audience. His choice of subjects fit a basic pattern of people who lived close to nature. On the whole there were more similarities than dissimilarities in his work.

It is also true that Flaherty allowed room for discovery, his own and the audiences'. Too much, however, has been made of his role as an explorer. His desire to make films originally grew out of a desire to explore the off beat corners of the world. He never remained an explorer in the true sense of the word, though he always claimed he was. After the <u>Nanook</u> experience his days of hard journeying in open country came to an abrupt end. He never became deeply versed in any other culture but that of the Eskimos. The fiction of exploration served to conceal a lack of treatment for his films until he was well into production. It served also to distance him from the sometimes pretentious world of filmmakers and film critics. He could ignore them by claiming another vocation.

Flaherty was an artist whose temperament antagonized corporations, institutions, and government agencies. He needed someone to intercede on his behalf in order to protect him from the practicalities of film sponsorship and production. The lack of a script, prolonged shooting schedules, and consistently going over budget did not endear him to many cost-conscious producers. He never worked for the same sponsor twice. Perhaps he deserved what he got in the way of these difficulties. Yet one has to admire his stubbornness, his uncompromising independence, his self-direction, his pursuit of his own obsessions and personal interests in spite of the hard and fast world of the sponsored film. Flaherty took the money but felt little obligation to the sponsor, only to his conscience as an artist.

Flaherty, a maverick in the documentary movement, had even less in common with Hollywood and the feature entertainment industry. It seems slightly absurd and somewhat ironical to entomb him in a pantheon of moviemakers the way Andrew Sarris and several French writers have done. Flaherty was the supreme antagonist of the Hollywood which these critics revere. One would be hard pressed to find any favorable utterance toward Hollywood or its films in the totality of Flaherty's life. To him feature films were artificial; they used exotic locations only as a backdrop. He couldn't stomach their crassness, their tawdry sensationalism, the ignorance of the world that they reflected, and their total indifference to the nobility, strength, and character of people who lived close to nature. A more fitting pantheon for Flaherty should include filmmakers like Alberto Cavalcanti, Joris Ivens, and Humphrey Jennings who also created poetry on film out of the real world.

NOTES

1. The same principle applies for several early British films.
See Rachel Low, The History of the British Film: 1918-1929 (vol. 4).
London: Allen & Unwin, 1971, p. 289.
2. Boston: Small, Maynard, 1923, pp. 3-8.
3. The New Republic, 26, No. 401 (9 August 1922), 306-307.
4. Let's Go to the Pictures. London: Chatto & Windus, 1926,
p. 57 and note.
5. New York: W. W. Norton, 1927, pp. 67-68. Arthur Calder-
Marshall, p. 96, misconstrues the gist of Stefansson's criticism.
6. The Seven Lively Arts. New York: Harpers, 1924, pp. 331-332.
7. New York: Simon and Schuster, 1926, p. 600. And Ramsaye's
"Flaherty Great Adventurer." Photoplay Magazine, 33, No. 6 (May 1928),
58; 123-126. Reprinted in George C. Pratt, Spellbound in Darkness:
A History of the Silent Film. New York: New York Graphic Society,
1966; revised ed. 1973, pp. 349-354.
8. "Another View of Nanook," translated by Harold J. Salemson
from Canudo's L'Usine aux images. Paris, 1927, and reprinted in
Lewis Jacobs (comp.), The Documentary Tradition: From Nanook to
Woodstock, pp. 20-21.
9. Griffith, The World of Robert Flaherty, pp. xiv-xv.
10. New York Sunday Times, 3 May 1953. Quoted in Rotha and Wright
manuscript, pp. 47-48.
11. Paul Rotha, Documentary Film, 1952 ed., p. 82.
12. Rotha and Wright, "Flaherty Biography," p. 62.
13. Flaherty, The Drawings of the Enooesweetok of the
Sikosilingmiut Tribe of the Eskimo. 1915. Republished as Anerca:
Drawings of Enooesweetok, edited by Edmund Carpenter. Toronto:
J. M. Dent & Sons, 1959.
14. Edmund Carpenter, "Notes on Eskimo Art Film." Robert Flaherty
Foundation, n.d., quoted in Calder-Marshall, pp. 69-72. See also
Carpenter's Eskimo. Toronto: University of Toronto Press, 1959,
and Rotha and Wright MS, pp. 62-63.
15. See for example, Henri Agel, pp. 13-18.
16. Marcel Martin, "Flaherty," Supplement to L'Avan-scene du
cinema (March 1965), reprinted in part in Henri Agel, pp. 153-156.
17. The term nonfiction film includes a multitude of genre including newsreel and the March of Time, but recent histories only relate
to documentary film.
18. Jacobs, pp. 8-9.
19. Richard Meran Barsam, Nonfiction Film: A Critical History.
New York: E. P. Dutton, 1973, pp. 128-129.
20. Ibid., p. 135.
21. Erik Barnouw, Documentary, pp. 33-45.
22. Karl Heider, Ethnographic Film. Austin and London: University of Texas Press, 1976, pp. 22-23.
23. Panorama du film ethnographique et sociologique. Paris:
UNESCO, 1962, reprinted in part in Henri Agel, pp. 151-153. See
also De Heusch's, "The Flaherty Tradition and the Participating

Camera," in his The Cinema and Social Sciences. Paris: UNESCO, 1962, pp. 35-39.

24. Quoted by Ernestine Evans, "New Movies." National Board of Review Magazine (January 1943), an issue published in part as a salute to Flaherty.

25. Quoted in Barnouw, "Barnouw's File," p. 166.

26. Ibid., p. 167.

27. Extract printed in Barnouw, p. 176; also, Griffith, p. 71.

28. 3 March 1926, pp. 46-47.

29. "Moana of the South Seas." The Arts, 8, No. 5 (November 1925), 255-262.

30. In an interview conducted toward the last years of Grierson's life he said: "I suppose I coined the word in the sense that I wasn't aware of it's [sic] being used by anybody else. I mean, to talk about a documentary film was new, and I know I was surprised when I went over to Paris in 1927 and found them talking about 'film documentaires.' Now, I must have seen that before, but I wasn't aware of it. When I used the word 'documentary' of Bob Flaherty's Moana, I was merely using it as an adjective. Then I got to using it as a noun: 'the documentary'; 'This is documentary.' The word 'documentary' became associated with my talking about this kind of film, and with me a lot of people around me." Elizabeth Sussex, The Rise and Fall of British Documentary: The Story of the Film Movement Founded by John Grierson. Berkeley: University of California Press, 1975, p. 3.

31. Reprinted in Jacobs, The Documentary Tradition, pp. 25-26.

32. Frances Flaherty, "The Camera's Eye." National Board of Review Magazine, 2, No. 4 (April 1927), 405. Reprinted in Pratt, pp. 344-347.

33. Rotha, Documentary Film, p. 83.

34. Richard Corliss, "Robert Flaherty: The Man in the Iron Myth." Film Comment, ix, No. 6 (November-December 1973), 40.

35. Barsam, pp. 138-139.

36. Quoted in Henri Agel, p. 39.

37. "Experimental Cinema in America, 1921-47." Hollywood Quarterly, Vol. 3, No. 2 (Winter 1947-48), 111-124, and Vol. 3, No. 3 (September 1948), 278-292. Reprinted in Jacobs, The Rise of the American Film: A Critical History. New York: Columbia University Teachers College Press, 1968, 2nd ed., pp. 543-582. Also reprinted in Roger Manvell (ed.), Experiment in the Film. London: Grey Walls Press, 1949, pp. 113-152.

38. "Lost Paradise: Tabu." Creative Art, 8, No. 6 (June 1931), 462-463.

39. Tabu. National Board of Review Magazine, 6, No. 4 (April 1931), 9-11.

40. Maurice Scherer, "La Revanche de L'Occident." Cahiers du Cinema (May 1953), cited by Griffith in his "Flaherty and Tabu." Film Culture, No. 20 (1959), p. 13. Note: Floyd Crosby won an Academy Award for his cinematography on Tabu.

41. Lotte H. Eisner, Murnau. Berkeley: University of California Press, 1973.

42. Agel, 44.
43. Grierson, "The Man I Killed by Ernst Lubitsch," Everyman (18 February 1932), reprinted in Hardy (ed.), pp. 69-70.
44. Quoted by Paul Rotha, Documentary Diary, p. 58.
45. Ibid., pp. 57-58.
46. "Romance, and Reality: Man of Aran." New Statesman and Nation, 7 (28 April 1934), p. 638.
47. Observer (6 May 1934), quoted in Calder-Marshall, p. 165.
48. Cinema Quarterly, 2, No. 4 (Summer 1934), 245-246.
49. Cinema Quarterly, 3, No. 1 (Autumn 1934), 7-9.
50. "Flaherty's Man of Aran." New Masses, 13 (30 October 1934), pp. 29-30.
51. "Robert Flaherty's Escape." New Theatre (December 1934), p. 29.
52. "John Grierson Replies." Cinema Quarterly, 3, No. 1, (Autumn 1934), 10-11.
53. Man of Aran. Sight and Sound, 3, No. 10 (Summer 1934), 70-71.
54. Rotha and Wright, p. 228.
55. Letter dated 5 February 1935, quoted in Rotha and Wright, p. 217; Calder-Marshall, p. 168.
56. Griffith in Rotha's Film Till Now, pp. 521-522.
57. Agel, pp. 49-56.
58. Spectator, 16 April 1937.
59. "Flaherty and the Films." The New Republic (21 April 1937), p. 323.
60. John Grierson, "The Course of Realism," in Charles Davy (ed.), Footnotes to the Film. London: Lovat Dickson and Reader's Union Ltd., 1938, reprinted in Hardy, p. 204. See also World Film News, No. 12 (12 March 1937).
61. Griffith, "The Land." National Board of Review Magazine, 16, No. 9 (December 1941), 11-12.
62. Griffith in Rotha, Documentary Film, p. 320.
63. "New Movies," National Board of Review Magazine, 13, No. 1 (January 1943), 7 and 15.
64. Calder-Marshall, pp. 199-200.
65. Quoted in Griffith, The World of Robert Flaherty, pp. 142-143.
66. "Robert Flaherty: The Man in the Iron Myth," p. 42. Corliss also states that "the film was effectively suppressed, and to some degree remains so today." It was suppressed during the war but 16mm prints have been available from the Department of Agriculture and National Audiovisual Center for many years.
67. "More Seeing, Less Selling." Saturday Review (9 October 1948), p. 61.
68. Harold Clurman, "Flaherty's Louisiana Story." Tomorrow (October 1948); reprinted in Jacobs, The Documentary Tradition, pp. 230-232.
69. "Movies," The New Republic (11 October 1948), pp. 30-31.
70. Griffith, "American Documentary," in Rotha's Documentary Film, 3rd ed., p. 32.
71. Rotha and Wright, p. 312.
72. 28 August 1948, quoted in Calder-Marshall, pp. 225-226; also, Time (20 September 1948), pp. 94-96.

73. Agel, pp. 76–79.

74. Claude Mauriac, "Le Cinéma de Decouverte: Robert Flaherty," in his L'amour du cinéma. Paris: Editions Albin Michel, 1954, pp. 163–168.

75. Barsam, p. 151. His comments for the most part consist of an extensive description of the film.

76. Barnouw, pp. 217–219.

77. "Flaherty," Artwork, 7 (Autumn 1931), pp. 210–215; reprinted in Hardy, pp. 139–144.

78. Grierson, "First Principles of Documentary." Cinema Quarterly (Winter 1932); reprinted in Hardy, pp. 145–153.

79. Grierson, "Postwar Patterns." Hollywood Quarterly, 1 (1945–1946), 159–165.

80. Grierson, "Robert Flaherty: An Appreciation." New York Times (29 July 1951).

81. Grierson, "On Robert Flaherty." The Reporter, 5, No. 8 (16 October 1951), 31–35. See also his article "Flaherty as Innovator." Sight and Sound, 21, No. 2 (October–December 1951), 64–68, in which Grierson enumerates Flaherty's photographic innovations, including the mobility of the camera, panchromatic film, long lenses, lighting techniques, and so on.

82. Griffith, "Flaherty and The Future," p. 6.

83. Quoted in an interview by Harrison Engle, "Thirty Years of Social Inquiry." Film Comment (Spring 1966). Reprinted in Jacobs, The Documentary Tradition, p. 359.

84. "Robert Flaherty and the Naturalistic Documentary." Hollywood Quarterly, 5, No. 1 (Fall 1950), 41–48.

85. "The Understood Antagonist and Other Observations." Film Quarterly, 12, No. 4 (Summer 1959), 16–23.

86. Van Dongen, "Robert J. Flaherty," pp. 213 and 228.

87. Frances Flaherty, "The Camera's Eye," reprinted in Pratt, p. 344; and her Odyssey of a Film Maker, pp. 10–11; 43.

88. Kracauer, Theory of Film: The Redemption of Physical Reality. New York: Oxford University Press, 1960, pp. 204 and 247–249.

89. José Clemente, Robert Flaherty. Madrid: Ediciones Rialp, 1963, pp. 19–32.

90. Fuad. Quintar, Robert Flaherty et le Documentaire Poetique. (Etudes Cinematographiques No. 5). Paris, 1960.

The Films: Synopsis, Credits and Notes

1 <u>NANOOK OF THE NORTH</u> (1922)

   This film depicts Eskimo life in the Arctic typified by the
daily routine of Nanook and his family. It begins with the
title: "No other race could survive...yet here live the most
cheerful people in all the world--the fearless, lovable, happy
go-lucky Eskimo." Using a map, it shows the Ungava Peninsula,
bordering on the eastern shore of Hudson Bay where Eskimos
struggle for the necessities to sustain life. Closeups intro-
duce the principal personnages: Nanook, the hunter, and his
wife Nyla. Later, the whole family is introduced one by one
as they emerge from a kayak with apparently limitless capacity.
The next few scenes show some typical survival techniques of
Eskimo life such as using moss for fuel and the making and
repairing of kayaks.
   The Eskimos make their annual trek to the trading post
first by carrying their <u>omiak</u>, a large canoe-type boat, over
to the shore and paddling it down the river. At the post
Nanook displays his prized skins and furs--and his husky pup-
pies; Nyla displays her newly born child. The trader demon-
strates a grammophone for Nanook, who is so curious and
mystified by the music's source that he tests the record with
his teeth. The children are treated to sea biscuits, lard,
and castor oil.
   From the trading camp the Eskimos make their way across the
ice-bound Arctic wilderness. Nanook paddles his kayak in between the ice flows and also is shown walking over difficult
ice fields with great agility. Nanook then gives a demonstration of his fishing skill by dangling a piece of bait through
an ice hole and spearing the fish that are lured to the
surface.
   The next major sequence shows the harpooning of a walrus.
The wounded monster makes his way toward the water to escape
his hunters, now engaged in a tug of war. Sadly, the walrus'
mate tries to rescue him but in vain. The Eskimos, sledging
across rugged terrains of ice and snow, continue on their
winter journey. Nanook removes a small white fox from a trap
that he had set earlier.

With the skill of a construction engineer, Nanook proceeds to build an igloo to shelter his family for the night. First he tests the snow, cuts blocks of ice with his long knife, and builds an igloo from the inside, cutting his way out and showing no little pride in his accomplishment. To cap off his achievement he cuts a block of translucent ice for a window and a block of snow to reflect the sunlight. He has time to pass some of his skill on to his small son. The family ensconces itself for the cold night ahead.

The journey begins again the next day. Nanook spears a seal through a widened breathing hole in the ice. The seal is too much for him to pull through the ice until the other members of his group come to the rescue. The Eskimos skin and gut the seal, enjoy a feast of raw meat, and throw the scraps to the ferocious sledge dogs. The winds howl and blow as the Eskimo family searches for another shelter. Good fortune brings them an abandoned igloo and the family prepares to bed down in their communal bed, leaving the snow-blanketed dogs outside to the mercy of the icy wind.

Credits

Production:	Revillon Frères
Producer, Director, Scenario, Photography, and Editing:	Robert Flaherty
Assistant:	Captain Thierry Mallet
Titles:	Carl Stearns Clancy, Robert Flaherty
Assistant Film Editor:	Charles Gelb
Personnages:	Nanook, Nyla, Allee, Cunayou
Filmed on location in the Hudson Bay region of Canada beginning August 1920–August 1921.	
Distribution:	Pathe Pictures Exchange
Copyrighted:	17 May 1922
Running time:	75 minutes, silent
Premiered:	11 June 1922, Capitol Theater, New York City

Note: Sound version released by United Artists, July 1947; Producer: Revillon Frères; Sound Version: Herbert Edwards; Narration: Ralph Schoolman; Narrator: Berry Koeger; Original Music: Rudolph Schramur; Supervisor of Sound: Edward Craig; Original Document: Robert J. Flaherty

Note: New sound version with music track only and restored original footage released by International Film Seminars, Inc., 1976. Restored by David Shepard.

The Films: Synopsis, Credits and Notes

2   THE POTTERYMAKER (1925)

An elderly woman and a young girl, dressed in period cos-
tumes, enter the potter's studio. The girl accidentally dam-
ages a vase in progress on the potter's wheel. Shown in one
basic shot, the potter begins to shape another vase. Occasional "cutaways" show the old woman and girl watching his
work with avid interest. The potter carefully molds the shape
of the vase, applies a glaze, and places it in a kiln which he
has bricked shut. The film ends here, rather abruptly. Presumably some footage has been lost.

Credits

Sponsor:	Metropolitan Museum of Art, New York City
Financed by:	Maude Adams
Scenario, Direction, and Photography:	Robert J. Flaherty
Running time:	14 minutes, silent

Note: No credits appeared on the film viewed at the Museum
   of Modern Art.

3   MOANA: A ROMANCE OF THE GOLDEN AGE (1926)

Set in the Samoan Islands, Moana is the story of a Polynesian youth, named Moana, his family, friends, and relations,
how they live their everyday lives, and how Moana in particular gains manhood and the respect of his community. The film
begins with shots of tall palm trees against a sky filled with
white clouds. The barebreasted Fa'angase, surrounded by lush
foliage, bundles leaves for her house. Tu'ungaita looks for
her son Pe'a among the broad leaves. Moana is shown, young
and muscular, dressed in a sarong, with a wreath in his hair.
Several scenes show how they gather the taro root, fruit,
leaves, and bark. Gathering these gifts of nature, the Samoans
leave the forest, and the camera tilts up to the trees that began the story.
Stopping along the jungle trail, Moana constructs a giant
snare trap for the jungle's only dangerous animal, the wild
boar. Moana finds a vine, which contains cool, fresh water,
and gives his mother a drink. They continue on their journey
down to Safune, the village by the sea.
Now the first shots of the sea and the lagoon are shown.
The village huts are large and stately, domed with grass, open
and airy. Meanwhile Moana and his companions return to the
snare trap, pushing away the leaves to reveal a charging wild
boar, caught by the leg. After braining him, they tie his
legs together and carry him down to the village on a pole.

Moana goes spear fishing, diving from his outrigger canoe.
The water is clear to the bottom in the shallow reefs.
Fa'angase holds up a giant clam that she found in the water.
Moana comes along in a boat and they all return with the
bounty, first from the land, now from the sea.

Tu'ungaita, the mother, makes a large piece of cloth from a
strip of mulberry bark. The entire process is shown, including the pounding of the strip, separating layer after layer,
the making of dyes, drawing patterns, and finally making a
dress called a "lavala." Pe'a, aptly meaning Flying Fox,
scales an enormously tall palm tree with a rope hitch between
his ankles; he shakes the coconuts loose for Moana below.

Now Moana and his brothers return to the sea. High waves
roll in and there is a blowout in the far distance. They pad-
dle over and through the waves, but the outrigger is overturned. They fish along a rugged part of the shore; the waves
engulf them but not menacingly. Pe'a makes a fire by rubbing
wood and smokes out a giant robber crab from between the rocks.
Moana captures a giant sea turtle with his bare hands, attempts
to turn it over and into the boat; it escapes but they retrieve
it. In the mother's cook house a great feast is being prepared:
coconut meat wrapped in leaves, bread fruit, and bananas are
placed over heated stones and covered with broad leaves.

At the end of the day Fa'angase puts a flower in Moana's
hair and annoints him with perfumed oil in preparation for
the siva dance. Moana is mostly shown dancing alone, with
grace and style, and Fa'angase slowly moves into the frame.

All this is preparation for a great event, Moana's rite of
manhood. The tattooing of Moana begins with the tattooist and
others in attendance. The inking and drawing are done tap by
tap with bone needles, a little at a time, for the pain is
hard to bear; and occasionally Moana can be seen grimacing.
The villagers dance the siva outside in honor of Moana. When
the ordeal is over Fa'angase and Moana dance the siva
together.

Credits

Production:	Famous Players—Lasky
Director:	Robert J. Flaherty
Assistant Director:	Frances H. Flaherty
Producers:	Robert J. and Frances H. Flaherty
Production Assistant:	David Flaherty
Technical Assistant:	Lancelot N. Clarke
Editor and Titles:	Julian Johnson (Robert and Frances Flaherty)
Personnages:	Pe'a, Fa'angase, Ta'avale (Moana), Tafunga, Tu'ungaita

Filmed on Savaii, Samoa,
a British New Zealand
mandate, April 1923–
December 1924.

Distribution: Paramount Publix
Copyrighted: 24 February 1926
Running time: 85 minutes, silent
Premiere: 7 February 1926, Rialto Theater,
                         New York City
Note: Premiered in New York City as Moana: The Love Life of
  a South Sea Siren.

4   TWENTY-FOUR DOLLAR ISLAND (1927)

     A camera impression of New York focusing almost exclusively
on Manhattan skyscrapers and harbor activities. The film
opens with antique maps of the Western hemisphere and drawings
of New Amsterdam, the former Dutch colony. Next appears a
classic shot of the Manhattan skyscrapers looming over the
New York harbor. A title reads: "New York symbol of industry,
finance, power, where men are dwarfed by the immensity of that
which they have conceived--machines, skyscrapers--mountains of
steel and stone." A waterfront teeming with activity is
shown: construction, ferries, tugboats, and the Brooklyn
Bridge seen through a mesh of wires. The camera, then, shows
enormous skyscrapers, some in various stages of construction.
The camera moves up and down them like a steeplejack. Toward
the end, other shots of the harbor are contrasted with
Manhattan buildings.

Credits

Production: Pictorial Films Inc.
Scenario, Photography,
and Direction: Robert J. Flaherty
Editor: John D. Pearmain
Distributor: Pathe Pictures
Copyrighted: 12 December 1927
Running time: 15 minutes, silent

5   TABU: A STORY OF THE SOUTH SEAS (1931)

     This is the story of a young couple whose love for each
other violates a sacred tabu which ultimately brings them to
their fateful end. Set in the mountainous South Sea Island of
Papeete, the film opens on Matahi, a muscular young Polynesian,
spear fishing with his companions. Afterwards, they bathe under a gentle waterfall where Matahi finds a wreath of flowers
that had tumbled down. He places it on his head, goes to the
top of the fall, and discovers a group of Tahitian girls frol-
icking in a pool. In lusty playfulness he grabs one of the
girls. He sees Reri and approaches her; her jealously is
awakened when she sees the wreath on his head. The other girl

approaches and she and Reri claw and grab at each other in the
water before Matahi breaks it up by dumping the other girl
down the cascade.

The arrival of the island schooner "Moana, Papeete" is
shouted in the village. Hundreds of men and women rush to
their outrigger canoes to greet the ship. Matahi is clearly
leading the race but turns around to pick up his little
brother left on the shore. The Tahitians climb all over the
ship in great merriment. The old priest Hitu bears a message
from the head chief of the islands naming Reri as his new
sacred virgin. "No man must touch her nor cast upon her the
eye of desire--for in her honor, her virginity, her purity,
resides the honor of all her race." Reri, therefore is de-
clared tabu. Matahi, just arriving, playfully throws a wreath
on Reri's head. An old woman dashes it to the deck. Matahi,
bewildered by the news, leaves the ship in despair.

Back in the village, islanders make ready for a reception.
The young men prepare to dance and Reri is attended to by
several women. While Reri dances Matahi jumps in and joins
her, exchanging smiles in defiance of the tabu. Hitu puts an
end to the ritual and takes Reri away to the boat for safe-
keeping. But during the night Matahi steals her away.

One of the few titles indicates that the lovers have fled
to the "islands of the pearl trade where whitemen rule." The
next scene shows Matahi and Reri, shipwrecked on the shore,
being discovered by the island residents. In another scene
Matahi is carried on the shoulders of a crowd of half-castes
who are celebrating at his expense the discovery of a pearl.
The Chinese tradesmen carefully note each bottle and are certain to get the unsuspecting Matahi to initial the bills.
Nevertheless, Matahi and Reri dance in their temporary happiness. The arrival of the "Moana" sends them into hiding.
An island policeman finds their hut and serves them with an
arrest warrant issued by the island government, because of
the disturbance they have caused between tribes in violating
local laws. Reri bribes the policeman with a pearl, and he
destroys the warrant. The boat leaves the island without
them but Reri is haunted with fear.

A diving scene shows how one unfortunate pearl diver is
killed by a shark; there have been other incidents like this,
and the policeman places this location under tabu from further
diving. Hitu returns to the hut in the night but only Reri
sees him. He threatens Matahi with death unless Reri leaves
with him. Matahi, later, sees the opportunity to leave the
island on another boat. At the ticket office the Chinese
merchants take his money and apply it toward the bill he
accumulated during the pseudo-celebration. He cannot bear
to tell Reri and decides to go diving for big pearls in the
tabu lagoon. He leaves Reri in the night, goes diving, fights
off a shark, and in the end manages to find a pearl. Meanwhile, Reri has left with Hitu, leaving Matahi a note which

tells him that she must go so that he may live. Matahi, upon
discovering the note, rushes to his canoe to catch up with
Reri and Hitu who are now under sail in a small craft. At one
point, Matahi must dive in the water and swim after them.
Virtually exhausted, he reaches them and grabs on to a rope
hanging over the side. With a heart of stone, old marble-
face Hitu cuts the rope. Left in the boat's wake, Matahi is
too tired to continue or has lost his will. He disappears
beneath the surface.

Credits

Production:	F. W. Murnau, Robert J. Flaherty
Director:	F. W. Murnau
Script:	F. W. Murnau, Robert J. Flaherty
Photography:	Floyd Crosby, Robert J. Flaherty
Music:	Dr. Hugo Reisenfeld
Associate Producer:	David Flaherty
Assistant Director:	W. M. Bainbridge
Cast:	Reri--Anne Chevalier; Matahi--the boy; Hitu--the old chief; Jean--the policeman; Jules--the captain; King Ah--the Chinese trader
Released by:	Motion Picture Sales Corp.
Copyrighted:	3 August 1931 by Paramount Publix
Note:	Film credits indicate: "Told by: Robert Flaherty."
Premiere:	18 March 1931, New York
Running time:	82 minutes, sound--music track only

6   INDUSTRIAL BRITAIN (1933)

This documentary film has as its principal theme the continuity between the old skills and crafts of the English
worker and the quality and workmanship of modern industrial
products manufactured in Great Britain. The old crafts and
trades were represented by scenes of a windmill in operation,
weaving with a loom, and towing a barge along a canal.
Scenes of steam and smoke in industrial towns represent the
modern world. In some crafts, however, methods have not
changed. Pottery and glassmaking are used as examples to
show the continuity of skills. There are details of goblet
making and lens grinding. The narrator says industrial towns
are not drab: beautiful things are being made.
From here the film moves into larger industries. Steel-
making is shown with dramatic shots of fire and moulten metal.
The individual skills behind the making of an airplane engine
are shown. The film concludes with shots of heavy industries
whose products are supplied to the world.

Credits

Production:	Empire Marketing Board Film Unit
Producer:	John Grierson
Directors:	John Grierson, Robert J. Flaherty
Principal photography:	Robert J. Flaherty
Other photography:	John Grierson, Basil Wright, Arthur Elton
Editing:	John Grierson, Edgar Anstey
Distribution:	Gaumont-British Distributors Ltd.
Running time:	21 minutes, sound
Production Manager:	J. P. R. Golightly
Production Assistant:	John Taylor
Narration spoken by:	Donald Calthrop
Premiered:	November 1933, London

Note: Basic photography completed in 1931 but sound not added until 1933, along with five other films which comprised the "Imperial Six" series. The viewing print (35mm) in the Museum of Modern Art indicates only one personal credit: "Production: John Grierson, Robert J. Flaherty."

7   MAN OF ARAN (1934)

This film portrays daily life in the Aran Islands, some thirty miles off the western coast of Galway, Ireland. It portrays life as it existed in the early 1930s and as it may have existed a hundred years before. Mikeleen, the Boy, is seen along the shore. His mother is rocking a cradle in a typical Aran cottage, made of limestone and a thatched roof. The sea is ferocious and unrelenting as it smashes against the rocky shore in furious rhythm. Maggie and Mikeleen go to the cliffs to observe Tiger King and his crew trying to land their curragh, a light-weight boat. As they near the treacherous shore, the boat is almost wrecked. Maggie goes to help them, tries to save the nets, and is almost swept under. Fragments of English are heard on the sound track. Even walking home along the shore, the sea is a constant menace.

The next few scenes show how the Aran Islanders manage to eke out their living from their barren, rock-covered land. They must make their own soil from seaweed, sand, and fertilizer. But first Tiger King must clear the rocks from his small patch of land. He crushes them with a sledge hammer or with other rocks. Maggie searches for seaweed and soil. Another scene shows how cloth, tar, and flame are applied to a curragh in order to repair a hole.

Mikeleen fishes from the edge of a cliff, high above the water, oblivious to the danger of falling. Closer to the water now, the boy sees something in the water--a basking shark, slow moving, ugly, with a large amorphous mouth. The audience experiences the excitement and terror through the boy's eyes.

Here follow rapidly, edited scenes of shark fishing: the
boat, the men, ropes, a harpoon, waves, and glimpses of the
giant shark. These scenes capture the speed of the chase.
Maggie and Mikeleen watch from the shore. Harpooned, a shark
pulls the boat along in a calm sea. Maggie keeps vigil through
the night waiting for the men's return. When the fishermen
return with their prize catch, the villagers give them a tri-
umphant reception. A cauldron is readied for rendering the
shark liver into oil. The shark is butchered. Later a boat
goes out to meet a school of sharks. Mikeleen wants to go but
is ordered back.

As Maggie struggles to carry her unwieldy load of seaweed,
she and the boy watch the sea apprehensively. A storm is
coming. Tiger King and two others are trying to return to
shore in heavy seas. The boatmen need skill and precision to
stay atop the high seas. Waves explode against the shore.
Finally one wave carries them in, but the boat is quickly
overturned and slapped around like a piece of driftwood. They
must act quickly to save themselves and the gear. The family
greets the men; they pick up harpoons and ropes and stare at
the sea in disbelief. The man, woman, and child are silhouetted atop the cliffs as they make their way home.

Credits

Production:	Gainsborough Pictures Ltd., of Gaumont-British Picture Corporation Ltd.
Directed by:	Robert J. Flaherty
Collaborators:	John Goldman, Frances H. Flaherty
Assistant Director:	Pat Mullin [sic]
Laboratory:	John Taylor
Recordist:	H. Hand
Editor and Scenarist:	John Goldman
Musical Score:	John Greenwood; under the direction of Louis Levy
Characters:	Colman "Tiger" King--A man of Aran; Maggie Dirrane--His wife; Michael Dillane--Their son; Pat Mullin [sic], Patch Ruadh ("Red Beard"), Patcheen Flaherty, Tommy O'Rourke--The shark hunters; Patcheen Conneely, Stephen Dirrane, Mac McDonough--The curragh men

Note: The above credits are as indicated on a 16mm print
distributed by the Museum of Modern Art. Filmed on location
in the Aran Islands, 1932-1934. David Flaherty can be
credited as a production assistant and for additional
photography.

Premiered:	25 April 1934, London; 18 October 1934, United States

Running Time: 76 minutes, sound
Distribution: Gaumont-British Distributors Ltd.

8   ELEPHANT BOY (1937)

   This is a dramatized feature film based on Rudyard Kipling's
children's story, "Toomai of the Elephants." Set in the jun-
gles of India, it is the story of a boy who wishes to achieve
recognition and manhood among the community of elephant hunters
who make up his world. In a prologue Toomai, played by Sabu,
explains the importance of the elephant in Indian life. The
first few scenes establish parallels between animal life and
human life. Toomai awakes from sleeping in tall grass. Kala
Nag, his father's elephant, mimics his awaking motions.
Toomai, lifted by the great elephant's trunk, rides Kala Nag
down the village path. An infant is seen in the middle of the
path, but carefully Kala Nag steps over it. Toomai and Kala
Nag are completely at home in their natural habitat.
   Toomai guides Kala Nag to the river where there are other
elephants bathing in the river water and being tended by their
mahouts. They make fun of Toomai, injuring his pride.
   The Government of Mysore announces a wild elephant drive
and recruits mahouts and their elephants for the hunt. Two
Englishmen, one a commissioner, actually plan the hunt and
take charge of the recruiting. Toomai's father and Kala Nag
are hired. Impressed by Toomai's handling of the elephant,
the commissioner allows the young boy to come along. Toomai
later gives thanks for his good fortune to his god represented
by a huge monolith.
   In the jungle the drivers build a stockade out of a tree
trunks and straps. But after six weeks they have been unable
to capture any wild elephants. Commissioner Peterson is at
the end of his rope. The mahouts still continue to mock little
Toomai who wants to be accepted as a hunter. They say he will
be a hunter only when he has seen the elephants dance, which
to them is some kind of a joke. Toomai, incredibly, believes
them.
   A tiger comes to the camp in the evening. The English
commissioner and Toomai's father go to shoot it. Petersen
shoots it but Toomai's father approaches it too soon and is
mortally injured by the wounded beast. Toomai searches for
his father during the commotion. The crowd opens to let
Toomai through. A funeral follows and he burns his father's
corpse on a pyre. Kala Nag grieves, and to make matters worse
an evil mahout whips him with a chain. The elephant goes on a
rampage, injuring his new master, demolishing small buildings.
Only Toomai is able to stop Kala Nag. The injured man, however, wants Kala Nag shot. In a judgment worthy of Solomon,
the commissioner forces the man to accept payment instead.
Nevertheless, Toomai steals away in the night believing his
elephant will be shot.

Toomai and Kala Nag discover a herd of wild elephants in the river, and later that evening Toomai witnesses the mythical dance of the elephants. The hunters and trackers find Toomai, who leads them to the wild herd. They organize a stampede and steer the elephants down the river toward the camp.

Afterwards in a ceremony Toomai is honored by the hunters and is given the name of Toomai of the Elephants. His happiness causes him to cry.

Credits

Production:	London Film Productions Ltd.
Producer:	Alexander Korda
Directors:	Robert J. Flaherty, Zoltan Korda
Supervising Director:	William Hornbeck
Screenplay:	John Collier, based on Rudyard Kipling's short story "Toomai of the Elephants"
Assistants:	David Flaherty and Frances H. Flaherty
Photography:	Osmond H. Borradaile
Screenplay Collaboration:	Akos Tolnay and Marcia de Silva
Production Manager:	Teddy Baird
Sound Recording:	W. S. Bland, H. G. Cape
Editor:	Charles Creigton
Distribution:	United Artists
Copyrighted:	In U.S., by London Films Productions, 22 April 1937
Running time:	85 minutes, sound
Music:	John Greenwood
Music Director:	Muir Mathieson
Characters:	Sabu: Toomai; W. E. Holloway: His Father; Walter Hudd: Petersen; Allan Jeayes: Muchua Appa; Bruce Gordan: Tham Lahl; D. J. Williams: Hunter; W. Hyde-White: Commissioner
Premiered:	5 April 1937, New York; 7 April 1937, London

Note: Most exteriors filmed on location Mysore, India, 1935–1936, under the direction of Flaherty; studio scenes filmed in London studios under the direction of Zoltan Korda.

9   THE LAND (1942)

The Land begins with a foreword written by Wayne Darrow of the Agricultural Adjustment Agency:

> The strength that is America comes from the land.
> Our mighty war effort is the product of its land
> and people. Land: our soil, our minerals, our
> forests, our water-power. People: their skills,

their inventiveness, their resourcefulness,
their education, their health. Land and people, in war or in peace, this is our national
wealth.

This is the story of how rural America used
machines to achieve an unbelievable production--
but at a terrible cost to land and to people
through the wastes of erosion and poverty; the
story of freedom and abundance through the
workings of a democracy and through man's mastery of his own machines.

The film opens on a prosperous Pennsylvania farm and shows
a portrait of "Good people of the solid old stock that settled
this country three hundred years ago." But even in the rich
state of Pennsylvania, the narrator continues, "trouble has
crept in." Men walk over eroded fields and knolls. Rain and
rushing water wash away the soil. "When soil fails, life
fails."

Every state has been touched by the problem of erosion,
particularly the old cotton South. The camera shows scenes
of blacks in cotton fields, dilapidated shacks, and Southern
mansions that have seen better days. A malnourished girl
stares despairingly from a porch. The narrator tells us that
the soil was wasted by crops of tobacco and cotton, exhausted
by generation after generation. In one crumbling mansion an
elderly black man is bewildered by his isolation.

The people have gone West, but here too on the Great Plains,
wind and erosion have taken away the soil. Farms have blown
away in the dust. The people, forced to become migrants, are
homeless and landless. Entire towns have died. Once they
were called pioneers, but now migrants are forced to live in
roadside camps, dress in old clothes, and travel in broken-
down, patched together cars. They live on the road the best
way they can. One family who has given up its farm is shown
loading up a horse-drawn wagon with their pitiful belongings.
They are heading west toward a New Land, a New World as the
Europeans called America long ago.

In the West man has conquered the desert. Irrigation has
made the soil rich. Along the border country, men, women, and
children are glad to find work. They come from all over the
states. Filipino and Mexican workers are everywhere because
they work hard and cheap. We see them working in the fields.
The migrant labor camps are sad places. Old before her time,
a woman shows us a pathetic young boy sleeping; his hands are
moving as if he were still picking peas.

Machines can do the work of many men. A motorized cotton-
picker denudes bushes. A bulldozer clears the land with ease.
There are machines for almost every job, and they take many
jobs away. A displaced migrant worker remembers his Cumber-
land Mountain farm, and in his vision it looks like paradise.

Even in Iowa with good farms there is trouble. Farm prices are too low, farms fail, and former landowners become tenants. Farm laborers wait in lines for relief handouts of food, and they are glad to receive it.

In defense farmers are storing their harvest in giant granaries. Machines move grain like mountains of sand and load ships and barges; it is enough grain to feed the world. Wheat and corn surpluses are a source of this country's strength. America has great strength in the wheat fields and in the mountains and ranges where sheep and cattle graze. Farmers are trying to save the land by contour plowing to prevent run off. They are also strengthening the soil with fertilizers. They are talking their problems over, sharing their ideas. We can produce enough food to feed the world. But man must learn to live with his machines, control them. "The great fact is the land, the land itself, and the people, and the spirit of the people."

Credits

Production:	Agricultural Adjustment Administration, United States Department of Agriculture
Script, Direction, and Photography:	Robert J. Flaherty
Collaborator:	Frances H. Flaherty
Additional Photography:	Irving Lerner, Floyd Crosby
Production Manager:	Douglas Baker
Editor:	Helen van Dongen
Music:	Richard Arnell
Played by:	The National Youth Administration Symphony, under the direction of Fritz Mahler
Narration Written by:	Russell Lord, with Robert J. Flaherty
Narrator:	Robert J. Flaherty
Distribution:	U.S. Department of Agriculture
Running time:	43 minutes, sound
Premier:	April 1942, the Museum of Modern Art, New York City

Note: Production started August 1939. Shooting locations throughout the United States.

10 LOUISIANA STORY (1948)

This documentary, dramatized in part, portrays a state of mind, namely, a boy's infatuation with the bayou. The search for oil in his fantasy world brings the penetration of modern technology. It bemuses him at first, but he comes to admire it. And later it leaves his world untouched in its primeval beauty.

The opening sequence, one of the most famous in film history, takes place in the Bayou country of lower Louisiana. "It is the high water time of the year," the narrator (Flaherty) says, "the country is half drowned. We move through a forest of bearded trees. There are wild fowl everywhere in flight and swimming on the water. We are spellbound by all this wildlife and the mystery of the wilderness that lies ahead." Everywhere there is sort of a gliding movement: the water, an alligator, a snake. And from under the hanging cypress trees a young Cajun boy paddles his pirogue with the same effortless flow. He is at one with his world. His name is Alexander Napoleon Ulysses Latour.

But his world is disturbed when he hears a large, strange machine treading through the tall grass. This experience frightens him, for he already believes in werewolves and mermaids. He returns home. At the house, his father, speaking in a patois accent, talks about alligator hunting to an oil engineer. Alexander sees his father signing a document, a lease for the oilman. He enjoys some antics with his pet raccoon, set in the rich fauna and flora of the river. The oil men begin their surveys and bring their equipment. An oil rig is seen moving behind the trees like a skyscraper on wheels. When it is settled on its drilling site, Alexander approaches it timidly. The oilmen are kindly and paternal toward him. Alexander is shy and barely expresses himself in heavily accented English. He gives them a demonstration of how he catches catfish. But he is still too timid to go aboard the oil rig. Then one evening he musters enough courage, climbs aboard, steals into the heart of the apparatus, and watches the goings-on with avid interest. Long pipes twisted in place by heavy chains are drilled deep into the water and earth one after the other. The screeching of bare metal, hydraulic pumps, pulleys, pipes crashing and banging create a symphony of industrial sounds. The boy's father who has been searching for him comes to ward him away.

Alexander's enemy in the forest swamp is the alligator. Tying his raccoon to the boat, he goes to investigate an alligator's nest of eggs which so interests him that he neglects to hear the approaching alligator coming through the grass until it is almost too late. The alligator's frightful hiss, though, scares him away, and returning to the pirogue, he finds only a broken string instead of Jo-Jo, his pet raccoon. He observes an egret being caught by an alligator and of course imagines the worst for his pet. He plots revenge and sets a trap with a baited hook. The alligator takes the bait; a tug of war ensues between the boy and beast with the latter having the edge. Meanwhile, the father has been searching for him, hears the shouts and splashing, and rescues his son from being pulled under the slime-covered water. "He killed my coon!" he cries. The father says "never mind, we'll get him." And they do (off camera).

One day while fishing from the oil rig, Alexander hears a
great roar. It is a wildcat blow-out. Gas and water gush
from the well. The roar of the huge geyser is deafening.
Newspaper headlines tell the story, and the well is capped,
silent, temporarily dormant. When no one is looking the boy
sneaks over to the empty, dark, deep drill hole; he pours down
a bag of salt for luck. In another private moment he spits
down the well.

The boy is sad that the derrick will be taken away. A newspaper story tells that they finally struck oil. The family
shares in the prosperity. Alexander gets a new rifle and outside the house he is happily reunited with his raccoon spotted
in a tree. The well is capped for future use and only a con-
torted pipe is left standing in the water. Alexander and Jo-
Jo are seen climbing on the pipe as they wave good-bye to the
oil rig being barged away. He spits in the water again for
good luck.

Credits

Production:	Robert J. Flaherty Productions, Inc. (Standard Oil of New Jersey)
Producer and Director:	Robert J. Flaherty
Story:	Robert and Frances Flaherty
Associate Producers:	Richard Leacock, Helen van Dongen
Photography:	Richard Leacock (and Robert Flaherty)
Editor:	Helen van Dongen
Editorial Assistant:	Ralph Rosenblum
Music:	Virgil Thomson
Music Technical Assistant:	Henry Brant
Music Performed by:	Members of the Philadelphia Orchestra, Eugene Ormandy conducting
Sound:	Benjamin Donniger
Music Recording:	Bob Fine
Re-recording:	Dick Vorisek
Distribution:	Lopert Films (USA); British Lion Films Corp. (UK)
Copyrighted:	28 September 1948
Characters:	Joseph Boudreaux--The boy; Lionel LeBlanc--His father; El Bienvenu-- His mother; Frank Hardy--The driller; C. P. Guedry--The boilerman
Premiere:	September 1948, New York; 22 August 1948, Edinburgh Film Festival, Scotland
Running Time:	77 minutes, sound

11   GUERNICA (1949)--Unfinished

The film begins with a wide shot of two people silhouetted before Picasso's famous giant mural. The camera begins to dissect visually the components of this passionate work. Close-up after close-up magnify the pain and suffering of these barely representational figures. A close-up of a woman in anguish, a close-up of another, more abstract with fewer lines, human figures, their hands and feet distorted, a woman carrying her dead child. The camera pans across a horse's snarled jaw, suffering. Wider shots reveal the horse, a bull, a woman, tilting down to the dead. The film ends as it began with the wide shot of the mural and the seated couple.

Credits

Production:	Museum of Modern Art, New York City
Direction and Photography:	Robert J. Flaherty
Editing:	David Flaherty
Introductory Titles:	Richard Griffith
Running time:	12 minutes, silent

12   THE TITAN: THE STORY OF MICHELANGELO (1949)

Using murals, paintings, sculptures, drawings, and architectural structures, this film biography traces the inimitable life of Michelangelo. It shows the artworks that inspired him, it recreates the political and religious events that are reflected in his own work. It tells of Michelangelo's early career in Florence and of his relationship to the Medici's, a powerful Renaissance dynasty, and to the Popes in Rome who commissioned some of his greatest work. A central argument of the film is that although Michelangelo believed that man and his art were deeply rooted in nature--indeed he was obsessed by physical beauty and perfection--he was driven to reaffirming his faith by criticism of the lack of spiritualism in art and by the challenge of the Reformation.

Credits

Production:	Robert J. Flaherty in Association with Robert Snyder and Ralph Alswang
Producer:	Robert Snyder
Director and Editor:	Richard Lyford
Writer:	Norman Borisoff
Camera:	Harry Ringger
Sound:	Robert Vincent
Music:	Alois Melichar
Art Interpretation:	Michael Sonnabend

Voices: Peter Campbell, Joe DeSantis
Told by: Frederic March
Running time: 67 minutes, sound
Note: Adapted from the Curt Ortel film <u>Michelangelo: The
   Life of a Titan</u> (1940), Pandora Films, Zurich, Switzerland,
   made in the German language.
Distributor: Contemporary Films (1950)

13   A FILM STUDY OF ROBERT FLAHERTY'S LOUISIANA STORY (1962)

   Consists of the opening sequence of <u>Louisiana Story</u> in the
final version, the related outtakes or portions not used in
the final cut, and ends with a repetition of the edited opening sequence. During the showing of the outtakes Frances
Flaherty and Richard Leacock intermittently discuss the artistic considerations that went into the shooting of each scene,
the day-to-day physical conditions that confronted them, and
the sense of discovery that was essential to the Flaherty
method. This version is owned and circulated by the Museum
of Modern Art.

Credits

Sponsor: University of Minnesota, made pos-
                           sible by a grant from Louis W. and
                           Maude Hill Family Foundation

Study Material Prepared
and Assembled by: N. H. Cominos
Study Project under the
Direction of: George Amberg
Narrators: Frances Flaherty and Richard Leacock
Running time: 114 minutes, sound
Note: The outtake footage assembled under this title in the
   custody of the University of Minnesota is 1,000 minutes.
   <u>See</u> Part VI, Archival Sources.

Writings about Robert Flaherty, 1904-1976

1904

14 SYNGE, J. M. Riders to the Sea, in A Treasury of the Theatre.
    Edited by John Gassner. New York: Simon and Schuster,
    1960 ed., pp. 628-732.
        In the Man of Aran Flaherty tried to put into visual
    images a story of men against the sea. Synge's tense drama,
    which Gassner calls the greatest one-act tragedy of the
    English-speaking theatre, provided inspiration to Flaherty
    if not exactly a model. Synge's drama of life and death
    among deceptively simple fisherfolk takes place on as is-
    land off the west coast of Ireland which is, in fact, in
    the Aran Islands.

1907

15 _____. The Aran Islands. London: George Allen & Unwin Ltd.,
    166 pp.
        The famous writer describes his stay on the Aran Islands,
    furnishing insightful information on the landscape and the
    Gaelic-speaking people. A book Flaherty read in prepara-
    tion for the making of Man of Aran.

1922

16 ANON. "Nanook of the North: A True Story of the Arctic."
    Visual Education (September), pp. 327-331.
        An extensive description of the film.

17 ANON. "Nanook of the North." Moving Picture Herald (24 June),
    p. 707.
        An article about the exhibits and publicity relating to
    the film's opening.

*18 ANON. "Nanook of the North." Exceptional Photoplays, No. 1
    (November), pp. 1-3.
        Cited by Wolfgang Klaue. See entry 254.

19   ANON. "Nanook of the North." World's Work, 41 (April), 426.
     A brief description of the film.

20   PATTERSON, FRANCES TAYLOR. "Nanook of the North." The New
     Republic, 26, No. 401 (9 August), 306-307. Reprinted in
     Pratt (see entry 262), pp. 342-344.
        One of the most cogent contemporary reviews of this film
     in which the reviewer makes an important distinction between
     Nanook and the travelogues and educational films that pre-
     ceded it.

21   TIDDEN, FRITZ. "Nanook of the North." Moving Picture World,
     56, No. 8 (24 June), 735.
        Describes it as a film which defies classification but
     concludes, significantly, that it is a "true human
     document."

                              1923

22   FREELICK, L. "New Movie Prophet." Asia, 23 (June), 396.
        Article about Flaherty in connection with the release of
     Nanook of the North. Magazine's interest in "Asian" peoples
     is very broad indeed, extending to the fringes of Asia and
     beyond.

23   SHERWOOD, ROBERT E. "Robert Flaherty's Nanook of the North,"
     in his The Best Moving Pictures of 1922-23. Boston: Small,
     Maynard, pp. 3-8. Reprinted in Jacobs (see entry 275),
     pp. 15-19.
        One of the first important critical reviews of Nanook
     which recognized the director's unique contribution to the
     originality of the film; includes Flaherty's production de-
     tails and difficulties in finding a distributor.

24   TALBOT, FREDERICK A. Moving Pictures. Philadelphia:
     Lippincott.
        Contains production details of Nanook of the North.

                              1924

25   O'DELL, SCOTT. Representative Photoplays Analyzed. Hollywood:
     Palmer Institute of Authorship, pp. 369-371.
        Contains synopsis and scenario analysis of Nanook of the
     North.

26   SELDES, GILBERT. "An Open Letter to the Movie Magnates," in
     his The Seven Lively Arts. New York: Harper's, pp. 397 ff.
        Contains rather naive critical references to Nanook of
     the North.

1925

27   ANON. "Along the Trail with the Editor." Asia (May), p. 375.
     Introduction to Frances and David Flaherty's series on
     the making of Moana.

28   ANON. "Moana." Exceptional Photoplays, 6, No. 2 (November-
     December).
     A favorable review which emphasizes the film's acceptance
     of life and its photographic and overall production
     qualities.

29   BILBY, JULIAN. Nanook of the North. London: Arrowsmith,
     319 pp.
     Although this volume uses the title and includes illus-
     trations from the film, it is a story in narrative form of
     a typical Eskimo named Nanook rather than the one known by
     Robert Flaherty.

30   FLAHERTY, DAVID. "Serpents in Eden." Asia (October),
     pp. 858-869, 895-898.
     The director's brother describes some of the unpleasant-
     ries not presented in Moana; describes a South Sea trader
     and island resident commissioner, who conspired against the
     film project, as figures of exploitation.

31   FLAHERTY, FRANCES HUBBARD. "Setting up House and Shop in
     Samoa." Asia (August), pp. 639-651, 709-711.
     Describes finding a suitable location; setting up a
     laboratory in a cave; refurbishing a residence; acquiring
     food; first encounters with Samoan customs; explaining the
     film project to Samoans; changing concept of the film; and
     the discovery of the value of panchromatic film.

32   _____. "Behind the Scenes with our Samoan Stars." Asia
     (September), pp. 747-753, 795-796.
     Describes locating cast of principal characters; several
     trying experiences with native actors.

33   _____. "A Search for Amimal [sic] and Sea Sequence." Asia
     (November), pp. 954-962, 1000-1004.
     Describes adventures and misadventures in Samoa during
     the making of Moana: the search for "sea monsters"; shark-
     fishing; endless ceremonies and feasts; and Robert Flaherty's
     illness on location.

34   _____. "Fa'A-Samoa." Asia (December), pp. 1085-1090,
     1096-1100.
     Describes how the filmmakers developed an appreciation
     for the Samoan culture which shaped the film; photographic
     problems; and the tattoo sequence.

35   L. D. F. "Moana of the South Seas." Asia (May), pp. 389-392,
     450.
     Impressionistic and detailed description of the film.

36   SELIGMANN, HERBERT J. "Moana of the South Seas." The Arts
        8, No. 5 (November), 255-262.
            An effusive review which appreciates the use of shapes,
        movement, and textures not unrelated to the discoveries
        painters had made in these islands.

37   STALLINGS, LAURENCE. "Moana." New York World (18 February).
        Compares film to The Golden Bough; epic and graceful.

                                1926

38   ANON. "Censor has banned film which artists acclaim as wonder-
        ful picture." Toronto Star (4 February).
            Regarding absurd censorship of Moana in Canada.

39   ANON. "Moana." Cinema Art (April), p. 50.
            A description of Moana, including a few favorable impres-
        sions by the reviewer.

40   BARRY, IRIS. Let's Go to the Pictures. London: Chatto &
        Windus, 270 pp.
            A critic's guide to the movies. Shows influence of the
        criticism of Nanook of the North as an inexact picture of
        Eskimo life.

41   GRIERSON, JOHN. "Flaherty's Poetic Moana." New York Sun
        (8 February). Reprinted in Jacobs (see entry 275),
        pp. 27-28.
            By now Grierson's most famous review, written anony-
        mously, in which he first used the term documentary to
        describe a film; stresses its beautiful pictorial elements,
        cinematic techniques, and its truthfulness to life.

42   HALL, MORDAUNT. "Nanook of the South (Moana)." New York Times
        (8 February), p. 24.
            The reviewer believes that the film captures the spirit
        of Polynesians, their happiness and naturalism. The film
        is a poem free from sham.

43   LITTELL, ROBERT. "Moana." The New Republic (3 March),
        pp. 46-47.
            A favorable review which admires the patience that went
        into the film, "crafted from life itself," but sees the
        struggle for life (absent in the film) as essential to
        civilization.

44   RAMSAYE, TERRY. A Million and One Nights: A History of the
        Motion Picture Through 1925. New York: Simon and Schuster,
        1964 re-issue, 868 pp.
            A classic history of motion pictures from primitive be-
        ginnings through the high point of the silent era. In con-
        nection with Flaherty, see for description of industry and

for films contemporary with <u>Nanook of the North</u> and <u>Moana</u>.
<u>Moana</u> not mentioned and <u>Nanook</u> just barely but useful for
contrast.

45 SHERWOOD, ROBERT E. "Moana." <u>McCalls's</u> (6 May), pp. 27-28.
    Reviewer is delighted by the film's visual beauty.

1927

46 CANUDO, RICCIOTTO. "Another View of Nanook," in his <u>L'Usine</u>
    <u>aux images</u>. Paris. Translated by Harold J. Salemson and
    reprinted in Jacobs (<u>see</u> entry 275), pp. 20-21.
        Exuberant, personal interpretation stressing the theme
    of <u>Nanook of the North</u> as representative of Man pitted
    against the Elements, eventually dominating them, but fate-
    fully isolated in his mastery.

47 CLARKE, DONALD H. "Producer of Nanook joins Metro-Goldwin."
    <u>New York Times</u> (26 June), Section 8, p. 2. Reprinted in
    Pratt (<u>see</u> entry 262), pp. 347-348.
        An interview with Flaherty on the occasion of his de-
    parture for California en route to the production of <u>White</u>
    <u>Shadows in the South Seas</u>. Most of the interview, however,
    concerns <u>Twenty-four Dollar Island</u> in which Flaherty talks
    about his film work and impressions of New York. One of
    the more informative pieces on one of his most obscure
    films.

48 FLAHERTY, MRS. ROBERT J. (Frances Hubbard). "The Camera's
    Eye." <u>National Board of Review Magazine</u>, 2, No. 4 (April),
    4-5. Reprinted in Pratt, (<u>see</u> entry 262), pp. 344-347.
        Contrasts the making of <u>Nanook</u> and <u>Moana</u>. In both films
    the camera, with its capacity for infinite detail, sought
    out reality. Describes efforts to present quite different
    races of people. Concludes with comparison to <u>Potemkin</u> and
    optimistic prognosis for "documentary" film, a term which
    she actually uses only one year after Grierson's historic
    review of <u>Moana</u>.

49 WELLER, S. M. "Interview." <u>Motion Picture Classic</u>, 26
    (October), 25.
        Cited by Mel Schuster. <u>Motion Picture Directors: The</u>
    <u>Bibliography of Magazine and Periodical Articles, 1900-1972</u>.
    Metuchen, N. J.: Scarecrow Press, 1973.

1928

50 ANON. "Stark Love and Moana." <u>MovieMaker</u> (November). Re-
    printed in Jacobs (<u>see</u> entry 275), pp. 27-28.

117

Compares handling of two films about "racial minorities."
Former is about mountain people of Tennessee. It is rushed
compared to Moana, which catches the essence of a people
and their daily lives.

51   GLASSGOLD, C. ADOLPH. "The Films: In the Antipodes." The
     Arts (September), pp. 166-167.
          A favorable review emphasizing the theme, acting and
     photography in White Shadows in the South Seas.

52   NEEDHAM, WILBUR. "The Future of American Cinema." Close-Up,
     2 (June), 48-49.
          An appreciation of Nanook and Moana.

53   O'BRIEN, FREDERICK. White Shadows in the South Seas. New
     York: Grosset & Dunlap.
          Best seller upon which the film was based. Originally
     published in 1919; several editions since.

54   RAMSAYE, TERRY. "Flaherty, Great Adventurer." Photoplay
     Magazine 33, No. 6 (May), 58, 123-126. Reprinted in
     Pratt (see entry 262), pp. 349-354.
          Mainly a biographical article on Flaherty by a major
     film historian. Develops the theme of Flaherty's connec-
     tion with 17th century explorers who first traveled the
     North region. Includes discussion of the making of Nanook
     of the North, Moana, and White Shadows in the South Seas.

55   STEFANSSON, VILHJALMUR. The Standardization of Error. London:
     Kegan Paul, Trench, Trubner, 83 pp.
          A rambling essay on knowledge by an explorer and prolific
     writer who deplores the acceptance of myths and half-truths
     as knowledge. Unfortunately Nanook of the North is one of
     his examples of myth portrayed as truth. The author does
     not concern himself with art, only scientific accuracy.
     (Note especially pp. 66-72.)

                              1930

56   ROTHA, PAUL. The Film Till Now. London: Jonathan Cape.
     With Additional Section by Richard Griffith in 1967 ed.
     Middlesex: Hamlyn Publishing Group Ltd., 831 pp.
          A classic, critical survey of the world's films contain-
     ing numerous references to Flaherty. Rotha discusses the
     contribution of Nanook of the North and Moana as they re-
     late to the beginnings of the documentary movement. Addi-
     tional material by Griffith includes mainly critical
     reception of Flaherty's work.

57 ROWE, NEWTON. <u>Samoa Under the Sailing Gods</u>. London and New
York: Putnam.
A former agricultural inspector in Samoa, 1922-26, describes the social ills and the maladministration of the
islanders under the mandate of the New Zealand Government
that Flaherty chose to ignore in his film <u>Moana</u>.

1931

58 COWLEY, MALCOLM. "Tabu." <u>The New Republic</u>, 66 (1 April), 183.
A review which resents the imposition of a Hollywood plot
and treatment on Polynesian life.

*59 FERGUSON, FRANCIS. "Tabu." <u>Bookman</u>, 73 (August), 634.
Cited by Wolfgang Klaue. <u>See</u> entry 254.

60 GRIERSON, JOHN. "Flaherty--Naturalism and the Problem of the
English Cinema." <u>Artwork</u>, 7 (Autumn), 110-215. Reprinted
in Hardy (<u>see</u> entry 273), pp. 139-144.
A critique of the English cinema with a plea to follow
the naturalism of Robert Flaherty rather than the artifice
of Hollywood.

61 HAMILTON, JAMES SHELLEY. "Tabu." <u>National Board of Review
Magazine</u>, 6 (April), 9-11.
Generally a favorable review of <u>Tabu</u> but criticizes
contrivances, studio atmosphere, and staginess.

*62 MURNAU, F. W. "L'Etoile du Sud." <u>Revue du Cinéma</u>, Nos. 23-25
(June).
Cited by Henri Agel. <u>See</u> entry 257.

63 POTAMKIN, HARRY ALAN. "Lost Paradise: Tabu." <u>Creative Art</u>,
8, No. 6 (June), 462-463.
An unfavorable review based on the argument that the
film's failure is the "failure of motion picture 'art industry' to respect the experience of a people as something
to draw upon seriously for the theme and plot."

1932

64 GRIERSON, JOHN. "First Principles of Documentary." <u>Cinema
Quarterly</u> (Winter). Reprinted in Hardy (<u>see</u> entry 273),
pp. 145-153.
Flaherty's approach to filmmaking illustrates some of
Grierson's basic principles: that a documentary rejects
acted stories and artificial backgrounds; that individuals
cast in their everyday roles rather than actors are better
guides to a screen interpretation of the modern world; and

that "materials and stories" taken from reality can be more real philosophically than the acted article.

1934

65   ANON. "Primitive Life on Aran Islands." New York Herald Tribune (24 June), Sec. 5, p. 3.
      Includes brief history of Aran Islands and reviews Man of Aran, emphasizing Flaherty's failure to reveal much of island life. Since the "spiritual factor" is missing, the reviewer calls the film a "materialistic conception of cinematography."

66   BOND, RALPH. "Man of Aran." Cinema Quarterly, 2, No. 4 (Summer), 245-246.
      Critical review arguing Flaherty's escapism and irrelevance to modern social problems.

*67 BRAUN, B. VIVIAN. "Flaherty's Man of Aran." Film Art, 2 (Spring), 17.
      Cited by Paolo Gobetti. See entry 243.

68   CARTER, HUNTLEY. "Man of Aran." London Observer (6 May), p. 13.
      Letter criticizing C. A. Lejeune's review of 29 April.

69   DAVY, CHARLES. "Man of Aran." London Spectator (4 May), p. 697.
      Criticizes the social omissions in the film.

70   ELLIS, PETER (pseud.). "Robert Flaherty's Escape." New Theatre, 1, No. 9 (December), 29.
      Flaherty's failure to exploit social implications of his subject matter ultimately supports fascism.

71   FERGUSON, OTIS. "Rock and Water." The New Republic, 80 (November 7), 366.
      Ferguson appreciates some of Man of Aran's technical elements but finds the total impact disappointing on artistic grounds.

72   FLAHERTY, MIRIAM R. "Sentimentality and the Screen." Commonweal, 20 (5 October), 522-523.
      Poses Flaherty as the answer to Hollywood's commercialization of "cinematic art."

73   GRENVILLE, VERNON. "The Play and the Screen." Commonweal (9 November), p. 66.
      An extremely favorable review of Man of Aran in which the principal actors "move through the film with a naturalness, a power and a grace which is superb. In their

struggles with the sea and the soil we seem at the core of
life itself."

74   GRIERSON, JOHN. "Flaherty." Cinema Quarterly, 3, No. 1
     (Autumn), 12-17.
          A critical review of Flaherty's work defending his
     approach to filmmaking over Hollywood's. Applauds achieve-
     ments of Man of Aran despite commercial cinematic demands.

75   GWYNN, STEPHEN. "Flaherty's Film of Aran; the Island, its
     People." London Observer (13 May), p. 10. Also published
     in Boston's Living Age (July), pp. 455-456.
          A film review and description of Aran life. The film is
     a good illustration of Synge's "Riders to the Sea."

76   HAMILTON, JAMES SHELLEY. "Man of Aran." National Board of
     Review Magazine, 9, No. 8 (November), 8-10.
          "Man of Aran is ourselves when we had to feed ourselves."

77   HERRING, ROBERT. "Man of Aran." London Mercury, 30, No. 176
     (June), 169-170.
          Criticizes film for not presenting a broader view of
     island life but admires courage presented in the film and
     Flaherty's craftsmanship.

78   KENNEDY, ED (pseud.). "Man of Aran." Film Front, 1
     (24 December), 6-7.
          Unfavorable review based on socio-political grounds.

79   LEJEUNE, C. A. "Man of Aran." London Observer (29 April),
     p. 24; and (6 May), p. 13.
          Criticizes lack of narrative and omission of island
     social conditions.

80   MONTAGU, IVOR. "Man of Aran." New Statesman and Nation, 7
     (28 April), 638.
          Views film as a poetic document but criticizes omission
     of struggle of man with man.

81   O'NEIL, BRIAN. "Man of Aran." New Masses, 13 (30 October),
     29-30.
          Accuses film of reflecting prevailing ideology of
     capitalist class. Flaherty's portrayal of the islanders
     is out of touch with reality.

*82 PASINETTI, FRANCESCO. "Man of Aran." Il Ventuno (August).
          Cited by Paolo Gobetti. See entry 243.

83   ROTHA, PAUL. "Man of Aran." Sight and Sound, 3, No. 10
     (Summer), 70-71.

Describes this as Flaherty's best film but reviewer is
sure to point out that documentary can take other paths.

84   SCHRIRE, DAVID. "Evasive Documentary." Cinema Quarterly, 3,
      No. 1 (Autumn), 7-9.
      Argues for stronger criticism of Man of Aran because it
      diverts public attention from social struggles and conflict.

*85   SEGAL, MARK. "Man of Aran." Filmliga, 7, No. 8, pp. 290-293.
      Cited by Wolfgang Klaue. See entry 254.

86   SENNWALD, ANDRE. "Man of Aran." New York Times (19 October),
      p. 27.
      He is overwhelmed by the reality of the film but doubts
      ability of American audiences, numbed by false dramatiza-
      tions, to respond to the film intellectually.

87   TROY, WILLIAM. "Film: Pure Cinema." The Nation, 139,
      No. 3617 (31 October), 518.
      An ambivalent review of Man of Aran in which the reviewer
      praises the film's photography and nonnarrative structure,
      a form of "pure cinema" that departs from Flaherty's pre-
      vious films, but criticizes Flaherty's essential failure
      to get close to the people as James Middleton Synge and
      Liam O'Flaherty have done.

                              1935

88   ACOTT, G. M. "Men and Women of Aran." London Catholic Herald
      (1 November).
      Cited by Mary Mainwaring. See entry 210.

89   GREENE, GRAHAM. "The Cinema." Spectator (25 October), p. 663.
      Critical review of Man of Aran.

*90   HOBSEN, H. "Man of Films." Christian Science Monitor Magazine
      (6 November), p. 8.
      Cited by Mel Schuster. See entry 49.

*91   LEECH, CLIFFORD. "Definitions in Cinema." Cinema Quarterly,
      13, No. 3 (Winter), 79-80.
      Cited by Mary Mainwaring. See entry 210.

92   MULLEN, PAT. Man of Aran. New York: E. P. Dutton, 286 pp.
      Highly anecdotal, autobiographical narrative of the
      culture, history, family life, and hardships of the Aran
      Islands by one who grew up there and acted as the go-between
      for Flaherty and the island people. Describes the making of
      the film in vivid detail though somewhat removed from aes-
      thetic considerations of film art. Reprinted by Massachu-
      setts Institute of Technology Press.

93 TROY, WILLIAM. "Films: Behind The Scenes." The Nation, 141,
    No. 3563 (10 July), 56.
        A review of Pat Mullen's book Man of Aran (see entry 92),
    which is called a supplement to Flaherty's film and il-
    lustrates how ethnographic films are put together.

                            1936

94 MEYERS, SIDNEY. "An Event: The Wave." New Theatre
    (November). Reprinted in Jacobs (see entry 275), pp.
    pp. 118-122.
        Mainly a discussion of Paul Strand's film with reference
    to Flaherty, who is criticized because of his escapism and
    anachronistic attitude. Meyers prefers social commitment
    of The Wave.

^95 MICHELI, ITALO. "L'Uomo di Aran." L'Italiano, No. 30.
    Cited by Henri Agel. See entry 257.

                            1937

96 ANON. "La Danza degli Elefanti." Bianco e Nero, No. 9
    (September), pp. 81-84.
        Plot summary and review of Elephant Dance, stressing
    documentary elements which Flaherty imposed on a literary
    work.

97 FERGUSON, OTIS. "Flaherty and the Films." The New Republic
    (21 April), p. 323.
        Generally unfavorable review of Elephant Boy which
    points to fairly obvious shortcomings of the film.

98 FLAHERTY, FRANCES. Elephant Dance. New York: Scribner,
    136 pp.
        Contains the letters of Frances Flaherty to her daughters
    in England during the making of Elephant Boy. The letters
    contain detailed descriptions of location filming, problems
    of working with the crew, cast, and elephants. Totally
    from Frances' viewpoint though she writes as if her hus-
    band's thoughts were the same.

99 _____. Sabu: The Elephant Boy. New York: Oxford University
    Press, unpaginated.
        A short, profusely illustrated narrative of Sabu's dis-
    covery as an actor, his relationship with elephants, and
    his charming, courageous, and sometimes mischievous exploits
    during the making of Elephant Boy.

                            123

100   GREENE, GRAHAM. "Elephant Boy." London <u>Spectator</u> (16 April),
       p. 707.
           Criticizes film's structure and poor adaptation of
       Kipling's story and lack of suspense.

101   GRIERSON, JOHN. "Elephant Boy." <u>World Film News</u>, 1, No. 12
       (March), 5.
           Grierson defends Flaherty's role, especially evident in
       the jungle footage. However, the studio takes over with
       its Oxford accents, makeup, and costumes and reality is
       not realized.

                                1938

102   DAVY, CHARLES, ed. <u>Footnotes to the Film</u>. London: Lovat
       Dickson and Reader's Union Ltd. Reprinted by Arno Press
       and the <u>New York Times</u>, 1970, 334 pp.
           Contains Grierson and Greene's criticisms of Flaherty
       films.

*103   EISENSTEIN, SERGEI M. "My i oni." <u>Kino</u> (5 December).
           Cited by Wolfgang Klaue. <u>See</u> entry 254.

104   GREENE, GRAHAM. "Subjects and Stories," in <u>Footnotes to the
       Film</u>. Edited by Charles Davy. New York: Arno Press,
       pp. 61-62.
           Critical comments on <u>Man of Aran</u>, which "did not even
       attempt to describe truthfully a way of life." Greene,
       one of the most influential critics, dismisses the film
       because of its poor adaptation, ellipses, and staginess.

105   GRIERSON, JOHN. "The Course of Realism," in <u>Footnotes to the
       Film</u>. Edited by Charles Davy. New York: Arno Press,
       pp. 137-161. Also reprinted in Hardy (<u>see</u> entry 273),
       pp. 199-211.
           This essay traces the history of actuality film, criti-
       cizing newsreels but praising <u>The March of Time</u>. It dis-
       cusses documentary in Germany, France, Russia, Britain, and
       the United States, citing examples of major directors like
       Flaherty.

106   HOLMES, WINIFRED. "Evil Eye in Belgium." <u>Sight and Sound</u>,
       7, No. 26 (Summer), 113-155.
           An article about Henri Storck which includes several com-
       ments about Flaherty's influence on the Belgian filmmaker.

107   LORD, RUSSELL. <u>Behold Our Land</u>. Boston: Houghton Mifflin,
       310 pp.
           Lord collaborated with Flaherty on the script for <u>The
       Land</u>. This book focuses on the mistreatment of the land

                                124

from an ecological point of view, thus sharing a common
theme with the film that Flaherty made later on.

1939

108   JACOBS, LEWIS. <u>The Rise of the American Film: A Critical</u>
      <u>History</u>. New York: Harcourt, Brace, 1939. Second ed.
      New York: Teachers College Press, Columbia University,
      1968, 613 pp.
         A classic history of American cinema. See for very
      brief assessment of Flaherty's films as of 1939. Clearly
      Jacob's focus is on the feature film and he speaks of docu-
      mentaries essentially in terms of their influence on
      features.

1941

109   ANON. "Documentary Daddy." <u>Time</u>, 37 (3 February), 69.
         Short biographical piece on Flaherty, recounting his
      film career.

110   GRIFFITH, RICHARD. "The Land." <u>National Board of Review</u>
      <u>Magazine</u>, 16, No. 9 (December), 11-12.
         Griffith tries to defend <u>The Land</u>, despite its weak-
      nesses as a sign that Flaherty had come back to the modern
      world to work alongside the rest of the documentary film
      movement.

111   LORD, RUSSELL. "Robert Flaherty Rediscovers America: Editor-
      ial Notes and Forthcoming Moving Picture." <u>The Land</u>, 1,
      No. 1 (Winter), 67-75.
         Includes short biography of Flaherty and describes his
      travels through the United States while shooting <u>The Land</u>.

*112 NICHOLSON, IRENE. "Man of Aran." <u>Film Art</u>, No. 4 (Summer).
         Cited by Henri Agel. <u>See</u> entry 257.

113   STRAUSS, THEODORE. "The Giant Shinnies Down the Beanstalk:
      Flaherty's <u>The Land</u>." <u>New York Times</u> (12 October). Re-
      printed in Jacobs (<u>see</u> entry 275), pp. 197-199.
         An interview with Robert Flaherty in which he discusses
      his "rediscovery of America"; the problems of machines and
      labor; and the ideas that go into his films. Strauss er-
      roneously concludes that Flaherty is no longer a romantic.

1942

114   GRIFFITH, RICHARD. "The Land." <u>Documentary News Letter</u>, 3,
      No. 2 (February), 27.

Compares The Land to Lorentz's work, only Flaherty's
job was more complicated. The Land poses a national problem but offers no solution.

1943

115   . "Flaherty and the Future." New Movies (formerly
National Board of Review Magazine), 13, No. 1 (January),
4-7, 15.
In this anniversary issue twenty years after the release
of Nanook of the North, Griffith argues for greater recognition of Flaherty's talents during the war; criticizes
nondistribution of The Land and tries to explain how it is
needed for the war effort.

1945

*116   LEPROHON, PIERRE. "Un poete de l'exotisme: Robert J. Flaherty,"
in his L'exotisme et le cinema. Paris: Edition Jacques
Susse, pp. 132-142.
Cited by Henri Agel. See entry 257.

1946

117   GRIERSON, JOHN. "Post-War Patterns." Hollywood Quarterly, 1,
No. 2 (January), 159-165.
Restates his messianic conception of documentary that
looks for beauty in the daily work of man, and discusses
the film's relationship to sponsors like industry and
government. Flaherty's classicism is contrasted with
Grierson's more contemporary and publicly oriented views.

118   ROSENHEIMER, ARTHUR [pseud. Arthur Knight]. "They Make
Documentaries: Number One--Robert Flaherty." Film News,
7, No. 6 (April), 1-2, 8-10, 23.
A biographical survey of Flaherty's life, including an
interview with Flaherty, who comments on the making of his
films and their intended purpose.

*119   WEINBERG, HERMAN G. "Two Pioneers: Robert Flaherty, Hans
Richter." Index Supplement to Sight and Sound. 15 pp.

1947

120   BALCON, MICHAEL, et al. Twenty Years of British Film
(1925-1947). London: Falcon Press, 96 pp.

Survey of British feature films and documentaries by
leading figures in the British film industry. Flaherty's
Industrial Britain, Elephant Boy, and Man of Aran are
included.

121 BRINNIN, JOHN MALCOLM. "The Flahertys: Pioneer Documentary
Filmmakers." Harper's Bazaar, 81, No. 12 (December),
146-147, 187-188, 191.
Describes his first-hand observation of the shooting of
the night-time derrick scene in Louisiana Story. Emphasizes
the collaboration between Robert and Frances Flaherty and
their efforts to find children for their films.

*122 DiGIAMMATTEO, FERNALDO. "Flaherty: La Funzione del
documentario," in his Essenza del film. Torino. Edizione
de Il Dramma.
Cited by Paolo Gobetti. See entry 243.

*123 DIXON, CAMPBELL. "Is Nanook a Fake?" Daily Telegraph.
Revised criticism of the lack of authenticity in the
film. Cited by Arthur Calder-Marshall. See entry 249.

124 GOGARTY, OLIVER ST. JOHN. "My Friend Flaherty." Tomorrow
(March). Also reprinted in his book Mourning Became
Mrs. Spendlove. New York: Creative Age Press, 1948.
Charming tribute and appreciation of the Flaherty char-
acter; in anecdotal form.

125 JACOBS, LEWIS. "Experimental Cinema in America, 1921-47."
Hollywood Quarterly, 3, No. 2 (Winter 1947-48), 111-124;
No. 3 (September 1948), 278-292. Reprinted in his The
Rise of the American Film. New York: Columbia University
Teachers College Press, 1968 ed., pp. 543-582. Also in
Roger Manvell, ed., Experiment in the Film. London: Grey
Walls Press, 1949, pp. 113-152.
Contains appreciation of the photographic values of
Twenty-Four Dollar Island with quotations from Flaherty
on camera work.

126 ROSENHEIMER, ARTHUR [pseud. Arthur Knight]. "Un maitre du
documentaire: Robert Flaherty." Revue du Cinéma, No. 4
(January), pp. 42-51. Reprinted in part in Henri Agel,
Robert J. Flaherty. Paris: Editions Seghers, 1965, p. 165
(see entry 257).
The camera as an agent of discovery is the Flaherty
technique.

1948

*127   AGER, CECELIA. "A Lyric Journey Into Bayous with Flaherty."
        New York Star (September 29).
            Cited by Mary Mainwaring. See entry 210.

128   ANON. "Movie of the Week: Louisiana Story." Life (4 October),
        pp. 151, 154.
            An illustrated description of the film and Flaherty's
        colorful life. He lived with the people, entered into their
        daily routine, and made a film that seemed to come right out
        of it.

129   ANON. "Old Master." Time (20 September), pp. 94-96.
            A short story about Louisiana Story on the occasion of
        its winning a Venice International Film Festival award.

130   ANSTEY, EDGAR. "Industrial Britain," in Experiment in the
        Film. Edited by Roger Manvell. London: Grey Walls Press,
        1948. Reprinted in part in Sight and Sound, 21, No. 2
        (October-December 1951), 70.
            Contains rather perceptive criticism of Industrial
        Britain noting Flaherty's use of black and white patterns,
        low sunlight, and a camera movement that anticipates.

*131   CAMPASSI, OSVALDO. "Tabu." Cinema (Rome), No. 1 (October).
            Cited by Paolo Gobetti. See entry 243.

132   CLURMAN, HAROLD. "Flaherty's Louisiana Story." Tomorrow
        (October). Reprinted in Jacobs (see entry 275),
        pp. 230-232.
            Favorable review of the poetic aspects of Louisiana
        Story but Clurman, theater critic for The Nation, is unsure
        about the role of the oil industry.

133   GRIERSON, JOHN. "Louisiana Story." Documentary Film News, 7,
        No. 68 (September-October), 108.
            Capsule survey and review of Louisiana Story at
        Edinburgh Film Festival.

134   HATCH, ROBERT. "Louisiana Story." The New Republic
        (11 October), pp. 30-31.
            Rather unfavorable review which concludes that the film
        is neither a satisfactory lyric nor a convincing documenta-
        tion of progress and change.

135   KIPLING, RUDYARD. "Toomai of the Elephants," in his The
        Jungle Book, Vol. 2. Garden City: Doubleday, pp. 145-172
        (1st pub. 1895).
            This short story was the basis for the Flaherty-Korda
        film Elephant Boy.

*136   LOSEY, MARY. "Louisiana Story." Documentary 1948. London:
        Albyn Press.
             Cited by Henri Agel. See entry 257.

137   _____. "More Seeing, Less Selling." Saturday Review,
        (9 October), pp. 61-63.
             A favorable notice of Louisiana Story as an example of
        the improvement of sponsored films, which are beginning to
        serve the audiences.

138   ROULLET, SERGE. "Louisiana Story: nouveau film de Flaherty."
        La revue du cinéma, No. 12 (April), pp. 37-41.
             A favorable review of Flaherty's film with an explanation
        of its more superficial thematic elements.

*139   STERNFELD, FREDERICK. "Louisiana Story." Film Music Notes,
        7, No. 1 (September-October).
             Cited by Manvell and Huntley. See entry 221.

140   WEINBERG, HERMANN. "Louisiana Story and Melody Time." Sight
        and Sound, 17, No. 67 (Autumn), 119.
             With oil considered a force of nature, thus Flaherty
        answers his critics who have held that the theme of man
        versus nature was almost an anachronism in the modern world
        of technological progress.

*141   WRIGHT, BASIL. "Louisiana Story." Program of the Second
        International Festival of Documentary Films, Edinburgh
        (28 August).
             Cited by Woltgang Klaue. See entry 254.

142   _____. The Use of the Film. London: The Bodley Head.
        Reprinted by Arno Press, 1972, 72 pp.
             Written by a Flaherty scholar, this is a handbook on
        film from production to distribution with a special emphasis
        on the documentary though other types of films are covered.

                                    1949

*143   ALBERTINI, LAURA and MARIA PIA CARUSO. "Proiezione e
        interpretazione di immagini cinematografiche nei ragazzi:
        un esperimento con Nanook di Flaherty." Bianco e Nero,
        No. 5 (May).
             Cited by Paolo Gobetti. See entry 243.

*144   ANON. "Over the Magazine Editor's Desk." Christian Science
        Monitor Magazine (15 January).
             Cited by Mary Mainwaring. See entry 210.

*145   BESSY, MAURICE. "Robert Flaherty." Cinemonde (31 October).
          Cited by Mary Mainwaring. See entry 210.

*146   BROCHARD, A. "Louisiana Story--ou le don de la poésie."
          Le Peuple (Brussels).
          Cited by Wolfgang Klaue. See entry 254.

*147   CAMPASSI, OSVALDO. "Nanook of the North." Cinema (Rome),
          No. 18 (15 July).
          Cited by Henri Agel. See entry 257.

148   CARANCINI, GAETANO. "Louisiana Story." Bianco e Nero, No. 4
          (April), pp. 86-87.
          A favorable review in which the critic recognizes the
continuity of Flaherty's work, stressing the theme that
Flaherty is only comfortable with people in a primordial
state. Things of the city and the industrial world corrode
humanity. Flaherty makes no concessions to what is fashionable in cinema. Each scene reveals his style, creating
a climate of pure poetry.

*149   CARRIERE, PAUL. "Louisiana Story." Le Figaro (28 October).
          Cited by Mary Mainwaring. See entry 210.

150   CHARENSOL, G. "Louisiana Story." Les Nouvelles Litteraires
          (3 November), p. 4.
          To portray his subjects effectively Flaherty makes
them familiar and fraternal. Stresses unity of Flaherty's
work.

151   FOSTER, INEZ WHITELEY. "Partners and Pioneers." Christian
          Science Monitor Magazine (15 January), p. 5.
          A brief biographical article on Flaherty's career,
especially the role of his wife Frances, and their settling
down in Vermont.

*152   GOBETTI, PAOLO. "Robert Flaherty e il lirismo della camera."
          Cinema (Rome), No. 24 (October).
          Cited by Henri Agel. See entry 257.

153   JEANDER, M. "Louisiana Story." Liberation (Paris)
          (2 November), p. 4.
          Favorable review in which the writer sees conflicts as
old as humanity and as new as industrialization balanced
against one another.

154   LAFARGNE, ANDRÉ. "Louisiana Story." Ce Matin
          (29-30 October), p. 2.
          Sees love of nature as consistent theme in Flaherty's
work, and man in his naturalness threatened by civilization.

*155   MANVELL, ROGER. "Louisiana Story." <u>Records of the Film</u>,
           No. 18. London: British Film Institute.
              Cited by Wolfgang Klaue. <u>See</u> entry 254.

*156   NERY, JEAN. "Louisiana Story." <u>L'Ecran Francais</u>, No. 226
           (31 October).
              Cited by Wolfgang Klaue. <u>See</u> entry 254.

 157   REGENT, ROGER. "Robert Flaherty pour qui le cinema est une
           autre exploration." <u>L'Ecran Francais</u>, No. 226 (31 October),
           pp. 1-3.
              Cited by Henri Agel. <u>See</u> entry 257.

 158   TAYLOR, ROBERT LEWIS. "Profile of Flaherty." <u>New Yorker</u>
           (11, 18, and 25 June). <u>See also</u> his chapter "Flaherty-
           Education for Wanderlust," in his <u>The Running Pianist</u>.
           Garden City, New York: Doubleday, 1950, pp. 116-164.
              A major piece of biographical writing to bring Flaherty
           to the attention of the literary-minded public. Early edu-
           cation and experiences and anecdotes retold in lively
           style. Unfortunately does not use too many dates and many
           of the stories cannot be substantiated. But Flaherty was
           interviewed for these articles and he did not refute them.

                               1950

 159   ANON. "The Titan." <u>Time</u> (30 January), p. 84.
              Background story and favorable notice of this film.

 160   BROWN, JOHN MASON. "The Camera Creative." <u>Saturday Review</u>
           (25 March), pp. 26-28.
              Favorable review of <u>The Titan</u>.

*161   CECCHI, EMILIO. "Tabu." <u>Sequenze</u>, No. 9 (May).
              Cited by Paolo Gobetti. <u>See</u> entry 243.

*162   ECKARDT, J. "Robert Flaherty." <u>Film, Bild, Funk</u> (Stuttgart),
           No. 2, pp. 9-10.
              Cited by Wolfgang Klaue. <u>See</u> entry 254.

 163   GRAY, HUGH. "Robert Flaherty and the Naturalistic Documen-
           tary." <u>Hollywood Quarterly</u>, 5, No. 1 (Fall), 41-48.
              A defense of Flaherty's work against the criticism that
           he did not describe a truthful way of life. Describes
           naturalistic documentary as a dramatic form which may ex-
           tract some aspect of life from the actual world though not
           purely in a representational manner.

 164   HATCH, ROBERT. "Movies (The Titan)." <u>The New Republic</u>
           (30 January), p. 31.

                               131

A favorable notice of The Titan which recognizes the dramatic ability of the camera to present Michelangelo's masterpieces as fresh discoveries. The camera lets us vicariously experience the grandeur of his monuments.

*165   KRISHNASWAMY, M. V. "Louisiana Story." Fiche Filmographique (IDHEC-Paris), No. 42.
         Cited by Wolfgang Klaue. See entry 254.

166   LORD, RUSSELL and KATE, eds. and illus. Forever the Land: A Country Chronicle and Anthology. New York: Harper and Brothers, 394 pp.
         Based on the 1941 article in The Land (see entry 111), Lord describes Flaherty's character and his reaction to his "newly discovered America" after an absence of nine years. Also contains an earlier narrative script of The Land which is close to but not the same as the final version (pp. 29-36).

*167   PANDOLFI, VITO. "Documentare a lotta per la vita." Cinema, No. 52 (15 December).
         A discussion of The Land cited by Paolo Gobetti. See entry 243.

168   PICHEL, IRVING. "Stills in Motion." Hollywood Quarterly, 5, No. 1 (Fall), 8-13.
         Uses The Titan as a point of departure on the ability of the motion picture camera to create its own kind of motion from the still objects in the film. The camera and the process of editing add their own movement to Michelangelo's work.

169   ROBERTSON, E. ARNOT. "Louisiana Story," in The Cinema 1950. Harmondsworth: Penguin Books, pp. 98-102.
         A favorable review of a film described as typical Flaherty subject matter; especially appreciative of music. The oil crewmen do not stand up well as actors, but the boy is charming and convincing.

1951

170   ANON. Sight and Sound. "Flaherty in Review." 21, No. 2 (November-December), 70-71.
         Extracts from reviews of Flaherty films.

171   CASTELLO, GIULIO CESARE. "E'morto un poeta." Bianco e Nero, No. 7 (July), pp. 61-62.
         A eulogy to Flaherty, one of the few poets of the cinema; he remained pure and intransigent, free of the demeaning compromises demanded by the commercial industry. Louisiana Story was made at the height of his powers and represented the harmonization of two worlds.

*172 CHIARINI, LUIGI. "Significato di Flaherty." Cinema, No. 68
    (15 August).
        Cited by Paolo Gobetti. See entry 243.

173 FLAHERTY, FRANCES. "The Flaherty Way." Saturday Review
    (13 September), p. 50.
        How the eye and experience of the explorer enhanced the
    work of her husband.

174 GRIERSON, JOHN. "Flaherty as Innovator." Sight and Sound,
    21, No. 2 (October-December), 64-68.
        Sums up the major technical and aesthetic accomplish-
    ments of Flaherty, including his influence on the British
    documentary movement and on Grierson himself.

175 _____. "On Robert Flaherty." The Reporter, 5, No. 8
    (16 October), 31-35.
        A general summing up of Flaherty's life and art with
    some principal themes and motifs. Flaherty's influence on
    the British school; the differences between his poetic work
    and the social-propagandist filmmakers.

176 _____. "Robert Flaherty: An Appreciation." New York Times
    (29 July).
        A shorter version of Grierson's tribute in The Reporter.

177 KNIGHT, ARTHUR. "A Flaherty Festival." Saturday Review
    (6 January), pp. 27-28.
        On the occasion of a Flaherty retrospective at the
    Museum of Modern Art, Knight summarizes the Flaherty
    method, finding a great deal of unity in the way that each
    film was made; he calls them "camera explorations--explora-
    tions in human geography."

*178 LANOCITA, ARTURO. "Un poeta della lontananza: Flaherty, voce
    spenta." La Biennale, No. 5 (August).
        Cited by Paolo Gobetti. See entry 243.

179 MANVELL, ROGER and R. K. NEILSON BAXTER, eds. The Cinema.
    London: Penguin Books, 224 pp.
        An anthology which contains Helen Van Dongen's "Three
    Hundred and Fifty Cans of Film," pp. 56-78. See entry 188.

*180 M.T.L. "Gli uomini hanno fame mella terra de Flaherty."
    Cinema, No. 73 (November).
        An article on The Land cited by Paolo Gobetti. See
    entry 243.

*181 PANDOLFI, VITO. "Omaggio a Flaherty." Cinema, No. 71
    (1 October).
        Cited by Paolo Gobetti. See entry 243.

*182 PATALAS, ENNO. "Realist, Romantiker, Revolutionar--Leben und Werk von Robert Flaherty." Film Forum No. 1, pp. 8-11. Cited by Wolfgang Klaue. See entry 254.

183 SADOUL, GEORGES. "Hommage a Robert Flaherty." Les Lettres francaises, No. 379 (13 September), p. 6.
A general appreciation of Flaherty's major films. Sees Man of Aran as least satisfying because of its academic rigidity. Describes Flaherty as a victim of Hollywood.

184 SAMMIS, EDWARD. "Flaherty at Abbeville." Sight and Sound, 21, No. 2 (October-December), 68-70.
Personal, anecdotal description of location shooting on Louisiana Story.

185 SCHERER, MAURICE (pseud. Eric Rohmer). "Vanité que la Peinture." Cahier du Cinéma, 1, No. 3 (June), 22-29.
Compares painting and filmmaking, pointing out the number of choices available to the artist. Nanook of the North emerges as the first document to achieve the dignity of art. The beauty of man's struggle emerges from the Eskimo's daily routine.

186 STARR, CECILE. "The Film Forum: Documentary Masterpiece." Saturday Review (6 January), p. 28.
Belated review of sound version of Nanook of the North for 16 mm distribution purposes.

*187 TOEPLITZ, JERZY. "Robert Flaherty." Kwartalnik Filmowy (Warsaw), No. 3 (April).
Cited by Wolfgang Klaue. See entry 254.

188 VAN DONGEN, HELEN. "Three Hundred and Fifty Cans of Film," in Cinema 1951. London: Penguin Books, pp. 57-78.
The problems of editing Louisiana Story are discussed, such as working with non-professional actors, lack of a detailed script or continuity, the arrangement of shots for meaning, maintaining a point of view, and improvisation. Her advice is applicable for many film productions. Avoids the difficulties she had with Flaherty. Makes the production seem harmonious.

*189 VINCENT, CARL. "Robert Flaherty, 1' uomo e l'opera." Ferrania, No. 11 (November).
Cited by Paolo Gobetti. See entry 243.

190 WALD, MARVIN. "1950's Best Short Documentaries." Films in Review, 2, No. 6 (June-July), 11-14.
A survey of American and British documentaries submitted for Oscar nominations and awards.

191   WEINBERG, HERMAN G. "A Farewell to Flaherty." Films in
      Review, 2 (October), 14-16. Reprinted in his Saint Cinema:
      Selected Writings 1929-1970. New York: DBS Publications,
      1970, pp. 109-112.
          Weinberg recounts his last social meeting with Flaherty.

192   WRIGHT, BASIL. "The Documentary Dilemma." Hollywood Quarterly,
      No. 4, pp. 321-325.
          There are difficulties of sponsorship for documentary
      film but he sees hope in the United Nations.

                              1952

193   DICK, OLIVER LAWSON (deviced and written by). "Portrait of
      Robert Flaherty." BBC Broadcast, 2 September. Produced
      by W. R. Rodgers.
          A recorded radio tribute by Flaherty's friends and
      acquaintances in Britain.

194   GROMO, MARIO. Robert Flaherty: Nota biografica, filmografia
      e bibliografia... Parma: Edizione Guanda. 63 pp.
          A critical appreciation of Flaherty's contribution to
      film art such as personal integrity and a fierce independ-
      ence which made few concessions to popular tastes and com-
      mercial demands. Although he followed realism, his act of
      choosing images was an expression of his own poetic feel-
      ings. Also contains a biographical essay, film credits
      with a few lines about each film.

195   HUSTON, JOHN. "Regarding Flaherty." Sequence, No. 14,
      pp. 17-18.
          A personal reminiscence by the well-known director and
      friend of Flaherty; includes Flaherty's story telling; his
      "wonderful ways with primitive people"; and an incident with
      a mugger in which Flaherty saved the day.

196   KEMPE, FRITZ. "Robert Flaherty und seine Film." Film Bild
      Ton (Munich), No. 9 (December), pp. 311-314.
          History and background of five Flaherty films: Nanook
      of the North, Tabu, Man of Aran, Elephant Boy, and Louisiana
      Story.

197   MANVELL, ROGER. "Robert Flaherty," in Manvell and R. K.
      Nelson Baxter's, eds., The Cinema 1952. London: Pelican,
      pp. 126-129.
          Placed among the founders of the cinema, Eisenstein
      and Griffith, Flaherty's great gift to the film remains
      his observation of human expression; he patiently observed
      and photographed his subjects so that the smallest char-
      acteristics of movement and expression should not escape
      the screen. See entry 340.

                              135

198   ROTHA, PAUL. <u>Documentary Film</u>. In collaboration with Sinclair
       Road and Richard Griffith. New York and London: Hastings
       House Publishers, 1952 ed.; first published in 1935.
            This standard history of documentary film contains a
       favorable description of Flaherty's work but is critical
       of his method due to his lack of social awareness. Flaherty
       is placed squarely in the "Romantic Tradition," which Rotha
       essentially debunks. The best discussion is on <u>Nanook of
       the North</u>.

199   STARR, CECILE. "The Film Forum." <u>Saturday Review</u> (23 August),
       p. 34.
            Brief notice review of <u>The Titan</u>, which, according to
       Starr, at times becomes contrived and melodramatic.

                              1953

200   FLAHERTY, FRANCES. "How <u>Man of Aran</u> Came into Being." <u>Film
       News</u>, 13, No. 3, pp. 4-6.
            This is mostly on the making and shooting of the storm
       sequence. Provides some insight into Flaherty's way of
       working and how he was able to persuade his "cast" to per-
       form in front of the camera.

201   FREUCHEN, PETER. <u>The Vagrant Viking</u>. New York: Julian
       Messner, 422 pp.
            The famous explorer describes his first encounter with
       Robert Flaherty. Many of his experiences in the North
       paralleled Flaherty's.

202   GEORGE, GEORGE L. "The World of Robert Flaherty." <u>Film News</u>,
       13, No. 4, p. 19.
            A review of Richard Griffith's biography of Flaherty
       (<u>see</u> entry 203), which is called a faithful evocation of a
       sensitive craftsman.

203   GRIFFITH, RICHARD. <u>The World of Robert Flaherty</u>. New York
       and Boston: Duell, Sloan & Pearce, 165 pp. Reprinted
       1970 by Greenwood Press, Westport, Conn.
            Considered the major study of Robert Flaherty for many
       years, this book is more an anthology than a consistent
       scholarly study. The chapter on <u>Nanook of the North</u> con-
       sists mostly of extracts from Flaherty's diaries and notes,
       later embellished in his novels. He skips over the funda-
       mental dichotomy with Grierson's approach to documentary
       film and does not mention <u>Industrial Britain</u> as well as
       other projects. The chapter on the making of <u>Elephant Boy</u>
       consists of extracts from Frances Flaherty's book <u>Elephant
       Dance</u>; the chapter on <u>Man of Aran</u> consists of extracts from
       Pat Mullen's book <u>Man of Aran</u>. Griffith does not cite

exact sources, provides no analysis of films as such, and leaves large gaps in between films. Robert Flaherty read the bulk of the manuscript before his death and it was evidently approved by Frances and David Flaherty. It is not a critical study, though the reviews it received were fairly favorable.

204 LEE, ROHAMA. "Flaherty's Finest Film." Film News, 13, No. 3, pp. 4-5.
    A discussion of the making of Man of Aran. Defends the shark fishing sequence as indicative of the spirit of the Aran Islanders though not truly representative of their way of life.

205 REISZ, KAREL and GAVIN MILLER. The Technique of Film Editing. New York: Farrar, Stauss; 1968 rev. ed. London and New York: Focal Press and Hastings House. See Chapter 8: "Imaginative Documentary," pp. 135-155.
    This is a technical and aesthetic discussion of the editing of Louisiana Story consisting primarily of Helen Van Dongen's close analysis. Particular attention is paid to the film's opening sequence and to the oil drilling sequence. Shot lists are included. Van Dongen explains the meaning of many shots, the emotional statement they conveyed. Her advice is both practical and informative. See also Van Dongen's "350 Cans of Film" (entry 188).

*206 SCHEIN, HARRY. "Robert Flaherty, och dokumentarfilmen." Dagens Nyheter (15 August).
    Cited by Wolfgang Klaue. See entry 254.

207 SCHERER, MAURICE [pseud. Eric Rohmer]. "La Revanche de L'Occident." Cahier du Cinema, 4, No. 21 (March), 46-47.
    Includes the interesting argument that in Tabu, Murnau revenged Western Art by imposing traditional European imagery over the revolutionary concepts of Gauguin.

208 WYNKIP, M. H. "The Flaherty Memorial." Films in Review, 4, No. 2 (February), 105-106.
    A description of a Museum of Modern Art tribute to Robert Flaherty in which many of his friends and acquaintances participated.

1954

*209 CHEVALIER, J. "Louisiana Story." Image et Son (October).
    Cited by Henri Agel. See entry 257.

210 MAINWARING, MARY LOUISE. "Robert Flaherty's Films and Their Critics." Ph.D. dissertation, Indiana University, 219 pp.

Mainly a summary and paraphrasing of newspaper reviews
of Flaherty's films. Good bibliography of newspaper references, domestic and foreign.

211   MAURIAC, CLAUDE. "Le cinéma de la decouverte: Robert
      Flaherty," in his L'Amour du cinéma. Paris: Editions
      Albin Michel, pp. 163-168.
         Broad interpretation of Tabu which sees more Flaherty
      influence than most other critics and an appreciation of
      the poetic aspects of Louisiana Story.

212   STELLA, VITTORIO. "Flaherty, Clouzot, DeSica, Rossellini."
      Bianco e Nero, 3, No. 4 (April), 47-53.
         Includes a review of Mario Gromo's Robert Flaherty.
      See entry 194.

                              1955

*213 AGEL, HENRI. "Precis d'imitation: Louisiana Story." Fiche
      Filmographique. Paris: Editions l'Ecole.
         Cited by Henri Agel. See entry 257.

214   BARDET, FRANCOIS. "Man of Aran." Fiche Filmographique,
      Paris: Editions d'Ecole.
         Criticizes the lack of sociological sensibility in
      Flaherty's work.

215   MANVELL, ROGER. "Louisiana Story," in The Film and the Public.
      Harmondsworth: Penguin Books, pp. 170-173.
         A good deal of description with many words of praise for
      the photography, editing, and music. Sees the film as
      firmly rooted in the Flaherty tradition and explores some
      of the symbols that appear in the film.

                              1956

*216 A. F. "Pionier der Leinwand--Flaherty Werk als Sprache des
      Menschen." Berlin Telegraf (22 July).
         Cited by Wolfgang Klaue. See entry 254.

*217 GREMILLON, JEAN. "Robert Flaherty: A la trace de L'homme."
      Cinema, 2, Nos. 9 and 10 (October).
         Cited by Wolfgang Klaue. See entry 254.

218   STARR, CECILE. "Ideas on Film: Film Seminar in Vermont."
      Saturday Review (13 October), pp. 32-33.
         Describes objectives of the Flaherty Seminars: an ex-
      ploration of his world, seeing his films, talking with
      those who worked with him, and exchanging ideas about his
      methods.

1957

219 CBS News (Television). "Odyssey: The World of Robert
     Flaherty."
          Produced in cooperation with the Museum of Modern Art
     and broadcast on 17 February 1957. Producer: Charles
     Romine. Lilian Gish, Fred Zinnemann, Oliver St. John
     Gogarty, and Peter Freuchen offer their reminiscences
     matched against excerpts from Flaherty films. Script
     property of CBS Inc.

220 MANVELL, ROGER. "Robert Flaherty, Geographer." The Geograph-
     ical Magazine, 39, No. 10 (February), 491-500.
          Describes Flaherty as the first to put film to the ser-
     vice of geography in the sense of understanding man's
     intimate relationship with his environment. A general re-
     view of Flaherty's filmmaking career with reference to this
     theme.

221 MANVELL, ROGER and JOHN HUNTLEY. The Technique of Film Music.
     London and New York: The Focal Press, pp. 99-109. Re-
     printed 1967.
          Contains an analysis of Virgil Thomson's score for
     Louisiana Story. First seven shots are described in rela-
     tion to the music. Score is printed.

*222 MARCEAU, J. P. "Louisiana Story." Fiche Filmographique,
     No. 294. Also in Tele-Cine, No. 64 (March).
          Cited by Wolfgang Klaue. See entry 254.

                              1958

*223 BOLESLAW, MICHALEK. "Die Rolle der Kamera für die Dramaturgie
     der Filme Robert Flahertys." Reprinted in Wolfgang Klaue,
     comp., Robert Flaherty. Berlin: Henschelverlag, 1964,
     pp. 50-59.

                              1959

224 ANON. "Robert Flaherty." Bianco e Nero, 20, Nos. 8-10
     (August-October), 109-115.
          For Man of Aran and Elephant Boy, both of which won
     prizes at Venice Film Festivals, this listing includes
     credits, synopses, and numerous extracts from Italian
     reviews.

225 BACHMANN, GIDEON. "Bob." Film, No. 21 (September-October),
     pp. 23-27.
          Several film figures discuss Flaherty and his work.

                              139

*226 BEHER, HANJAKOB. "Robert J. Flaherty." <u>Der Filmberater</u>,
        No. 11 (June), pp. 85-88.
            Cited by Wolfgang Klaue. <u>See</u> entry 254.

227   CALLENBACH, ERNEST. "The Understood Antagonist and Other
        Observations." <u>Film Quarterly</u>, 12, No. 4 (Summer), 16-23.
            Discusses the structure and appeal of documentary films.
        With reference to Flaherty, Callenbach sees his major films
        as organized and structured around conflict.

228   CARPENTER, EDMUND, ed. <u>Anerca: Drawings by Enooesweetok</u>.
        Toronto: J. M. Dent and Sons, unpaginated.
            Drawings collected by Flaherty at Amadjnak Bay, 1913-
        1914, with Eskimo poetry selected by Carpenter. 1915 edi-
        tion first published by Flaherty under the title <u>The
        Drawings of Enooesweetok of the Sikosilingmiut Tribe of
        the Eskimo</u>.

229   _____. <u>Eskimo</u>. With Frederick Varley and Robert Flaherty.
        Toronto: University of Toronto Press, unpaginated.
            Text by Carpenter discusses Eskimo perception of the
        world with reference to artistic expression in their daily
        lives. Painting by Varley and sketches and photographs of
        Flaherty's collection of Eskimo carvings.

230   FLAHERTY, DAVID. "A Few Reminiscences." <u>Film Culture</u>, 20,
        No. 2, pp. 14-16.
            Flaherty's brother describes his collaboration with
        Murnau on the making of <u>Tabu</u>. Both Robert Flaherty and
        Murnau are portrayed as rebels against Hollywood. Murnau
        held purse strings on <u>Tabu</u>. He sees little Flaherty in-
        fluence in the final product.

231   FLAHERTY, FRANCES. "Explorations," in <u>Film Book I: The Audi-
        ence and the Filmmaker</u>. Edited by Robert Hughes. New York:
        Grove Press, pp. 61-65.
            Flaherty's major films contain the same theme--the spirit
        by which a people comes to terms with its environment.
        Describes "nonpreconception" as fundamental to the Flaherty
        method. Let the camera discover life; let it lead the
        search for truth.

232   _____. "Flaherty's Quest for Life." <u>Films and Filming</u>, 5,
        No. 4 (January), 8.
            The technique, philosophy, and making of <u>Nanook of the
        North</u>. Adapted from a recording of her lecture at the
        National Film Theatre.

233   GRIFFITH, RICHARD. "Flaherty and Tabu." <u>Film Culture</u>, No. 20,
        pp. 12-13.

The disagreement with Murnau and Flaherty on the production of <u>Tabu</u>. Flaherty was interested in the theme of the impact of Western Civilization on primitive culture for some time, but he rejected the romanticization imposed on the natural setting.

234 HUGHES, ROBERT, ed. <u>Film: Book I, The Audience and the Film-maker</u>. New York: Grove Press, 158 pp.
An anthology which contains Frances Flaherty's "Explorations" (<u>see</u> entry 231), and Charles Siepmann's "Robert Flaherty: The Man and the Filmmaker" (<u>see</u> entry 238).

235 MURNAU, F. W. and ROBERT FLAHERTY. "Tabu, A Story of the South Seas." <u>Film Culture</u>, No. 20, pp. 27-38.
<u>See</u> entry 341.

236 . "Turia, An Original Story." <u>Film Culture</u>, No. 20, pp. 17-26.
<u>See</u> entry 342.

237 ROTHA, PAUL and BASIL WRIGHT. "Flaherty Biography." Unpublished typescript, approx. 500 pp. Copies deposited in the Museum of Modern Art and in the "Flaherty Papers," Columbia University, Butler Library, New York City.
An admirable study that covers biographical and critical aspects of Flaherty's work written from the point of view of two filmmakers and scholars. Significant judgmental differences with the Calder-Marshall adaptation of the manuscript, which also largely excluded the critical reception owing to the wishes of the publisher. It is strongest on British aspects and weakest on the American, especially pertaining to <u>The Land</u>. Continental criticism mostly ignored and presumably not updated since 1959. A most authoritative work, however.

238 SIEPMANN, CHARLES R. "Robert Flaherty--The Man and the Filmmaker," in <u>Film Book No. 1: The Audience and The Filmmaker</u>. Edited by Robert Hughes. New York: Grove Press, pp. 66-75.
A description of Flaherty's personality as a key to understanding his work. Portrayed as a rebel against urbanization, conformity, and Hollywood.

1960

239 CAVALCANTI, ALBERTO. "Aus der Geschichte des Dokumentarfilms im Westen." <u>Deutsche Film Kunst</u>, No. 11, pp. 377-378.
Cavalcanti argues that the documentary form has been taken over by the media for advertising purposes, betraying Flaherty's intention of presenting the real world to a wide audience. Although the feature film has adopted some of

the documentary's techniques, reality is rarely achieved
Compares Flaherty to Chaplin, Griffith, and Eisenstein in
the aesthetic experience of film art.

240 DAVIS, GARY L. "Tabu." Film Heritage, 1, No. 3 (Spring),
35-37.
Program notes and review.

241 FARZANET, E. "Le film ethnographique."
Paper presented to the Institut des hautes etudes
cinematographique (IDHEC).

242 FLAHERTY, FRANCES (HUBBARD). The Odyssey of a Film-Maker:
Robert Flaherty's Story. Urbana, Illinois: Beta Phi Mu,
45 pp. Reprinted by Arno Press, 1972.
Discusses nonpreconception as Flaherty's method of
discovery. Discusses only Nanook of the North, Moana,·
Man of Aran, and Louisiana Story. A sweeping, panegyrical
tribute to her husband.

243 GOBETTI, PAOLO. "Robert Flaherty," in Quaderni Mensili di
documentazione cinematografica. Turin: Centrofilm.
Contains a European-oriented bibliography.

244 KRACAUER, SIEGFRIED. Theory of Film: The Redemption of
Physical Reality. New York: Oxford University Press,
364 pp.
Discussion of Flaherty for the most part can be found
in Chapter 11, "The Film of Fact," pp. 193ff., and Chapter
14, "The Found Story and The Episode," pp. 245ff.

245 QUINTAR, FUAD. Robert Flaherty et le Documentaire Poetique:
Etudes Cinematographiques No. 5. Paris, 318 pp.
A general interpretation of the poetry and visual style
in Flaherty's principal films. Defends Flaherty against
the materialist-sociological approach to documentary in
favor of the pantheistic mysticism in Flaherty's world and
the mystery of creation; a bio-filmography.

1961

246 STANBROOK, ALAN. "Louisiana Story." Films and Filming, 8,
No. 3 (December), 20-22, 42.
A critical discussion which sees the basic theme in the
film as a conflict between Cajun life and civilization.
Flaherty implies that they both can bring good to another
although his sympathies are with the Cajun boy. Stanbrook
felt the celebrated opening sequence was too rapid for the
tranquil atmosphere.

1962

247 DE HEUSCH, LUC. The Cinema and Social Science: A survey of
     ethnographic and sociological films. Paris: UNESCO.
     101 pp.
          Argues that Flaherty's films do have value for the study
     of ethnography. Flaherty brought artistic integrity to
     observation and made the camera participate in the film-
     making process. Flaherty discussed pp. 35-39.

*248 TURCONI, DAVIDE. "Il film proibito di Flaherty." Bianco e
     Nero, No. 2, pp. 23-33.
          An article on The Land, cited by Wolfgang Klaue. See
     entry 254.

1963

249 CALDER-MARSHALL, ARTHUR. The Innocent Eye: The Life of
     Robert J. Flaherty. Based on research material by Paul
     Rotha and Basil Wright. London: W. H. Allen; Baltimore:
     Pelican Books, 1970.
          Adaptation of the Rotha-Wright manuscript, see entry 237.

250 CLEMENTE, JOSE L. Robert Flaherty. Madrid: Ediciones Rialp.
     115 pp.
          Book-length Spanish introduction to Flaherty's major
     films. Little or no new factual information. Brief inter-
     pretation of their achievements. Argues against social
     critics: not appeared to be concerned with authenticity.
     Describes Flaherty's role as an artist searching for the
     essence of life.

*251 FERNANDEZ CUENCA, CARLOS. Robert Flaherty. Madrid: Filmoteca
     Nacional de Espana. 61 pp.
          Cited in the Catalog of the Book Library of the British
     Film Institute. Boston: G. K. Hall.

252 SARRIS, ANDREW. "Pantheon Directors; Filmography." Film Cul-
     ture, No. 28 (Spring). Reprinted and revised in his The
     American Cinema: Directors and Directions 1929-1968. New
     York: E. P. Dutton, pp. 42-43.
          Notable that Flaherty is included among the "pantheon"
     of feature film directors.

1964

*253 BERNARDINI, ALDO. "Robert J. Flaherty--una testimonianza di
     autentica umanita nel cinema." Milan Letture (March).
          Cited by Wolfgang Klaue. See entry 254.

143

254   KLAUE, WOLFGANG, comp. <u>Robert Flaherty</u>. Berlin (East):
        Henschelverlag, 300 pp.
           An important anthology of writings relating to Flaherty
        translated in German. Includes general critical articles,
        a selection of his writings, and critical and background
        material relating to specific films. The extensive bib-
        liography includes numerous references to European news-
        paper items on Flaherty.

*255   LEYDA, JAY. "Das Flaherty-Erbe," in <u>Robert Flaherty</u>. Com-
        piled by Wolfgang Klaue. Berlin (East): Henschelverlag,
        pp. 46-49.

*256   TOEPLITZ, JERZY. "Die Schopferische Methode von Robert
        Flaherty," in <u>Robert Flaherty</u>. Compiled by Wolfgang Klaue.
        Berlin (East): Henschelverlag, pp. 7-22.

1965

257   AGEL, HENRI. <u>Robert J. Flaherty</u>. Paris: Editions Seghers.
        192 pp.
           A critical study of Flaherty's major films. Most bio-
        graphical data taken from Griffith whom he rather liberally
        quotes. An extreme personal reading of Flaherty films.
        Extracts of critical writing appended to book. Good French
        and Italian bibliography.

258   ENGLE, HARRISON. "Thirty Years of Social Inquiry." <u>Film Com-</u>
        <u>ment</u> (Spring). Reprinted in Jacobs (<u>see</u> entry 275),
        pp. 343-360.
           An interview with Willard Van Dyke.

259   MARTIN, MARCEL. "Robert Flaherty." <u>Anthologie du Cinema</u>.
        Paris: L'Avant-Scene du Cinema, Vol. 1, pp. 121-172.
        Reprinted in part in Agel (<u>see</u> entry 257), pp. 153-156.
           Refutes social critics by arguing that a dialectic
        vision of the world conflicts with Flaherty's sense of
        pure imagery.

260   VAN DONGEN, HELEN. "Robert J. Flaherty, 1884-1951." <u>Film</u>
        <u>Quarterly</u>, 18, No. 4 (Summer), 2-14.
           Describes the personal and aesthetic conflicts in work-
        ing with Flaherty on <u>The Land</u> and <u>Louisiana Story</u>. De-
        scribes his method of work, his feelings, and his
        compulsions. Explains her own role in structuring film;
        she achieves a fine balance between her own feelings as an
        artist and Flaherty's control as a director. One of the
        more important articles on Flaherty.

1966

261   FLAHERTY, DAVID. "Poet of the Cinema." Columbia Library
        Columns, 15, No. 2 (February), 3-12.
              Written on the occasion of depositing the "Flaherty
        Papers" in the Butler Library of Columbia University, a
        short narrative by Flaherty's brother on the making of
        Robert Flaherty's major films and his contributions to
        "cinematic art."

262   PRATT, GEORGE C. Spellbound in Darkness: A History of the
        Silent Film. New York: New York Graphic Society (Revised
        ed. 1973), pp. 342-354.
              Contemporary reviews of Nanook of the North, an article
        by Frances Flaherty, and newspaper and feature articles on
        Robert Flaherty.

263   WEINBERG, HERMAN G. The Innocent Eye. Film Culture, No. 41
        (Summer), pp. 92-93.
              Favorable notice of Arthur Calder-Marshall's biography
        of Flaherty.

1967

264   BAZIN, ANDRE. What is Cinema?: Berkeley and Los Angeles:
        University of California Press, pp. 50-51.
              Essays selected and translated by Hugh Gray. Brief dis-
        cussion of seal hunting sequence in Nanook of the North
        and of the alligator sequence in Louisiana Story. Trans-
        lated from "The Virtues and Limitations of Montage,"
        Cahier du Cinema (1953 and 1957).

265   SADOUL, GEORGES. "A Flaherty Mystery." Cahier du Cinema in
        English, No. 11 (September), pp. 46-51.
              Louisiana Story as discovered through the personalities
        of Frances and Robert Flaherty.

266   THOMSON, VIRGIL. Virgil Thomson. London: Weidenfeld and
        Nicolson, pp. 393-394.
              The music critic and composer describes his contribution
        to the making of Louisiana Story for which he composed music
        sound track and score.

1968

267   LENNIG, ARTHUR. "Robert Flaherty," in Persistence of Vision:
        A Collection of Film Criticism. Edited by Joseph McBride.
        Madison: Wisconsin Film Society Press, pp. 179-184.

268 SNYDER, ROBERT L. Pare Lorentz and the Documentary Film.
     Norman: University of Oklahoma Press, pp. 131-140.
     Origin and production problems of The Land, based on
     Lorentz's personal papers, including letters written by
     Lorentz and Frances Flaherty. Writing consists largely of
     extracts and paraphrases in dissertation style. But no
     analysis of film, nor of production problems after the
     film was transferred from the U.S. Film Service to the
     Agricultural Adjustment Administration of the Department
     of Agriculture.

                              1969

269 JACOBS, LEWIS, ed. The Emergence of Film Art. New York:
     Hopkinson and Blake, Publishers, pp. 215-221.
     Contains Flaherty's article on Nanook, see entry 344.

                              1970

270 FONDILLER, HARVEY V. "Bob Flaherty Remembered." Popular
     Photography (March), pp. 98-102.
     Recaptures his first interview with Flaherty in October
     1948 in which they discussed cameras and camera work on the
     making of Nanook of the North and Louisiana Story. Rambles
     over Flaherty's career, emphasizing his personality.

                              1971

271 DARROW, WAYNE. "The Land." Unpublished memorandum dated
     8 October.
     Former AAA official recounts his experiences with
     Flaherty, filling in some gaps that cannot be found among
     the official records of AAA.

272 GEDULD, HARRY M., ed. Film Makers on Film Making.
     Bloomington: University of Indiana Press, pp. 56-64.
     Contains Robert Flaherty's "How I Filmed Nanook of the
     North," see entry 303.

273 HARDY, FORSYTH, ed. Grierson on Documentary. Praeger: New
     York, 411 pp., revised 1966.
     Contains an essay on the Flaherty method, background on
     Industrial Britain, and other writings. Essential for un-
     derstanding how Grierson's views compared with those of
     Flaherty's. A standard text, marred only by the lack of
     dates and unclear citations.

*274 ISSARI, M. ALI. "Robert Flaherty's Biofilmography." Cinema
     Verité, pp. 184-188.

275 JACOBS, LEWIS, comp. The Documentary Tradition: From Nanook
     to Woodstock. New York: Hopkinson and Blake, Publishers,
     530 pp.
          An excellent anthology of writings on documentary film
     by filmmakers, critics, and historians, arranged chrono-
     logically and introduced by Jacobs. See especially,
     Sherwood's review of Nanook of the North, pp. 15-19
     (entry 23); Ricciotto Canudo's essay "Another View of
     Nanook," pp. 20-21 (entry 46); Grierson's review "Flaherty's
     Poetic Moana," pp. 25-26 (entry 41); and an anonymous re-
     view of Stark Love and Moana, pp. 27-28 (entry 50);
     Flaherty's "Filming Real People," pp. 97-99 (entry 316);
     Meyer's "An Event: The Wave," pp. 118-122 (entry 94);
     Strauss's review "The Giant Shinnies Down the Beanstalk:
     Flaherty's The Land," pp. 197-199 (entry 113); and Clurman's
     "Flaherty's Louisiana Story," pp. 230-232 (entry 132). All
     of these articles are cited under their original dates of
     publication.

276 LEVIN, G. ROY. Documentary Explorations: 15 Interviews with
     Film-makers. Garden City, New York: Doubleday, 420 pp.
          Basil Wright and Richard Leacock discuss the Flaherty
     method.

277 LOW, RACHEL. History of the British Film. 1918-1929, Vol. 4.
     London: Allen & Unwin, 544 pp.
          This standard history contains a few scattered refer
     ences to Flaherty as his films affected British developments.

278 MUNDEN, KENNETH, ed. The American Film Institute Catalog of
     Motion Pictures Produced in the United States: Feature
     Films 1921-1930. New York and London: Bowker, 2 vols.
          Volume 1 contains synopses and production credits for
     Nanook of the North (p. 536), Moana (p. 519), and White
     Shadows in the South Seas (p. 895). Naively categorizes
     Moana as a "Travelog."

                              1972

279 BARNOUW, ERIK. "Robert Flaherty (Barnouw's File)." Film
     Culture, Nos. 53-55 (Spring), pp. 161-185.
          A file of correspondence between Flaherty and Barnouw's
     father on a proposed film in Bali, 1929; also financial
     details about Nanook of the North and Moana.

280 GRIECO, MARIE D. "Frances Hubbard Flaherty: A True Seer."
     Pamphlet, 15 pp.

Memorial tribute presented 29 August 1972, at the 18th
Annual Robert Flaherty Film Seminar, Brattleboro, Vermont.

281 LEACOCK, RICKY. "Remembering Frances Flaherty." Film Comment
(November-December), p. 39.
An affectionate memoir of Robert and Frances Flaherty.

282 MOULD, DAPHNE D. C. POUCHIN. The Aran Islands. London:
David Charles.
A popular introduction to the flora, fauna, geography,
and people of the Aran Islands. The references to Flaherty
are mostly taken from Pat Mullen's Man of Aran (see entry
92). A bibliography for more detailed reading is included.

283 WERNER, P. "Frances Flaherty: Hidden and Seeking." Film
Makers Newsletter, Nos. 9-10 (July-August), pp. 28-30.
The director of a film about Frances Flaherty tells how
it was made.

284 SIEPMANN, CHARLES A. "Robert Flaherty's Brief Career as a
Radio Announcer." Film Culture, Nos. 53-55 (Spring),
pp. 185-190.
Describes Flaherty's work with the BBC and includes a
response from Frances Flaherty and amplification by the
BBC, including a list of programs with dates.

1973

285 BARSAM, RICHARD MERAN. "The Humanistic Vision of Robert
Flaherty," in his Nonfiction Film: A Critical History.
New York: E. P. Dutton, pp. 124-159.
Largely based on Calder-Marshall's book (see entry 249)
for factual materials. Very much an interpretive reading
of Flaherty films from the viewpoint of the 1970s.

286 CORLISS, RICHARD. "Robert Flaherty: The Man in the Iron
Myth." Film Comment (November-December), pp. 38-42. Reprinted in Barsam (see entry 296), pp. 230-238.
A critical, impressionistic evaluation of Flaherty's
major films. Favors Nanook of the North and some aspects
of The Land. Dislikes direction of Flaherty's career toward
being a photographic technician and toward ornamentation.

287 EISNER, LOTTE H. Murnau. Berkeley: University of California
Press, 286 pp.
Argues that Murnau controlled the making of Tabu from
beginning to end and that the film was a valid extension of
his personality.

*288 HELMAN, A. "Robert Flaherty albo rytual odkrywania formy."
       Kino, 8, No. 3 (March), 62-64.
          "Nanook as seen from today's point of view with refer-
       ence to Bazin's theory of film." Cited in Karen Jones,
       International Index to Film Periodicals: 1973 (Interna-
       tional Federation of Film Archives [FIAF]). New York and
       London: St. Martin's and St. James Press. 1973.

289   ROTHA, PAUL. Documentary Diary: An Informal History of the
       British Documentary Film, 1928-1939. New York: Hill and
       Wang, 305 pp.
          Detailed discussion of the making of Industrial Britain
       (pp. 50-59) by the leading Flaherty scholar. References to
       Flaherty throughout book.

290   STAPLES, DONALD E., ed. The American Cinema (Voice of America
       Forum Series). Washington, D.C.: U.S. Information Agency,
       pp. 191-212.
          Hugh Gray interviewed by VOA correspondent Edwin Gordon
       on the subject "Father of the American Documentary." A
       general overview of Flaherty's work with a brief discussion
       of the making of his films and their themes. Several errors,
       the most glaring being the confusion of Nanook of the North
       for Moana in connection with Grierson's famous review coin-
       ing the term "documentary."

                              1974

291   ARMES, ROY. "Flaherty and the Idea of Documentary," in his
       Film and Reality: An Historical Survey. Baltimore:
       Penguin, pp. 30-37.
          A critical but superficial introduction to Flaherty's
       work; describes primarily Nanook of the North, Moana, and
       Man of Aran, based evidently on Calder-Marshall. "His work
       lights up certain of the basic issues of documentary," and
       concludes that Flaherty remained at heart an explorer, not
       a propagandist.

292   BARNOUW, ERIK. Documentary: A History of the Non-Fiction
       Film. New York: Oxford University Press, 332 pp.
          For Flaherty, the best discussion is on Nanook of the
       North (pp. 33 ff.); the other films (Man of Aran, pp. 97-
       99, and Louisiana Story, pp. 216-219) are briefly mentioned.
       Includes the biographical influences upon Flaherty's work,
       his relationship with Grierson, and his place in the his-
       torical development of documentary film. The book has be-
       come the standard historical survey of documentary film.

                              149

1975

293   NAPOLITANO, ANTONIO. <u>Robert J. Flaherty</u>. Florence: La Nuova
      Italia, 109 pp.
         A short history and interpretive guide to Flaherty's
      work. Does not cite sources of information except for some
      generous quotations.

294   SUSSEX, ELIZABETH. <u>The Rise and Fall of British Documentary:
      The Story of the Film Movement Founded by John Grierson</u>.
      Berkeley: University of California Press, 219 pp.
         A compilation of interviews with leading figures of
      British documentary. In "The Spell of Flaherty," pp. 23-24,
      they repeat what they have said in their writings, in more
      detail, of Flaherty's personality and of <u>Industrial Britain</u>.
      References to Flaherty throughout.

1976

295   ACHTENBERG, BEN. "Helen Van Dongen: An Interview." <u>Film
      Quarterly</u>, 30, No. 2 (Winter), 46-57.
         Traces Van Dongen's long career as an editor on what
      have become classics of the documentary genre and as a
      filmmaker in her own right. Assisted Joris Ivens for many
      years and Flaherty on <u>The Land</u> and <u>Louisiana Story</u>. She
      offers personal observations of Flaherty's character, how
      it influenced his art, and her own criticisms.

296   BARSAM, RICHARD, ed. <u>Nonfiction Film: Theory and Criticism</u>.
      New York: E. P. Dutton, 382 pp.
         Anthology of articles on "nonfiction" film. Contains
      Van Dongen's "Robert J. Flaherty, 1884-1951" (<u>see</u> entry
      260); and Corliss's "Robert Flaherty: The Man in the Iron
      Myth" (<u>see</u> entry 286).

297   EAGLE, ARNOLD. "Looking Back...at <u>The Pirogue Maker</u>, <u>Louisiana
      Story</u> and the Flaherty Way." <u>Film Library Quarterly</u>, 9,
      No. 1, pp. 28-37.
         The author was a still picture photographer with
      Flaherty during the making of <u>Louisiana Story</u>. Offers
      some anecdotes and insight into working with Flaherty.
      Explains origin of <u>The Pirogue Maker</u>, film for which
      Flaherty was given credit, posthumously.

298   HEIDER, KARL G. <u>Ethnographic Film</u>. Austin and London: Uni-
      versity of Texas Press, 166 pp.
         There are several references to Flaherty's films, <u>Nanook
      of the North</u> and <u>Moana</u>, throughout the book but most may be
      found on pp. 20-26. Heider acknowledges Flaherty's pio-
      neering contributions to ethnographic film and the use of

film for the study of cultural anthropology. Flaherty totally immersed himself in these cultures; however, his reconstructions detract from the ethnographic value. On the other hand, Flaherty's subjects participated in the filmmaking process.

299   ZINNEMANN, FRED. "Remembering Robert Flaherty." Action (May-June), pp. 25-27.
      Zinnemann was hired by Flaherty in 1930 to work on a possible film in the Soviet Union. Zinnemann recalls those days in Berlin waiting for permission to enter Russia.

Writings, Performances
and Other Film-Related Activity

1915

300   <u>The Drawings of Enooesweetok of the Sikosilingmiut Tribe of</u>
<u>the Eskimo</u>. Unpaginated. The drawings were collected by
Robert Flaherty at Amadjuak Bay, 1913–1914. Republished as:
<u>Anerca: Drawings by Enooesweetok</u>. Edited by Edmund
Carpenter. Toronto: J. M. Dent & Sons, 1959. Unpaginated.
<u>See</u> entry 228.
    Eskimo poetry selections added by Carpenter.

1918

301   "The Belcher Islands of Hudson Bay: "Their Discovery and Exploration." <u>Geographical Review</u>, 5, No. 6, pp. 433–458.
    Flaherty describes his discovery of a large land mass
that was previously thought to be just small islands.

302   "Two Traverses Across Ungava Peninsula, Labrador." <u>Geograph-</u>
<u>ical Review</u>, 6, No. 2, pp. 116–132.
    Flaherty describes his expedition of 1911 across an
unmapped wilderness.

1922

303   "How I Filmed Nanook of the North." <u>The World's Work</u>
(September), pp. 553–560. Reprinted in <u>Film Makers on Film</u>
<u>Making</u>. Edited by Harry M. Geduld. Bloomington: Indiana
University Press, 1971, pp. 56–64 (<u>see</u> entry 272).
    Discusses origin of <u>Nanook of the North</u>, major influ-
ences, and principal events during shooting.

304   "Indomitable Children of the North." <u>Travel</u>, 39, No. 4
(August), 16–20.
    Photographs of Eskimo life during the making of <u>Nanook</u>
<u>of the North</u> with lengthy captions presumably supplied by
Flaherty.

305   "Life Among the Eskimos." <u>The World's Work</u> (October),
          pp. 632-640.
              Describes the conditions of Eskimo life in Ungava, the
          filming of the igloo building sequence, whaling with Nanook,
          and praises the mechanical skill of Eskimos.

                                    1923

306   "Wetalltook's Islands." <u>The World's Work</u> (February),
          pp. 422-433.
              Narrates the origin of the Belcher Islands expedition on
          the suggestion of an Eskimo named Wetalltook.

307   "Winter on Wetalltook's Islands." <u>The World's Work</u> (March),
          pp. 538-553.
              Flaherty, in a tale of survival, tells how he finally
          reached the Belchers and of the winter he spent there.

                                    1924

308   <u>My Eskimo Friends</u>. Garden City, New York: Doubleday, Page,
          170 pp.
              In collaboration with Frances Hubbard Flaherty. Details
          of Flaherty's four principal expeditions to the Hudson Bay
          area and his fifth trip for the purpose of making the film
          <u>Nanook of the North</u>.

309   "Picture Making in the South Seas." <u>Film Daily Yearbook--1924</u>,
          pp. 9-13.
              Flaherty recounts his initial difficulty of adjusting to
          Samoan life, with its climate, pageantry, rituals, and
          festivals and his delicate confrontations with local cus-
          toms. Eventually he comes to respect and admire the Samoans.

                                    1928

310   "Acoma." 17 pp.
              Unpublished scenario of abortive film for Fox Studios
          dealing with the Acoma Indians of New Mexico; based on story
          by Randall H. Faye. "Flaherty Papers," Box 29, Columbia
          University.

                                    1931

*311   "Wie Tabu enstand." <u>Die Filmwoche</u> (Berlin) No. 22, pp. 690-691.
          Cited by Wolfgang Klaue. <u>See</u> entry 254.

*312 "Zum Amateurfilm schaffen." Film und Alle, 5, No. 5 (May),
      125.
           Cited by Wolfgang Klaue. See entry 254.

                              1932

313   Samoa. Berlin: R. Hobbing, 179 pp.
           Detailed account of the making of Moana, published in
      German. Discusses origin of film and search for purest ex-
      pression of Polynesian culture least influenced by white
      civilization. Based largely on Frances and David Flaherty's
      articles in Asia; see entries 30-34.

                              1934

314   "Account of Making the Film--Man of Aran." 23 pp. typescript.
           "Flaherty Papers," Box 31, Columbia University
           Flaherty recounts how he first learned of the Aran
      Islands, the initial distrust he encountered there, how he
      found a cast, shark hunting, fishing from cliffs, and the
      dangerous boat landing.

315   (Autobiography). Sunday Referee (London, 29 July-9 September).
           Autobiographical reminiscences of Hudson Bay exploration
      in seven installments, geared toward publicity of Man of
      Aran release.

316   "Filming Real People," Moviemaker (December). Reprinted in
      Jacobs (see entry 275), pp. 97-99.
           Excellent article on Flaherty's use of long focus lenses
      and their aesthetic role in his films up to Man of Aran.

317   "Robert Flaherty, Explorer, Engineer and Motion Picture Pro-
      ducer." BBC Broadcast (30 October).
           A radio interview largely concerning Man of Aran.

                              1935

318   "Robert Flaherty Tells How He Made Man of Aran." National
      Board of Review Magazine, 10, No. 1 (January), 5-7.
           Standard piece, though in less detail, on the making of
      the film.

319   "Living Dangerously in the Frozen North." BBC (January 22).
           A 15-minute radio broadcast. Transcript in "Flaherty
      Papers," Box 22.

*320   "Quelques instants avec Robert Flaherty." Intercine (March),
        pp. 5-7. Reprinted in F. DeGiamatteo's Essenza del Film.
        Turin: Il Dramma, 1947.
             An interview on Tabu, Man of Aran, and Elephant Boy,
        cited by Henri Agel. See entry 257.

                              1937

321   "The Captain's Chair." BBC Television. Broadcast of adapta-
        tion of novel. Narrator: Robert Flaherty. Adapted by
        Denis Johnston. Captain Grant played by John Laurie.
             One of the first television broadcasts to combine live
        performances with film.

*322   "La funzione del documentario." Cinema, No. 22 (25 May).
        Cited by Paolo Gobetti. See entry 243.

                              1938

323   The Captain's Chair: A Story of the North. London: Hodder &
        Stoughton, 314 pp.; also New York: Scribner's.
             A young man in his twenties (presumably Flaherty) re-
        ceives a commission to hunt iron ore in the heart of the
        Hudson Bay Company's domain around Hudson Bay, Canada.
        Written as a novel, the book describes his trips with
        Eskimos and includes survival tales told to him by the
        Eskimos. They cover over a thousand miles by canoe and
        sledge from Moose Factory up the coast of the Bay, across
        land to Leaf Gulf, and back to Cape Wolstenholme, where the
        young explorer finally meets up with Captain Grant's
        steamer.

324   "The Last Voyage of Captain Grant." BBC Radio Broadcast.
        Written by Flaherty; narrated by Geoffrey Tandy.
             Broadcasts based on the novel (dated 9, 23, and 30 July).

325   "North Sea." Sight and Sound, 7, No. 26 (Summer), 62.
        A brief review of a British documentary.

                              1939

326   White Master. London: Routledge.
             Flaherty's second novel about an explorer's life in the
        Hudson Bay region. A complex narrative within a narrative
        centering on a conflict between a chief trading post factor
        who exploits the people around him and a young "greenhorn."
        Filled with Flaherty's personal impressions of a savage
        land and intimate details gained through years of experience.

                              156

1942

327   "The Most Unforgettable Character I've Met." Reader's Digest,
      40, No. 239 (March), 41-44.
        Flaherty recounts the invaluable assistance of a young
      Samoan girl who acted as a go-between with the native
      chiefs during the production of Moana.

1948

*328   "The Story Behind the Louisiana Story." Film News.
      Cited by Wolfgang Klaue. See entry 254.

1949

329   "Louisiana Story." BBC. Third Programme (6 July; repeated
      26 July).
        A radio adaptation of the film narrated by Flaherty. In
      a preface to the program Flaherty described how the sound
      track had been created, particularly the oil drilling
      sequence.

330   "Making a Film in the Louisiana Bayous." Travel, 92, No. 5
      (May), 13-15, 32.
        A brief article on the origin, conception, and making
      of the film.

331   Man of Aran Programs. BBC. (17-18 December).
        Produced by Michael Bell; Flaherty, host and principal
      commentator. "The Painful Plough," about life and condi-
      tions on the Aran Islands; "Portrait of Aran," on the occa-
      sion of Flaherty's revisit to Aran; and "Aran and Some of
      its People," which contains Flaherty's accounts of his ex-
      periences on Aran, anecdotes about folklore, and the making
      of the film. Transcripts in "Flaherty Papers," Box 31.

332   "Odyssey of a film maker." BBC Home Service. (24 July).
        Flaherty talks about his journeys of exploration and his
      films.

333   "A Personal Impression." BBC (18 November).
        A television program about Flaherty's impressions of
      England after an absence of ten years.

334   Prerecorded Radio Talks. BBC.
        Those recorded 14 June and 24 July were about early
      prospecting expeditions; talk of 29 August concerned his
      experiences in the South Seas; also 5 September and
      1 October.

335   "The Grim, Gallant Story of Comock the Eskimo." Reader's
       Digest, 57, No. 339 (July), 169-180.
           Condensed from the BBC radio program. See entry 337.

                                1950

336   "Robert Flaherty Talking." The Cinema 1950. Edited by
       Roger Manvell. Harmondsworth: Penguin, pp. 11-29.
           A succinct autobiographical narrative which highlights
       the making of Nanook of the North, Moana, Man of Aran, and
       Louisiana Story. Flaherty discusses his first uses of the
       camera; his intentions in making a film of Eskimos; the use
       of panchromatic film in Samoa and his relationship with the
       Samoans; deriving a story from the location; working with
       nonactors; problems of distribution; music and sound and
       film; and his hope for the future.

337   "The Story of Comock the Eskimo." BBC. Five 15-minute broad-
       casts, 2-6 January, written and told by Flaherty.
           A story of survival learned from Comock himself. Accord-
       ing to one account these broadcasts were highly individual
       and very fascinating.

                                1951

338   "Film: Language of the Eye." Theatre Arts, 35, No. 5 (May),
       30-36.
           Recounts the making of Nanook of the North, Moana, and
       Louisiana Story.

*339   "L'occhio e la penna del nostro secolo." Cinema, No. 5
       (1 March).
           Cited by Paolo Gobetti. See entry 243.

                                1952

340   "The Story of Comock the Eskimo." The Cinema, 1952. Edited
       by Roger Manvell and R. K. Nelson Baxter. London: Pelican,
       pp. 100-125.
           An incredible tale of Eskimo survival that Flaherty
       learned on one of his expeditions and later embellished for
       publication.

                                1959

341   "Tabu, A Story of the South Seas." Film Culture, No. 20,
       pp. 27-38. Written in collaboration with F. W. Murnau.

                                158

The script in story form, closer to Murnau's completed film.

342   "Turia, An Original Story." Film Culture, No. 20, pp. 17-26.
Written in collaboration with F. W. Murnau.
The original outline story for the film, Tabu.

1968

343   The Story of Comock the Eskimo, as told to Robert Flaherty.
Edited by Edmund Carpenter. New York: Simon and Schuster,
95 pp.
One of the survival tales that Flaherty learned of and
from which he obtained a fair amount of literary mileage.

1969

344   "Nanook," in Lewis Jacobs, ed., The Emergence of Film Art.
New York: Hopkinson and Blake, Publishers, pp. 215-221.
Reprinted from Screen Director (February, 1951).
Describes how he developed an interest in film; the
making of Nanook of the North; and the problems of getting
it released for general exhibition.

1971

345   Nanook of the North. Edited from the film by Robert Kraus.
New York: Windmill Books, 32 pp.
Pictures and captions taken from the film.

Archival Sources

CLAREMONT, CALIFORNIA

354   <u>Claremont College</u>, School of Theology, The Robert and Frances
       Flaherty Study Center, Claremont, California, 91711.
       (714-626-3521)
           Claremont is the repository for the Robert and Frances
       Flaherty still photographic collection. Robert Flaherty
       shot the stills on location for <u>Nanook of the North</u> and he
       also shot some on Samoa during the making of <u>Moana</u>, but
       Frances Flaherty was responsible for originating most of
       the photographs after <u>Nanook</u>. There are also photographs
       relating to <u>Man of Aran</u>, <u>Elephant Boy</u>, and <u>Louisiana Story</u>.
       Although some of the photographs were used for publicity
       and publication, others were shot for production and may
       have been used for planning purposes. Study prints of
       some Flaherty films are also available at Claremont as well
       as outtakes of the <u>Man of Aran</u> footage. In addition, the
       collection includes oral interviews, especially with Frances
       Flaherty, a book collection chosen by her, and bibliographic
       aids.

MINNEAPOLIS, MINNESOTA

355   <u>University of Minnesota</u>, Audiovisual Library Service, 3300
       University Avenue SE, Minneapolis, Minnesota, 55414.
       (612-373-3842)
           The University has custody of 16mm reproductions of the
       outtake footage from <u>Louisiana Story</u>. Ninety reels of 35mm
       outtakes have been reduced to 29 reels of 16mm, amounting
       to about 1,000 minutes of viewing time. The original ni-
       trate negatives are still in the possession of the Library
       of Congress, however. The outtakes have been grouped to-
       gether following the continuity of the finished film and
       are described in a detailed subject list. Alternatively
       referred to as <u>A Film Study of Robert Flaherty's "Louisiana
       Story"</u> or the <u>Louisiana Story Study Film</u>, it allows for a
       comparison of the final edited film with the discarded foot-
       age. There are few opportunities like this for film study,

since documentary outtakes have been rarely treated with
such reverence. The university's copies are available for
study on premises by appointment.

NEW YORK, NEW YORK

356   Columbia University, Butler Library, New York, New York, 10027.
       (212-280-5153)
       The most valuable collection of manuscript materials is
       of course the "Robert J. Flaherty Papers" deposited in
       Columbia University by the Flaherty family and available
       for study purposes in the Manuscript Reading Room of the
       Butler Library. The papers consist of 92 archives boxes
       containing original manuscripts, correspondence, clippings,
       books, photographs, artwork, publicity materials, financial
       records, printed materials, and so on, arranged and inven-
       toried by the library. Contained in the first 15 boxes are
       general correspondence, 1916-1951, and family correspondence,
       which may only be used with written permission. Boxes 16-
       21 contain materials relating to Flaherty's explorations in
       Canada, including the Flaherty diaries. Boxes 22-53 con-
       tain scripts, correspondence, memoranda and other materials
       relating to his films, arranged by film title. Boxes 54-59
       contain material concerning Flaherty's publications, in-
       cluding contracts, correspondence, and reviews and other
       items. Boxes 60-67 contain miscellaneous materials ranging
       from interviews and awards to obituary notices. Box 68
       contains writings by Frances Flaherty, and Box 69 contains
       the Paul Rotha and Basil Wright manuscript study of Robert
       Flaherty adapted for publication by Arthur Calder-Marshall.
       Boxes 70-92 are essentially the records of the Robert
       Flaherty Foundation, later absorbed by International Film
       Seminars, Inc. The library permits copying of most of the
       papers for research and reference purposes. The "David
       Flaherty Papers" are also housed in the Butler Library.
       The Special Collections at the Butler Library include
       the Flaherty Oral History Collection. These are interviews
       conducted by Bruce Harding for International Film Seminars,
       Inc., 1973-1974, and permission is needed for access.

357   The Museum of Modern Art, Department of Film Studies, 11 West
       53 Street, New York, New York, 10019. (212-956-6100)
       "Notebooks" of Helen Van Dongen. Two cartons containing:
       Production diaries of Louisiana Story, August 1946-April
       1947; key number catalog of completed film and location
       maps; draft analysis of opening sequence; scripts and break-
       downs; narration and dialogue in final version; music score;
       final mixing logs; drafts of published articles on the edit-
       ing of the film; and letter to Willard Van Dyke, dated
       August 8, 1972, concerning her criticism of the Louisiana
       Story Study Film. Included for The Land are negative

catalogs and key number lists and several scripts at different stages. There are also files relating to News Review No. 2 (1943) which Van Dongen made for the U.S. Office of War Information; Calligraphy, the unfinished film project; The Gift of Green; and Pete-Roleum (1939). Permission required for duplication.

Paul Rotha and Basil Wright. "Flaherty Biography." Unpublished manuscript. November 24, 1959, Electrostatic copy of typescript. (See entry 237). Original research material for Arthur Calder-Marshall's book The Innocent Eye: The Life of Robert J. Flaherty. (See entry 249). Provides more detail on the critical reception of Flaherty's films. Rotha and Wright's own critical views are included; they are strongest on Flaherty's work in Britain and weakest on American aspects. (Carbon copy available among "Flaherty Papers," Box 69, Columbia University, Butler Library.) Permission for duplication required.

In addition, the Museum has study prints of all the Flaherty films listed in Part III, and some copies are available for rental as listed in Part VII. The Museum maintains a specialized book library relating to film history and a clipping file on microfiche accessible by personal names and film titles.

WASHINGTON, D. C.

358   The Library of Congress, Motion Picture Section, Washington, D.C., 20540. (202-426-5840)

The Motion Picture Section maintains a specialized collection of film reference materials, including bibliographies and texts, and a still picture file accessible by film title. Many of the publications needed for Flaherty research are available through the Library's Main Reading Room, though its collection of foreign periodicals is incomplete.

The Library also has several of the Flaherty films: the 1947 sound version of Nanook of the North; Moana, including the original work print; and Louisiana Story, including much of the outtakes for this and the Louisiana Story Study Film. The Library's films are not available for circulation but may be studied on its premises subject to the availability of viewing prints.

359   National Archives and Records Service, Washington, D.C., 20408. (202-523-3267)

The National Archives holds primarily government-related records. In connection with a study of Flaherty they include the records of the U.S. Department of Agriculture, which contain record copies of The Land, records of the Secretary of Agriculture Henry Wallace, and records of the Agricultural Adjustment Administration, which was the

specific sponsor of The Land. Unfortunately thorough and
repeated searches by archivists familiar with these records
have failed to turn up much significant documentation relating to either Flaherty or the film or both. One expla-
nation offered is that the AAA Division of Information
records were not preserved intact although some copies are
available in a central correspondence file. It was this
division that monitored the production for the government.

The records of the U.S. Film Service, also incomplete,
and of the Office of War Information contain several references to the making of The Land in its early stages. The
records of Pare Lorentz's office were not preserved as a
series, but as Professor Snyder had demonstrated in his
book, Pare Lorentz and the Documentary Film (entry 268),
some copies are contained in Mr. Lorentz's personal papers
which are still his property.

Film Distributors

360   Budget Films, 4590 Santa Monica Blvd., Los Angeles, California, 90029.

       Elephant Boy

361   Films Inc., 1144 Wilmette Ave., Wilmette, Illinois, 60091.

       Louisiana Story
       Nanook of the North (new sound version)
       Man of Aran
       Moana (under negotiations with Paramount)
       White Shadows in the South Seas

362   Indiana University Audiovisual Center, Bloomington, Indiana, 47401.

       Nanook of the North (1947 sound version)
       Louisiana Story

363   Ivy Films, 165 West 46th St., New York, New York, 10036.

       Tabu

364   Museum of Modern Art, Department of Film, 11 West 53rd St., New York, New York, 10019.

       Guernica
       Industrial Britain
       The Land
       Louisiana Story Study Film
       Nanook of the North (silent version)
       Moana

365   National Audiovisual Center, Washington, D.C., 20409.

       The Land

Note: Commercial distribution contracts are assigned for limited periods of time, making the above information subject to change. Many of these films may also be obtained in local public libraries.

Author Index

Author Index

N

Napolitano, Arturo, 293
Needham, Wilbur, 52
Nery, Jean, 156
Nicholson, Irene, 112

O

O'Brien, Frederick, 53
O'Dell, Scott, 25
O'Neil, Brian, 81

P

Pandolfi, Vito, 167, 181
Pasinetti, Francesco, 82
Patalas, Enno, 182
Patterson, Frances Taylor, 20
Pichel, Irving, 168
Potamkin, Harry Alan, 63
Pratt, George C., 262

Q

Quintar, Fred, 245

R

Ramsaye, Terry, 44, 54
Regent, Roger, 157
Reisz, Karel, 205
Robertson, E. Arnot, 169
Rohmer, Eric. See Scherer,
    Maurice
Rosenheimer, Arthur, 118, 126,
    177
Rotha, Paul, 56, 83, 198, 237,
    289
Roullet, Serge, 138
Rowe, Newton, 57

S

Sadoul, Georges, 183, 265
Sammis, Edward, 184
Sarris, Andrew, 252
Schein, Harry, 206

Scherer, Maurice, 185, 207
Schrire, David, 84
Segal, Mark, 85
Seldes, Gilbert, 26
Seligmann, Herbert J., 36
Sennwald, Andre, 86
Sherwood, Robert E., 23, 45
Siepmann, Charles, 238, 284
Snyder, Robert, 268
Stallings, Laurence, 37
Stanbrook, Alan, 246
Staples, Donald E., 290
Starr, Cecile, 186, 199, 218
Stella, Vittorio, 212
Stefansson, Vilhjalmur, 55
Sternfeld, Frederick, 139
Strauss, Theodore, 113
Sussex, Elizabeth, 294
Synge, J. M., 14, 15

T

Talbot, Frederick A., 24
Taylor, Robert Lewis, 158
Thomson, Virgil, 266
Tidden, Fritz, 21
Toeplitz, Jerzy, 187, 256
Troy, William, 87
Turconi, Davide, 248

V

Van Dongen, Helen, 188, 260, 295
Van Dyke, Willard, 258
Vincent, Carl, 189

W

Wald, Marvin, 190
Weinberg, Herman G., 119, 140,
    191, 263
Werner, P., 283
Wright, Basil, 141, 142, 192, 237
Wynkip, M. H., 208

Z

Zinnemann, Fred, 299

Film Title Index